THE MENTOR CONNECTION

THE MENTOR CONNECTION

STRATEGIC ALLIANCES
IN
CORPORATE LIFE

Michael G. Zey

With a new introduction by the author

Transaction Publishers
New Brunswick (U.S.A.) and London (U.K.)

Second printing 1993

New material this edition copyright © 1991 by Transaction Publishers, New Brunswick, New Jersey 08903.

Originally published in 1984 by Dow Jones-Irwin. © 1984 by Dow Jones Irwin.

Library of Congress Catalog Number: 90-40507
ISBN: 0-88738-865-5
Printed in the United States of America

Library of Congress Cataloging-in-Publication Data

Zey, Michael G.
    The mentor connection: strategic alliances in corporate life/Michael G. Zey; with a new introduction by the author.
        p.   cm.
    Reprint. Originally published: Homewood, Ill.: Dow Jones-Irwin, c1984.
    Includes bibliographical references and index.
    ISBN 0-88738-865-5 (pbk.)
    1. Mentors in business. 2. Success in business. I. Title.
HF5386.Z49   1990   90-40507
303.3'4—dc20   CIP

To my supporting cast

Contents

The Renewed Interest in Mentoring. How Prevalent Is Mentoring. Toward a Working Definition of the Mentor Concept. The Hierarchy of Mentoring. The Benefits Are Mutual. The Plan of This Book.

Level I—The Mentor as Teacher: *Teaching the Job. Drawing the Organizational Road Map. Career Guidance.* Level II—Personal Support: *Psychological Support. Confidence Building. Assistance with Personal Life.* The Thin Line. Level III—Organizational Intervention: *The Mentor Goes Public. Protection. Marketing the Candidate. Access to Resources.*

Level IV—Promotions Direct and Indirect: *Direct Promotion. The Subtle Approach. Position of Mentor.* Mentoring as Transformation. If the Mentor Never Existed. Life without a Mentor. The Effects of Organizational Type on Mentoring.

The Mentor: *Career Enhancement. Intelligence/Information Systems. The Trusted Adviser. Psychic Rewards. The Risks of Mentoring.* The Organization: *Integrating the Individual. Reduction in Turnover. Organizational Communication. Management Development. Managerial Succession. Productivity. Socialization to Power.*

Mentoring and the Barriers to Women: *The Image of Women in the Workplace. Are Male Managers Threatened by Female Managers? Are Women Prepared?* Male Mentors versus Female Mentors: Does It Make a Difference? *The "Comfort" Factor.   The Organizational Power of the Mentor.* Involvement and Innuendo. A Rival for Spouse? The Future of the Female Protege.

Introduction to the Transaction Edition

In the last few years, the concept of the "mentor" has become part of the common parlance: There seems to be an increased awareness of just how critical mentoring is to an individual's success. Articles in the popular press, as well as in academic journals, seem to cite ever greater evidence that mentors play a major role in people's career development. Research is demonstrating that mentors help young managers to become more successful, assist neophyte scientists in reaching their potential, and nurture budding musicians and artists.

Open a newspaper or book these days and somewhere you will encounter the term "mentor." In interviews, Hollywood superstars are only too quick to inform the public how some director or producer helped them reach stardom. Sports heroes regularly describe the role that a college or minor-league coach played in their development. The world of politics is rife with recountings of an older, established politician grooming a younger man or woman for a position on the national stage.

Surprisingly, not more than a decade ago one would be hard put to find more than a few articles about this subject. Now the field has become so rich that any literature search in social science or popular periodical data bases will uncover hundreds of citations about this new phenomenon. Dozens of dissertations and masters theses on mentoring have been written in the last few years in a wide range of fields, including medicine, management, social science, nursing, organizational behavior, psychology, and history.

By the mid-1980s, interest in the field had finally grown to "critical mass." Researchers and practitioners, needing to communicate with each other, began to hold conferences and meetings in which participants exchanged information and began to seriously build a knowledge base for the field. One of the earliest was the 1986 International conference on Mentoring in Vancouver. The International Association of Mentoring, which sponsored the event, found the response to the conference so encouraging that it quickly scheduled another.[1]

In the late 1980s a variety of mentoring organizations emerged in different parts of the U.S. and Canada. The International Mentoring Association, based at Western Michigan University, is one of the most active, combining the efforts of educators, business people, practitioners, and professionals to study this subject and perhaps foster mentoring activities. The Uncommon Individual Foundation in Radnor, Pennsylvania is fostering much research and activity in the field; in 1988 this organization sponsored a meeting of scholars in the field to discuss a number of issues related to mentoring.

Additionally, mentoring has not escaped the notice of the more established human resources/organizational-development groups. For instance, the American Society of Training and Development, the key trade association in human resources, has increasingly scheduled sessions around the issue of mentoring.

Various issues have arisen in the literature and at academic conferences. The literature features numerous discussions concerning the definition of "mentor," how the relationship works, and whether people should even retain a mentor in later parts of their early careers. Several articles have been written about male-female mentor pairs, the specific roles that mentors play in career development, historical examples of mentor-protegé partnerships, and the psychodynamics of mentoring.

One positive result is that over the decade researchers have developed a greater understanding of the mentoring process itself. Of course, as is typical in social science, different researchers emphasize different aspects of the relationship.

For instance, some researchers concentrate on the "stages" of the relationship. This stage theory of mentoring seeks to discover the predictable phases through which most mentor relationships pass. Though various researchers apply different labels to these phases, most of the theories claim that the typical mentor relationship can be broken down into three distinct phases. There is usually an initiation phase, in which the mentor and protege get to know each other and their needs. This is followed by a full-blown developmental stage, during which both parties experience most of the benefits. Many of these theories also posit a termination stage of the relationship; though they debate the reasons for the end of the relationship, they seem to agree that there is an element of rejection of the mentor by the protege, often because the protege no longer needs the relationship.[2]

The model that I developed for this book is closer in emphasis to social exchange theory. My Mutual Benefits Model is based on a belief that people enter into, and remain part of, relationships in order to meet certain needs. In this case, the mentor and protege engage in the mentoring relationship because each perceives that he or she will gain certain benefits from doing so.

While each may outgrow these needs, and hence the relationship, this is in no way a predetermined occurrence, as stage theories presume. Since the relationship may meet certain of the protege's needs indefinitely, this social exchange model assumes no predetermined termination point in a given relationship.

However, my model also makes an additional claim. Whereas, traditionally, mentoring was seen as a tool to benefit the mentor and the protege, I emphasize that the organization that contains the two members—a school, a corporation, or a government agency—will also greatly benefit from this interaction.

The Growth of Formal Mentoring Programs

As we shall soon see, the latent benefits of mentoring for the organization are many. Generally, many different organizations have begun to realize that, since mentoring is such a useful key to success and personal development, perhaps the relationships could somehow be fostered and its powers tapped. By the mid-1980s diverse organizations—in nursing, education, the arts, and industry—had independently begun to look for ways to formally link mentors and proteges.

A formal mentor program is simply one in which a mentor and protege, usually preselected, are linked either by the organization or a department within the organization, and are expected to continue in this relationship for an agreed-upon length of time. Of course, the company or organization usually hopes that these relationships will eventually take wing and thrive on their own, and will extend far beyond the official "time limit" placed on such relationships. In fact, one way to judge whether a program is successful is to see whether the formal relationships last beyond the specified time commitment.

The types of organizations that implement such programs, and the reasons that they start them, are varied. In Australia, for instance, the public school system has in place a fully operational system in which mentors help underachievers meet their full potential. The New York City public school system has also adopted such a program to help its students get better grades.

And in a southern U.S. city the police department has developed a mentor program to guide and train its new recruits.

The New Jersey Institute of Technology uses mentoring to solve adjustment problems confronting female engineers. It assigns already established female engineers to its junior and senior women engineering students as mentors, hoping that these veterans can prepare the neophytes for some of the problems they may face in the male-dominated world of high technology.

One of the most innovative applications of the concept of mentoring to problem solving is illustrated by the case of HOSTS Learning Systems, a West Coast-based learning-technologies company. This company has developed mentor programs to help combat the well-publicized problems that American youths have in the reading and math areas, deficiencies that even many experts feel are overwhelming in a great many cases. HOSTS has found that by assigning a mentor/tutor to a young student in the company's computer-oriented reading and math programs, they are able to increase the child's scores considerably. The key variable was found to be the individualized attention, and hence caring, that the volunteer mentors were providing.[3]

Some cities, such as New Brunswick, New Jersey, are developing programs that link older mentors with junior high school students in the hope that the adult guidance will keep them on the straight and narrow life path. One of the primary considerations is the belief that mentors might serve as a positive influence on the youngsters, perhaps dissuading them from involvement with drugs or engaging in criminal activity. The New York-based "I Have a Dream Foundation," started by philanthropist Eugene Lang, uses mentors as guides for disadvantaged students to encourage them to complete high school. For the proteges who *do* finish high school and go on to college, this foundation provides mentors drawn from big business to help them in the difficult transition into university life.[4]

There are several different sociological reasons for this interest in formalized mentoring. In the case of school systems and townships adopting such programs, certainly the recent changes in the family structure in America have prompted the initiation of any number of steps to help youths cope with personal problems. Schools increasingly have become involved in many functions previously relegated to the family, including "ego building," confidence building, and counseling. In that sense, it is not unexpected that schools, townships, and youth organizations would look for parental substitutes, such as formal mentors, to introduce stability into students' lives.

Society as a whole is experimenting with a variety of new support systems. Regardless of a person's problem, he or she can find a formal support group to solve it. Sometimes these groups provide nothing but companionship, like a type of group explored weekly on such television programs as "Dear John." People form support systems through computerized bulletin boards or by using 900-number "chat lines." Mentor programs are, in essence, part of a broader sociological trend.[5]

There also seems to be alive in the U.S. a new helping impulse. Call it the "kinder and gentler" spirit wafting over the land, but it just seems that more people want to improve the condition of others, society, or the environment. Certainly, in the school and tutoring systems retirees have a new-found sense of purpose in being able to share their knowledge and skills, and wisdom, with those younger. It gives a sense of empowerment to the mentors to know that they can help shape the next generation through these unique one-on-one relationships.

The Formal Corporate Mentor Program

While various civic and educational concerns have experimented with this innovation, nowhere has there been a wider adoption of formal mentoring than in the world of business. Hundreds of companies in North America, including such notables as Johnson and Johnson, Bellcore, NCR Corporation, Allstate, Pacific Telesis, and Merrill Lynch, to name just a few, are adopting formal mentoring programs. Let's look at a few of the reasons why.

Informal mentor relationships have been the basis of many corporate success stories. This is hardly a secret to managers and employees. Most know that the relationship can help the individual mentor or protege. The mentor, by guiding, counseling, protecting, and even sometimes promoting that protege, literally oversees the development and career of the junior member. In return, the protege helps advance the mentor's career in a multitude of ways: The protege may offer the mentor vital information about the lower echelons of the company, serve as a sounding board for the mentor's ideas, and, very often, directly pitch in when the mentor needs help finishing a project.

However, there has been an increased awareness of just how these relationships can benefit the organization that employs the mentor and the protege. As I point out in this book, mentoring often contributes to the development of corporate managers, and even facilitates the process of managerial succession. It has been found to be instrumental in increasing productivity, reducing turnover, and enhancing communication among the levels and sectors of the organization. Mentors also help integrate the individual into the organization and build his or her sense of belonging.

Hence, increasingly corporations have sought to tap the benefits of such relationships by establishing formal mentoring programs that link senior executives to junior employees. Varied in form, these programs differ according to their length, method of selecting and matching participants, and stated goals. The more structured programs may require that the mentor and protege meet regularly, and suggest that the mentor introduce the protege to top management or instill in his or her the values and norms of the corporate culture.

The programs vary. Bell Labs, the research arm of AT&T, utilizes a mentor program to orient new technical recruits to the corporation. Motorola, in southern Florida, has instituted three different mentoring program-new graduate mentoring, technical mentoring, and secretarial mentoring-all of which look to reduce turnover and better develop the participants' talent. In Indiana, AT&T's Consumer Products Lab has established three different formal programs as part of various career-development programs. Hoechst-Celanese, based in New Jersey, is establishing formal mentor programs to help in the areas of management development and is now beginning to establish mentor programs for its lower-level employees, nonprofessional technicians, and secretaries.[6] Johnson and Johnson's Ortho-Pharmaceutical Division has another successful program.

Even government is beginning to utilize formal mentoring for its management development programs. The U.S. Postal Service is utilizing mentoring as a way to develop its up-and-coming administrators. The State of Missouri is beginning to incorporate mentoring into its systems, and the State of New York's Governor's Office has utilized mentoring as a developmental tool.

How many programs exist in the United States? While it has been estimated that over 1,000 currently exist, no one seems certain of the actual number. It can be said, however, that many companies are incorporating formal mentor systems into their management development system.

Formal Programs Are Quickly Improving

Obviously, as this nascent organizational-development tool is adopted by more and more companies, researchers, human resources professionals, and practitioners are learning better ways to construct and maintain these programs. While the rudiments of building a successful program are explained in Chapter 10, I would like to make some points here about what our recent experience has taught us about building and sustaining good programs in organizations.

For one thing, most practitioners have learned that, when developing such a program, the corporate culture must be a prime consideration. Some cultures are just more conducive to one-on-one relationships than others, or a culture may not be receptive to the intimacy and sharing inherent in formal mentor programs.

We have also discovered that while there are many people who make good mentors, others should clearly be discouraged from participating in such programs. The person chosen as a mentor should be a good motivator and teacher, a high performer, unthreatened by others' success, and reflective of the company's values and culture. Companies learn over time that this checklist is very useful in determining the success of a program.

And increasingly, it is becoming apparent that "cross-functional mentoring" is extremely useful as a way of transmitting skills. At one time, program formulators thought it best that only marketing people mentor other marketing proteges, engineers mentor engineers, etc. Now we realize that the cross-pollination of ideas inherent in "interfunctional mentoring" (e.g., finance professionals mentoring technicians) is extremely helpful in teaching the protege how other parts of the organization work. The mentor also gains insight into operations at the lower levels.

And research and practice reveal that mentors and proteges in these programs can, and should, be trained for participation in the program. Training that involves a full discussion of the issues involved, role playing, and grappling with the issues can slice months off the "learning curve" for both members of the relationship. Additionally, training that demystifies the "first meeting" can spell success rather than failure not only for the relationship but the program itself.[7]

Also, programs are beginning to become more structured than they were during the mid-80s. Companies are realizing that they must develop mechanisms to ensure that program administrators can touch base with the participants at regular intervals, if only to let them know that the company is interested in the relationship's progress. Companies also are becoming more careful about who is paired with whom, taking into account such issues as chemistry, personality, and mutual need.

We are additionally becoming cognizant of the fact that there are sometimes unintended consequences to these programs. There is growing evidence that these programs are beginning to affect the culture of the organization is serendipitous ways. For instance, my own research has indicated that the proteges in these programs begin to adopt mentoring behaviors in regard to others in the organizations. If proteges happen to be a supervisors, they report that very often they start to replicate the mentoring behaviors of their formal sponsors.

We are also beginning to notice a great amount of upward communication occurring in these programs. Originally, we conceived of mentoring as a method of instilling the corporate culture into the protege, and perhaps teaching the person career and technical skills. We are beginning to realize proteges have many original ideas to contribute about the company and its overall direction. Mentor programs are facilitating the process by which proteges' ideas can be transmitted up the organizational hierarchy.

Mentoring and Future Corporate Problems

What is the future role of mentor programs? Certainly, formal mentor programs will continue to fulfill the functions we have already discussed. They will help companies transmit aspects of the corporate culture, and will serve to orient new members of the organization to company practices. Also, as shown, mentor programs will always help organizations transmit skills and develop a cadre of new managers, technicians, and all-around leaders.

However, as U.S. industry begins to face new challenges in the 21st century, several major social and economic trends may encourage corporations to turn to these programs to deal with a greater number of organizational problems.

Let's look at some of the needs that mentor programs may help meet in the 1990s and in the next century.

The Coming Labor Shortage

In most industrialized countries, labor-market growth is slowing down, leading to what some see as an emerging sellers' market for labor. Nowhere is this more striking than in the United States. During the 1970s, many new job hunters, members of the 1946-64 Baby Boom, quickly outstripped the available jobs and found themselves facing unemployment or underemployment. That situation now has changed dramatically. Lowered fertility after 1964 produced the so-called "Baby Bust," which now has employers in the position of having to compete for labor.

For example, during the 1970s the work force grew by 2 percent per year. During the 1980s, however, this annual increase became smaller and smaller, a change mostly affected by the decrease in the number of new workers available. While the number of entry-level workers aged eighteen to twenty-four increased by 22 percent in the 1970s, this group declined in the 1980s by 15 percent.[8] The drop in available entry-level workers accelerated so quickly that in one brief period, 1983-88, the size of the 18-to-24 year-old group decreased by two million people. Some estimate that by 1990 there are 4.5 million fewer entry-level workers than in 1980.[9]

Nowhere is the shortage more pronounced than in the high-skilled areas. Companies are quickly finding an increased need for workers to fill the technical, professional, and managerial positions so important in the global economy. Shortfalls in the high-skilled labor pool are forcing companies that must compete for the best college graduates to devise more creative methods of recruiting and keeping the quality worker.

The modern corporation is thus continually devising more creative methods of attracting and retaining quality employees. We are seeing companies offer "flextime," innovative career-development plans, child care assistance, and outright bribery to get people to work for them.

Mentoring programs can help companies retain such workers in this new socioeconomic climate. The role that both formal and informal mentoring relationships play in reducing turnover is based on several factors. First, an employee who has a mentor generally feels more closely interwoven into the organization's cultural fabric. The greater the protege's integration into the corporate culture, the less likely he or she is to leave the organization. Second, the mentor, by communicating to the protege the company's plans for his or her future, can reduce the protege's sense of uncertainty, and make him or her less prone to quit. Third, by helping the protege weather early career storms, the mentor reduces the chance that the protege will become frustrated or disillusioned and consequently leave the organization.

Mentor programs can help companies on the recruitment end, as well. It is apparent that companies are going to have to do more to make themselves attractive to this dwindling labor supply: they will have to show a worker that they care about him or her. Some are already demonstrating their concern for the worker with stock-option plans, employee-assistance programs, and day care centers. Mentoring programs fulfill the same function. A company that provides a guide, a coach, and/or a teacher, is showing that it cares about employees' careers. What worker wouldn't strongly consider joining a company that provides a senior person to oversee his or her development and career during the difficult early stages?

Increased Diversity of the Work Force

The composition of the American work force, like the U.S. population in general, is undergoing a massive transformation.[10] The growing presence of women, blacks, and other minorities in the corporate world is one of the major socioeconomic trends confronting modern business.

But corporations are having problems bringing these workers into positions of power and fitting them into the corporate social structure. How often do we witness corporations whose females and blacks are clustered at middle and lower levels of the corporate hierarchies?

What is preventing women and minorities from moving up the highest rungs of the corporate ladder? Observers have suggested a number of reasons: the lack of experience of these workers, the short-term nature of many of these employees' work-force participation, and the resistance of the entrenched traditional workers, usually white males, to these new groups.

Research shows that a major force inhibiting these groups' movement up the corporate ladder is the fact that they have had difficulty gaining entry into the "old boys" network; being a member of such a network ensures exposure to top management and access to information about organizational politics and "the right way of doing things," all necessary tools in the climb up that ladder.

Since this manpower bottleneck is clearly depriving corporations of such groups' talents and skills, companies are increasingly employing formal mentoring programs as a mechanism to develop the careers of females and blacks. By assigning mentors to key minority individuals, corporations are able to make sure that these people become known by top management and socialized into the norms and values of the company. These employees are then able to contribute their skills at the very highest levels of their organizations. Without such a program, however, many minority members will be, quite simply, left out of the power structure.

The Quest For Innovation

It is now an accepted fact that companies that want to remain competitive must find a way to foster innovation within their ranks. Observers have blamed lack of innovation for a range of economic problems, from the decline of U.S. Steel to the unfavorable balance of trade.

Corporations are hungry for ways to generate innovation among their ranks: A flourishing cottage industry has arisen to help corporations in that quest. Over the last several years, books addressing this problem, which usually feature in their titles such words as "intrapreneurship" and "innovation," have rolled off the presses.[11] Corporations even hire outside consultants to teach their employees "creative thinking" in the hope that the workers will develop new ideas that might lead to better products.

As will become clear in this volume, mentor relationships can play a strong role in generating innovation and entrepreneurial behavior within an organization. The relationships between mentoring and creativity, though subtle, is quite powerful.

According to the managers that I have interviewed, a mentor provides for the protege an environment in which he or she can develop ideas that can later be introduced into the corporate mainstream. In the best-case scenario, the mentor makes sure that the protege has ample time and freedom to develop his or her ideas and innovations.

In addition, the exchange of ideas between the two partners acts as a catalyst for innovation; the mentor and protege often stimulate each other's thinking through brainstorming and other techniques. A good example of the role of the mentor in the creative development of the protege is currently unfolding in many scientific R and D labs. In hi-tech and scientific fields, the 40-or-50-year-old physicist or astronomer has usually been considered "over the hill" in terms of his ability to make original contributions to the field. Hence, many of these senior people are given administrative positions. Now there is evidence of a growing tendency to link up these seniors with the company's recent Ph.D.'s in their creative prime. The seniors who are assigned to the younger scientists as their mentors give them advice and technical assistance on projects, and very often oversee the new person's intellectual development.

Since formal mentor programs can facilitate the linking of creative types in any organization, they have an important role to play in developing innovation and nurturing the "intrapreneur." Since the quest for innovation is a major trend, businesses will benefit from adopting such programs.

The Merger Explosion

Corporation mergers have become a fact of business life; we see examples of companies like Allied Corporation and Texas Air enormously increasing their net size by acquiring several companies in rapid succession.

One of the more curious aspects of the merger explosion is the fate of managers in the acquired company. Most companies simply assume that they must fire the top executives who currently manage the acquired company. There are two reasons that they believe that this is so. One is that companies assume that duplication of functions will abound if they retain the acquired company's top management, but the reason more often cited is that these managers will have problems adapting to the corporate culture of the new parent organization.

The net result is that the acquired company's management is often forced to resign. While the parent company does maintain some semblance of continuity by placing its people in the other corporation's key positions, it also loses something vital–the talent and skills of the purchased company managers. The case could be made that these old-line managers generally have a better idea of how to produce and market a product than those managers whom the parent corporation puts in their places.

There is every possibility that companies would be willing to retain those skilled workers and managers if they thought they could teach these employees their values and style. But how?

A formal mentoring program may be the answer. By simply assigning a mentor to each manager of the bought company, the parent corporation can pass on the culture to these new managers. Similarly, after a merger, the parent company's senior executives could serve as mentors to the manager-in-place in the absorbed company, to advise them on the customs, practices, style, and expectations of the parent company.

The Emergence of the Cross-Cultural Corporation

Increasingly companies are establishing subsidiaries in foreign countries. They very often staff these companies at the middle-and upper-middle management ranks with "foreign nations," natives of the host country.

These cross-cultural corporations face many manpower problems. For instance, many Japanese companies are having difficulty retaining American managers at their U.S. subsidiaries. Some of the major Japanese corporations are complaining that as many as 50 percent of their American managers quit within the first few years after their hiring.

Cross-cultural companies are often bewildered by the difficulty that the foreign-national managers have adapting to the style and practices of the employer. For example, Americans expect that their management positions ought to be accompanied by all the trappings of power: the office, the secretary, and a good degree of deference from subordinates. After joining a Japanese company, they are shocked when they find themselves in a participatory, "democratic" environment in which the outward trappings of power and rank are de-emphasized or completely eliminated.

A formal mentoring program is a good way to help the new manager adapt to this new culture. Instead of learning about the culture through trial and error, the protege could be guided by a mentor who would teach him the nuances of the Japanese company. The mentor could teach the new manager not just what the norms are, but why they exist. He or she could also intervene in any conflicts that might arise between the new manager and his or her new colleagues.

Not just the "protege" would benefit from such a program. In a recent *Wall Street Journal* article on American subsidiaries of Japanese companies, Japanese senior executives admitted that they knew little of the values and expectations of the American managers they employed. Worse, they had no idea of how to develop channels of communications.[12]

Because of this need to increase mutual understanding, cross-cultural corporations will begin to develop formal mentoring programs. This communication modality should increase productivity and reduce turnover.[13]

While not a panacea, formal mentoring should certainly be considered a major tool for solving a number of problems introduced by the above trends. It can help the creative employee develop his ideas and will make the corporation with such a program more likely to attract and retain quality workers than one without such a program.

Regardless of the particular problem that a mentor program is supposed to solve, however, these programs will grow because they conform to a whole new approach to organizational and employee development being adopted by the American corporation. U.S. corporations are beginning to become aware of just what it is that makes people productive, and establishing a culture and structure that optimize the chances that people can express themselves, have their needs met, and simultaneously reach a higher state of creativity.

A quick survey of the changes in the way that American companies are managing demonstrates this point. Invariably in the management literature we hear of companies streamlining their bureaucracies by "delayering" and "decentralizing." Companies   now establish task forces composed of individuals from different functions in the hope that these multidisciplinary taskforces will facilitate a cross-pollinization of ideas. Companies such as Hewlett-Packard have developed techniques such as on-site brainstorming sessions that involve the entire employee pool in the process of the development of new ideas and marketing tools.

It is within this context that mentor programs are developing. Formal mentor programs will be part of this larger matrix of techniques to improve management and nurture individual and organizational growth. It is quickly becoming apparent that by fostering mentoring, both formal and informal, companies are coming ever closer to discovering the secret of higher productivity.

Notes

1. For a full review of this conference, see *Mentoring, Aid to Excellence: Proceedings of the First International Conference on Mentoring.* International Association for Mentoring (Vancouver: 1986)
2. The "stage" theories of mentor relationships are presented in Kram, K.E., "Phases of the mentor relationships," *Academy of Management Journal*, 1983, 26 (4), pp. 605-625; Misserian, Agnes K., *The Corporate Connection*, Prentice-Hall (Englewood Cliffs: 1982); and Jones, Linda Philips, *Mentors and Proteges*, Arbor House, (New York: 1982)
3. Willbur, Jerald L. "Mentoring, achievement motivation, and the literacy challenge," *Mentoring International*, Summer 1989.
4. Hurley, Dan, "The Mentor Mystique," *Psychology Today*, May 1988.
5. For an examination of these newer support systems, see chapter 9, "The Expanding Universe of Formal Supports," in my *Winning With People*. J.P. Tarcher, Inc. (Los Angeles: 1990)
6. See Zey and Epstein, "Partners for Development," in the proceedings of the 1989 International Mentoring Conference. Western Michigan University.
7. Zey, Michael. "Building a Successful Formal Mentor Program." *Training and Development Yearbook*, Prentice-Hall (1990).

8. "Welcome, America, to the Baby Bust." *Time Magazine*, February 23, 1987.

9. Naisbitt, John, and Patricia Aburdene. *Reinventing the Corporation.* Warner Books (New York: 1985).

10. This change in the labor force is explored in "Beyond the Melting Pot," *Time Magazine*, April 9, 1990.

11. Two excellent examples of the "innovation" genre are Rosabeth Kantor's *The Changemasters*, Simon and Schuster: (New York: 1983) and Gifford Pinchot's *Intrapreneuring*, Harper & Row, (New York: 1985).

12. "Prior Adjustments: Japanese executives going overseas to take anti-shock course," *Wall Street Journal*, January 12, 1987.

13. Zey, Michael. "A mentor for all reasons." *Personnel Journal*, January 1988.

Preface
to the Original Edition

This book looks at the ways that connecting with a mentor affects people's careers, increases their chances of success, and enhances the quality of their work life. A mentor, a senior person in an organization who oversees the development and progress of a junior person, a protege, can have a powerful effect on the junior person's career. The aim of this book is to help the reader both understand the workings of the mentor relationship and learn how to apply that knowledge to improve his or her career.

My interest in this subject stemmed from several years of studying organizations and management and looking at how individual employees cope and thrive in the organizational environment. I found, however, that when the subject of success in an organization was dealt with, whether in my own research or in the literature, something was missing—the mentor relationship. In discussions with a circle of friends in business, I became curious about the influence that this "mentor connection" had on career progress.

This book, based on interviews conducted over a two-year period with dozens of managers in large and small corporations, examines mentoring and advises how mentoring can be employed as a means of gaining upward mobility. The book explores such issues as the strategies employed in acquiring a mentor, the factors important in selecting a mentor, and the handling of relationships with peers, co-workers, and direct supervisors. It also examines the pitfalls of these relationships and how to avoid them.

In short, this book is about politics in the modern corporation. And specifically, it looks at mentoring within this political environment.

While based on studies of managers, the book is not aimed only at that group. It is meant to help everyone who is currently working or plans to work, including business students and white-collar workers who want to improve their position. A mentor is useful at all levels, from top management down to clerical ranks.

Furthermore, my study reveals that the mentor relationship is not only important for the mentor and the protege. It also offers benefits to the employing organization. I have found that improvement in productivity, reduction in turnover, and a strengthening of the corporate culture are by-products of the mentor relationship. I therefore present guidelines and parameters for initiating a formal mentoring program within the corporation. Hence, this book should be useful to personnel departments, human resource specialists, and consultants involved in the areas of organizational development.

This book was written in the belief that my research into the mentor relationship could help the readers improve their chances for career success as well as expand their knowledge about the way the corporate world works. I hope that it will also encourage organizations to adopt formal programs to stimulate the development of mentor-protege relationships. Such programs, in turn, could positively affect productivity and management development.

Acknowledgments

A book of this type cannot be completed without the help of others. I would like to thank Maryanne DeVanna and Neil Plackcy of Columbia University, Cynthia Epstein and Gaye Tuchman of CUNY-Graduate Center, and Charles Nanry of Rutgers University for their guidance and assistance and Cathy S. Greenblat for her comments on early drafts of the research proposal.

A special thanks must go to Beth Cantor of the Association of MBA Executives for helping me acquire respondents for my study. Her tireless efforts in coordinating much of the research procedure made writing this book much easier. I would also like to thank Rose Silva of Baruch College-CUNY for her assistance in this study.

My wife, Cynthia Zey, gets special accolades for her help in revising the manuscript and her insights into the business world.

I would also like to thank Carol Ann Donchin, who "word-processed" this manuscript through its several stages. Her cooperation and efficiency made it possible to meet the various publishing deadlines.

This manuscript was completed while I was a fellow under NIMH Grant #5 T32 MH16373–03.

Michael G. Zey

1

Mentoring in the Modern Corporation

Under the guise of a single name, two parallel organizations exist. They act alike, speak alike, look alike, answer to the same label, and reside in the same building. One is the organization described by charts, newspaper clippings, reports to the stockholders, and management consultants. The other is a shadow organization, an all-too-real parallel entity based on power and politics that is only faintly reflected in the organization charts. The residents of this shadow organization are sometimes called contacts, insiders, or sponsors, but usually they are referred to as mentors and proteges.

To most of the corporation, the mentor relationship is a rumor. If the members of the firm know what that relationship is, not many know what it does, how it works, why its members become powerful, or how people gain access to it. This is not unlike the view that many citizens have of the dynamics of power in the government and society in general. They see bankers meeting in Geneva, an oil cartel convening in London, the queen of England horseback riding with the president of the United States, and they know that something important is taking place. But if you asked 100 of these observers exactly what was discussed, why, and how it would affect their lives, you would receive 100 different answers.

The operation and development of the mentor relationship is

exemplified by the career of Dan Garner. A Harvard MBA, Garner began his business career at the Communications Corporation* as a financial analyst and was soon promoted to financial manager.

After two years in the company, Garner received what he labels "the phone call" from the president (who had met him only in business situations), requesting that he take a temporary position as the president's "special assistant." Considered to be both a plush assignment and an acid test given only to a bright young executive, the position involved mopping up various loose ends of corporate affairs. But more important than the substance of the position was the fact that it afforded Garner a high degree of visibility.

> *"It was a year of enormous and intense congressional testimony in the communications area, which I prepared and was involved with. . . . I was our representative in working through all the issues with high government officials."*

The president of the domestic division of the Communications Corporation, pleased with Garner's work, promoted him to group director of planning. From that time on, the president acted as Garner's mentor, teaching him management skills, protecting him from competing organizational factions, and helping establish his legitimacy as a viable part of senior management. In other words, the president groomed Garner for a major policy position within the corporation.

The president eventually moved Garner up to vice president of planning and business development. Now, at a fairly young age, Dan Garner, having surpassed most of his peers and elders, is one of the eight senior people surrounding the president. In a comparatively short time he has assumed enormous responsibilities, including strategic planning and advising on all related issues regarding acquisitions, sales force allocations, and licensing.

Garner also serves as an internal consultant on issues relating to public policy in the communications field, helping to formulate corporate policy on such matters as communications law and image building among communications professionals. Available to him are a huge staff and outside resources, including a former presidential pollster and a director at one of the nation's largest public opinion research corporations. He is now functioning in both the financial and policy areas.

Dan Garner's experience with the mentor relationship is typical of the experience of the managers who appear in this book. A young

---

*The names of individuals and their employing organizations are fictitious in order to ensure confidentiality.

female whose career languished until she connected with a female vice president, a senior vice president who for 30 years underwent a sort of sequential mentoring by several individuals, a college English major who became director of personnel at a Fortune 500 company largely because she encountered her future mentor while participating in a senior-year internship program, a high-level advertising executive whose mentor helped him realize that his real strength lay in becoming a "corporate entrepreneur" instead of remaining an accountant—all stand as solid testimony to the power of the mentor relationship.

This book, based on over 100 interviews with senior and middle managers, shows how individuals are helped in their careers by mentors who advertise and market their proteges, protect them from organizational pressures, and serve as personal counselors and supporters. The book also examines the factors that cause a mentor relationship to fail and the special problems that female proteges face in the climb up the managerial ladder. In addition, it deals with the methods that managers and others have employed to connect with mentors, and it looks at the factors within the organization that affect the mentoring process.

The book is aimed not only at managers but at the wide array of people up and down organizational ladders who are interested in improving their careers and enhancing their chances of making the "mentor connection."

THE RENEWED INTEREST IN MENTORING

Traditionally, organizational literature has suggested a link between mentoring and career advancement. Eugene Jennings, in *Routes to the Executive Suite*, indicated that most company presidents have had sponsors who guided and promoted them, stating that "no one goes to the top rapidly without a sponsor."[1] In a *Harvard Business Review* article based on interviews with Jewel Tea Company executives, the point was emphasized that "everyone who makes it has a mentor".[2] This view is supported by Orth and Jacobs, who found that business people who could not identify a mentor or sponsor were reported as being less successful and less happy in their careers.[3]

In short, the connection between career success and having a mentor has been far from a well-guarded secret. But in the last few years there has been a substantial increase in the number of articles on mentoring appearing in the popular press, women's magazines, and business publications. The growing interest in the subject seems to have been generated by a combination of economic and sociological circumstances.

The heightened interest in mentoring as a method of achieving career success can first of all be viewed as a product of the demographic realities of our time. Members of the baby boom generation, having experienced overcrowded high schools, colleges, and dorms, housing shortages, and fierce job competition, are finally reaching the age at which individuals expect to assume an occupational position of authority and responsibility.

But according to Michael Wachter, this group is still haunted by the specter of shortages and overcrowding—this time in the area of career advancement.

> The baby boom children grew up in an atmosphere of continuing increases in real wealth and per capita income. Their aspiration levels, therefore, were affected not only by their parents, but also by the idea that upward mobility was a feature of American life. As they entered the labor market, however, they found conditions very different from those they had expected. Competing with a large group of entry-level workers, the baby boom generation found their relative wages down and their promotion possibilities reduced.[4]

According to a poll recently reported in *The Wall Street Journal*, a high proportion of the baby boom group expect to get their most immediate and meaningful life satisfaction from their jobs.[5] Part of job satisfaction lies in promotion, which has traditionally been contingent on education and ability. However, if Wachter is correct, education and ability, if unrecognized by the employing organization, will be insufficient for satisfactory upward mobility. In fact, many recent articles have reported that even the MBA degree is losing its effectiveness as a key to business success. A recent *New York Times* article reported that in 1982 over 58,000 men and women received their MBA degrees, compared to 21,000 only 10 years earlier and an average of 5,000 in the 1960s. The article indicated that within 20 years more than 1 million MBAs might be trying to reach the upper rungs of the business world.[6] Moreover, in addition to MBAs, countless others with claims of ability and experience will be trying to climb the corporate ladder. But there will just not be that much room at the top, so that methods other than obtaining educational credentials will have to be utilized to achieve success.

The *New York Times* article also claimed that "middle managers are getting squeezed out." Because many companies must run leaner operations, they are forced to lay off many middle managers. At times they even reach into the higher ranks to find dispensable employees. The auto and steel industries were singled out in this article, but such conglomerates as Allied Corporation in Morristown, New Jersey, and Scovill, Inc., in Connecticut, were also mentioned. The appearance of numerous executive placement firms and outplacement services also testifies to the fact that laid-off executives have to seek professional assistance in finding their next job, expecially since the companies to which they apply are probably undergoing their own middle-management squeeze.

Adding to the executive's woes has been the mushrooming of mergers and acquisitions. According to one account, almost 2,400 corporate mergers occurred in 1981 alone, possibly because, as with U.S. Steel's acquisition of Marathon Oil, it is far easier to buy a good company than to expand one's own. In much the same way that cutbacks imperil middle managers, mergers wreak havoc with the lives and careers of senior executives. A recent study of executives involved in corporate takeovers found that 52 percent of the "acquired" executives were fired within three years after the takeover.[7] There are two reasons for the devastating effect of mergers on executive careers. First, executives who opposed a merger while their company was still independent may be unwelcome in the merged organization. Second, and more common, executives may become redundant if their functions are being performed by persons in the acquiring company.

Complicating the situation of middle and senior managers alike is the recurring recessionary condition of the economy. Even companies that are not contracting operations may still not be expanding to any great extent, and this lack of growth signifies a stagnant opportunity structure in management. In these circumstances those managers who are gainfully employed cannot expect an organizational expansion that would provide the executive slots necessary for upward mobility.

So a variety of factors obstruct managers' chances for career growth: an oversupply of equally qualified members of the same age cohort, the elimination of managers who already populate the upper-middle executive rungs, mergers that eliminate positions at the top, and economic conditions that have generated a no-growth corporate environment.

For these reasons managers have become increasingly interested in a method for achieving success that transcends the standard routes to the top. Since during low-growth and recessionary periods there is a surplus of managers with quality credentials and experience, the inside track on career success provided by the mentor connection has become particularly important to managers. This book is devoted to exploring (and advising on) this mode of achieving upward mobility.

HOW PREVALENT IS MENTORING

Though much has been written on what a mentor is, what the benefits of having a mentor are, and how to acquire a mentor, there is very little hard data on the extent of the mentoring phenomenon.

Probably the most thorough quantitative study of mentoring was done by the international consulting firm Heidrich and Struggles. The study focused on 1,250 senior executives mentioned in the "Who's News" section of *The Wall Street Journal*, with questions centering on whether a person had ever taken an interest in the careers of these executives, guided them, and sponsored them for jobs.

Overwhelmingly, the respondents answered in the affirmative, two thirds claiming that at some point in their careers they had been mentored and one third claiming that they had had the allegiance of two or more mentors. The great majority of mentoring relationships had begun in the first 5 to 10 years of the proteges' business careers. The effects of mentoring were dramatic, the mentored group exhibiting higher gross salaries, higher percentage gains in salary during their careers, and higher bonuses and total compensation than did the unmentored group.[8]

The results of the Heidrich and Struggles study have often been interpreted as proof of the high incidence of the mentor relationship in industry. In reality, the data are misleading. As any reader familiar with the "Who's News" section of *The Wall Street Journal* can confirm, the executives it features represent, not the average manager, but a highly select group of business superachievers: chairmen or presidents of large firms, senior and group vice presidents of Fortune 500 companies, officers and presidents of the largest nonindustrial companies. Hence, the study, while confirming the belief that mentoring is an overriding factor in business success, does not paint a useful picture of the incidence of mentoring at all levels of business. From the data, we might mistakenly assume that two thirds of all managers, regardless of their organizational rank, are mentored.

The rarity of the mentoring process in the corporate world as a whole is striking. Fewer than one in three of my respondents had ever participated in this type of relationship, and fewer still had colleagues who were acting as mentors or proteges. From this it would seem either that mentoring relationships are kept well hidden (which is unlikely since part of the mentoring process is the open identification of the protege with the senior executive) or, more logically, that they occur very infrequently.

TOWARD A WORKING DEFINITION OF THE MENTOR CONCEPT

The concept of the "mentor" has been fraught with misunderstanding. People intermix the concepts of the coach, sponsor, teacher, "rabbi," and "godfather" with the concept of the mentor to such an extent that it is impossible to fathom what functions and entities they are referring to.

The mentor concept has been considered from a number of perspectives. The Woodlands Group divided overseeing roles into the roles of the coach, the sponsor, and the mentor. As a coach, a senior executive helps a subordinate meet specific growth needs; as a sponsor, he actively pursues promotional activities for a protege. In the mentor role, termed the most "significant" that a senior person could play, he guides, directs, and develops the protege.[9] Shapiro, Hazeltine, and Rowe also viewed the mentor role as the deepest form of supportive role and developed a continuum of supportive relationships that ran from peer through coach, sponsor, and finally mentor.[10] Daniel J. Levinson, in *The Seasons of a Man's Life*, perceived the mentor as a guide, teacher, and sponsor, an admixture of good father and good friend, who invited the young man into the adult world.[11]

My working definition of the mentor has been derived from both the literature on the subject and my own research. A mentor is a person who **oversees** the career and development of another person, usually a junior, through teaching, counseling, providing psychological support, protecting, and at times promoting or sponsoring. The mentor may perform any or all of the above functions during the mentor relationship.

As a teacher, the mentor imparts various organizational and occupational skills to the protege; instructs the protege in the power and political framework of the organization, perhaps divulging inside information; and gives the protege tips on corporate comportment and social grace.

As a counselor and source of psychological support the mentor generally tries to build the protege's sense of self through "pep talks," confidence building, and the like.

As an intervenor, the mentor actually intercedes on behalf of the protege, at some times protecting the protege when organizational pressures become too overbearing, at other times advertising the protege as a "good manager."

As a sponsor, the mentor either promotes the protege into a higher position (if the mentor has the power to do so) or influences the "powers that be" to promote the protege.

It is clear that these functions provide solid benefits to the protege: knowledge, personal growth, protection, and career advancement. The benefits that the protege receives through the mentor relationship will be explored and described in detail in Chapters 2 and 3.

THE HIERARCHY OF MENTORING

The protege's ultimate reason for participating in a mentor relationship is that the relationship helps him progress in his career. But although all four of the general functions referred to above—teaching, counseling, organizational intervention, and promotion—assist the protege in one way or another, the contributions that these functions make to his career progress are not of equal value. In fact, the functions can be arranged into a logical hierarchy according to the relative contribution that each makes to the protege's managerial development and advancement (see Table 1–1).

TABLE 1–1
The Hierarchy of Mentoring

Level	Mentoring Activity	Benefit to Protege	Primary Mentor Investment
IV	Sponsoring	Protege is recommended by mentor for promotion, more responsibility	Reputation/career
III	Organizational intervention	Mentor intercedes on protege's behalf in organizational setting; runs interference for protege where needed	Organizational relationships, reputation
II	Psychological counseling/ personal support	Mentor enhances protege's sense of self through confidence building, pep talks, may help protege's personal life on occasion	Emotion/self
I	Teaching	Protege receives instruction in organizational skills, management tricks, social graces; is given inside information	Time

For instance, when a mentor engages in teaching, he affords the protege the ability to perform his job better, expand his knowledge of the field, and learn the subtleties of organizational survival. Such mentoring is not equivalent in career importance to the mentoring in which the mentor actively intervenes on the protege's behalf. At this level in the mentoring hierarchy, the protege's abilities as a manager are being advertised rather than improved and the protege is being protected from organizational pressures that might become destructively overbearing without the mentor's assistance. And none of the mentor's other activities are as valuable to the protege as actual promotion by the mentor into a position of higher authority, salary, and status. Chapters 2 and 3 will present a full description of the ways in which the mentoring functions are actualized in the mentor relationship and of their effects on the protege's career.

A number of issues regarding the various mentoring functions must be addressed. I am not suggesting that these functions represent mutually exclusive stages in the mentor relationship, that the relationship necessarily moves from a teaching stage to an intervention stage to a promotion stage. Actually, the mentor can perform any or all of the functions whenever the need for them arises. The need (or lack of need) for the benefits of mentoring varies at different points in the protege's career, depending both on the protege's personal circumstances and on the organization itself.

Hence, overseeing another person's career often entails engaging, either simultaneously or sequentially, in teaching, counseling, and promoting. The mentor may act as a sponsor without offering psychological help or may act as a protector while offering only minor teaching assistance. One sees this especially in the case of older executives, whose needs vis-à-vis mentors have evolved over time. An older executive, with far less need for instruction than that of the executive fresh out of business school, may receive less mentoring in the teaching sense than in the interventionist or promotional sense. Thus, the help elicited from or offered by the mentor depends on the protege's stage of career development.

It should be indicated here that the higher the level of mentoring, and the greater its concomitant benefits, the greater the investment of the mentor.

When the mentor serves as a teacher, the primary element that he invests, or risks, is *time*. If the imparting of wisdom occurs on the job, the mentor will be required to utilize lunch hours or other time that he would ordinarily spend at his own activities. If it occurs during nonwork time, the mentor's social life or family life will be reduced by the time he spends on the mentor relationship.

At the personal support/counseling level, the mentor's primary investment is *emotion*. Here the mentor is giving of himself as well as his time. A substantial investment of emotion is required to help the protege work through off-the-job or on-the-job interpersonal problems, to bolster the protege against particular incidents of cold feet and general fears of failure, or to advise the protege on how to save a marriage that is crumbling under organizational and career pressures (and then to tell the protege's wife what he told the protege).

At the intervention level, the relationship between the mentor and the protege is "out of the closet." The mentor now announces to the organization that Joe Smith has a number of good qualities and that the mentor thinks enough of Joe to advertise and market him and to protect him from his peers if necessary. In publicly proclaiming the relationship, the mentor assumes a formidable risk. Now the mentor's judgment is on the line among fellow managers and seniors, the implication being that a poor judgment about a protege signifies an inability to judge not only people but also business trends and whole categories of business-related items. The mentor is risking his reputation.

However, the greatest risk to the mentor occurs at the sponsorship level. Here the mentor actually moves the protege into a position of responsibility. A senior manager would not sponsor a person unless absolutely sure of his ability to perform, but there is always the risk that the senior manager will miscalculate and that the sponsored person will fail in the new position. The consequence for the mentor may be more drastic than a tarnished reputation. The mentor may be demoted or even expelled from the organization.

THE BENEFITS ARE MUTUAL

It is obvious that at each of the mentoring levels the protege receives basic benefits. At Level I, he learns about job, organization, and career, and at the higher levels he receives the benefits of organizational advancement. Most analyses concentrate on the effect of the mentor relationship on the protege and refer only casually to the solid benefits that the mentor or the organization may receive from the relationship.

However, as will become apparent later on, the mentor does not engage in the relationship merely to satisfy an altruistic impulse. In fact, the career benefits of the relationship to the mentor may be as striking as the benefits that accrue to the protege. The protege helps the mentor do his job, serves the mentor as a source of organizational information and intelligence, and often becomes the mentor's trusted adviser.

And as will be detailed in Chapter 4, the organization may also derive benefits from the mentor relationship: a smoothly functioning managerial team, a properly socialized employee, an integrated worker. In fact, the main benefit of the mentor relationship to the organization may well lie in the fact that it provides a clear model of managerial succession, since it ensures the passing of organizational values and culture from one generation of managers to another.

As demonstrated in Figure 1–1, an exchange relationship exists between the mentor, the protege, and the organization. This three-way interrelationship is known as the *Mutual Benefits Model*. The arrows in the figure represent the benefits that are transferred. They

FIGURE 1-1
The Mutual Benefits Model

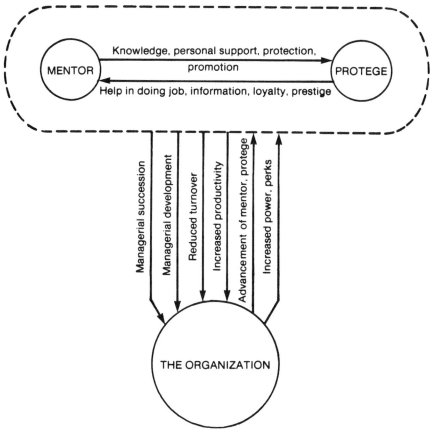

show that the mentor gives the protege support and protection and that the protege helps the mentor do his job, build his empire. The figure also indicates that the mentor relationship transfers benefits to the organization (a well-oiled management team, a well-developed manager, a protege able to maintain corporate traditions and values) and that in exchange for these benefits the organization advances the position and increases the power of both the mentor and the protege.

The model presented in Figure 1-1 is not an idealized depiction of the mentor relationship but a reflection of the way in which the mentor relationships presented in this book really work. The exchange of benefits will be explored at length in Chapters 2, 3, and 4.

Not all mentor relationships operate according to plan. As will be described in Chapter 6, when mentor relationships fail or deteriorate, this is usually because one or more of the parties perceive that they are not receiving benefits from the relationship, either because parties are unable to deliver the expected benefits or because the relationship is seen as not serving the organization.

Because most discussions about mentoring completely overlook the impact, whether negative or positive, that the mentor relationship can have on the organization, they do not take into account the fact that the relationship cannot survive unless the organization is a "willing partner" to it.

THE PLAN OF THIS BOOK

In this chapter I have presented a short introduction to the mentor relationship and its importance for the reader. Chapters 2, 3, and 4 detail the many benefits derived from the relationship by the mentor, the protege, and the organization. Case studies are utilized to illustrate those benefits.

A special topic in this book is the female protege, the subject of Chapter 5. The chapter examines the mentor's role in solving some of the problems encountered by female managers. Chapter 6 treats the negative side of mentoring. It shows why mentor relationships sometimes fail and the effects of such failures on the mentor, the protege, and the organization.

Chapter 7 deals with the mechanics and strategies involved in attracting, choosing, and keeping a mentor. It also describes the methods that members of the mentor relationship have developed to maintain good relations with peers and senior management. Chapter 8 looks to the future of industry and asks what role mentoring will play in the careers of the young managers who are now moving into positions in middle and senior management. It explores the possibility of establishing formalized mentoring programs as one response to industry's need for managerial and organizational development.

2

The Fast Track

Managers enter into mentor relationships for a variety of reasons and with a wealth of expectations, but their primary reason is that they expect to receive certain benefits from doing so. While friendship, chemistry, and empathy serve as motivators for establishing an alliance with a particular mentor or protege, at root the mentor relationship exists and thrives only to the extent that the participants expect their careers to be positively affected by it. In the next three chapters I will explore the benefits that the mentor and the protege receive from the relationship. I will also examine the positive implications of the relationship for the organization.

In this chapter we will see how the mentor puts the protege on the "fast track." Here the mentor's role is to make the protege more powerful, to facilitate the protege's access to various resources and skills that will enhance his ability to operate effectively within the organizational environment. We will be dealing with the first three Levels in the Hierarchy of Mentoring: the mentor teaches the protege, provides the protege with psychological support, and markets the protege and protects him from overbearing organizational pressures. (The next chapter will deal extensively with the Level IV function, the actual promotion of the protege.)

When I first began to investigate the mentor relationship, I had a general idea, gleaned both from readings and from friends and acquaintances in business, of the types of benefits that the protege could expect from having a mentor. What I did not realize was the depth of mentor relationships, the amount of time and energy involved in them, and the intricacies involved in helping a protege advance in an organization. "Training," the imparting of skills, seemed fairly uncomplicated. But as the case studies in this book will demonstrate, even training a protege requires an extraordinary commitment from the mentor.

LEVEL I—THE MENTOR AS TEACHER

This section will deal with the most basic level of mentoring, the teaching function. Since the classic concept of the mentor involved the functions of teaching, coaching, and overseeing the development of the protege, an analysis of the benefits of mentoring for the protege should rightly begin at this point. (For a summary of the teaching function, see Table 2–1.)

TABLE 2–1
Level I—The Teaching Function

Teaching the job	The mentor imparts a feel for the job, a knowledge of the skills needed to perform it, and information on trends in the field. The mentor also shows the protege the best methods for managing people in the organization and the importance of support from below.
Drawing the organizational road map	The mentor transfers information about non-skill aspects of organizational life: politics, the personalities of corporate managers, and the correct presentation of self. In general, the mentor transmits "state secrets" to the protege—information about corporate finances and other classified data.
Career guidance	The mentor provides the protege with a picture of the career paths available inside and outside the corporation. This often involves redirecting the protege from his chosen specialty into a field more suited to the protege's skills.

A major way to advance in an organization is to receive correct information about one's job, profession, career, and organization. Mentoring can benefit the protege by providing a wide array of instruction in these areas, through both indirect and direct mechanisms.

Teaching the Job

Any supervisor can teach a subordinate, and in fact by definition the supervisor's position requires a certain amount of teaching. But the mentor-protege relationship entails a degree of interaction of greater breadth and intensity than are usually present in the superior-subordinate interaction.

The success of the relationship depends in large part on the ability of the protege to learn. The protege must be a good listener and observer and must come to realize that being on the receiving end of the mentor's advice and instruction is not a sign of ignorance but a gateway to essential knowledge and eventual success.

The key to a fuller understanding of this process is the fact that while the supervisor teaches the subordinate to do the subordinate's job, the mentor teaches the protege to do the mentor's job. In short, the mentor is grooming a successor and must demonstrate all the care and attention required for that task.

The Transmission of Skills I was interested in learning exactly what contribution the mentor made to the protege's acquisition of job skills. I was surprised to find that the mentor directly intervened, at times to a dramatic extent, in the protege's on-the-job training.

In this age of the generalist, many managers are hired into their positions with only a minimum knowledge of the specific industry. They therefore need instruction in the employer's products, the employer's methods of manufacturing and distribution, and so on. Thus it is not uncommon for the mentor-protege relationship to initially assume a primarily teacher-student flavor. For instance, Dan Garner, the senior vice president of the Communications Corporation, whom we met in Chapter 1, had to ingest a huge amount of information about his concern's activities to advance so quickly. The communications industry is constantly beset by problems: the size of the communications companies and the power that a few giants wield over the entire industry tend to attract public attention and mobilize political opposition. In order to serve as a senior-level manager with both administrative and policy-related responsibilities, Garner had to undergo a period of apprenticeship. During this period, not only were marketing-type skills transmitted to him, but he was afforded an environment in which he could acquire a sense of the industry's unique public position.

"To say that my mentor taught me everything I know about the business is trite and not accurate. Let's just say that through observation and participation I've developed a facility with the industry and with the business that I'm amazed at. I'm amazed at what I know when I meet with other people,

*or when I'm down at the Hill in Washington these days. I'm truly amazed
at the process of osmosis, the kinds of things he's tugged me through and
involved me in."*

Rapid changes in any industry make the mentor's role as teacher particularly crucial. The many transformations in the banking industry have required its managers to continually develop new skills. A number of the persons interviewed who had been transferred from less technical areas of banking into more technical areas, such as loans, felt lost until they met their mentors. One of them said:

*"He's taught me how to negotiate a loan agreement, making sure things are
done right. His strength was in planning, especially from a marketing point
of view . . . how to approach a customer."*

This woman, now a vice president at a large bank, attributes her perception of her bank as primarily a marketing organization, with customers who must be satisfied, to her mentor's handling of her on-the-job training. She came into the loan department with a background in credit and a keen understanding of cash flows and ratios, but these skills were only a small part of being a lending officer. The mentor eased her transition into a marketing function, teaching her the mechanics of selling the bank's business.

John Levine, a former economics professor at a small midwestern college, underwent a rough transition when he entered the harsh and competitive world of management consulting within a major accounting firm. He claims that his confidence about his ability to perform is greater because his learning took place within a mentoring relationship that allowed him to painlessly assume ever greater responsibility.

*"You learn to be a consultant the way someone used to learn to read the law.
You watch someone else doing it for a while. Then you do it in little bits, with
somebody coaching you, viewing quite closely what it is you do. Then, as
you get better at it, you get to do bigger things with less coaching."*

The mentor offers shortcuts in the learning process. One respondent acquired a position as product manager at the Goodbrands Corporation with a good background in strategic planning, advertising, the media, and the creative side of business. However, she was a complete novice when it came to technical product research, packaging decisions, and so forth. The mentor, a vice president at the company, spent several months orienting her to the technical side of the business.

Often the mentor must impart a "feel" for the business or industry. David Dorwin, a recently promoted vice president at the Crandall Advertising Agency, a medium-sized firm, received a complete "conceptual reorientation" on the nature of advertising and the relationship between the agency and the client.

> *"He's taught me that in this type of relationship I must be the expert. Even though they are the client and they manufacture the product, I should know more about anything going on in this product than they do. In other words, I must make them need the agency."*

The skills garnered from this mentor-protege relationship have been invaluable. An unmentored account executive might have become a mere messenger between the agency and the client. The mentor taught Dorwin that the client needed direction and that the agency should conduct research on the needs of its industry, economic trends, and changes in consumer buying behavior. Since Dorwin's specialty is the highly competitive area of health care, this outlook is especially appropriate. His ability to read the client and to be better prepared than the client at strategic interactions is a product of the mentor-protege relationship.

Proteges, far from being passive recipients of knowledge, are often quite selective in the information and skills that they absorb from the mentor. As Dorwin confides, "I find I can take some of what's being offered to me, and take some of that and not use it." Dorwin's mentor, a senior vice president of the advertising firm, favors giving impromptu speeches at agency-client meetings, but David, realizing his own limitations and strengths, knows that he must get the "facts" before he enters a room.

> *"I'm a good presenter, but I must do homework and have all the facts straight. I don't get nervous when I speak because I know what I'm going to say and I know it better than anyone else sitting there."*

Hence, one can "learn" from the mentor by consciously not emulating some of his actions. In short, the mentoring experience presents an array of behavior, some acceptable for the protege, some not. Because the mentor and protege are different, some of the mentor's behavior is not adopted by the protege.

I think that the strength of the mentor relationship as a teaching device for the protege is that it gives the protege a source of information who accepts his lack of skills. All too often, what becomes important in business is having the right answers and not asking the wrong questions. At certain levels of the organization, "asking questions" is considered a sign of ignorance, and the young manager does so at his own risk. But the mentor-protege relationship expands the areas of inquiry permissible for the protege and thus accelerates his learning experience.

People Management If imparting knowledge about the technical side of a position falls within the realm of science, transferring wisdom regarding people management must be considered an art. Fresh from their MBA programs, many young managers are infused with the warm glow of cost-benefit analyses, econometric models, and sundry forms of financial wizardry, but the actual management of people is a skill that may elude them throughout their careers. Having a mentor can help them gain proficiency in this area of expertise and thus approach total managerial effectiveness.

Dan Garner, our senior vice president at the Communications Corporation, notes that his mentor "has marvelous traits of people management that I've tried to adopt." But how does the protege learn "people management"? Garner feels that simple observation can serve as a potent learning technique.

> "I've watched meetings where the participants have been polarized at the beginning of the meeting. My mentor will say virtually nothing at the meeting for an hour and a half. Here's an important person, impatient with time, efficiency, everything, who will just light up a cigar, just sit back and watch, let the group grind itself into consensus. He does this in such a way that no one loses face."

Since Garner's mentor allows him to sit near the seat of power and observe, Garner is afforded an opportunity to absorb management techniques that his mentor took 30 years to perfect. This method produces results that transcend those obtainable by mere verbal teaching.

> "I found myself doing many of the same things that he's done in meetings on very controversial issues. I found myself following the same patterns. Every now and then you'll stop yourself and say, 'My God, I'm doing exactly what my mentor would do if he were sitting in the room right now.' And you realize that it's not the behavior that would have come naturally eight years ago."

I asked Garner if he could describe what he claimed were radical changes in his managerial behavior. His answer reflected his growing awareness that management by consensus was much more effective and enduring than management by decree.

"Eight years ago, I would have walked in, pounded my fist on the table, and said, 'Well, goddamn it, we gotta arrive at a decision, so what's the answer?' I would never do that today."

Nan McKendrick, a general manager of merchandising who is being mentored by a powerful female vice president at the Woman-goods Corporation, has acquired similar insights into the management process.

"She taught me that one leads, not by authority, but by commanding respect —by showing that you try to do your best and respecting other people, rather than demanding."

Mentoring seems to help proteges understand that building a support team and infusing it with a sense of cohesiveness is the shortest route to an efficient operation. More important, they learn that if the support team feels that it is making a contribution and senses that this contribution is valued by the supervisor, it will perform in a cooperative and enthusiastic manner. John O'Hanlon, a senior vice president at Smith & Pitts, one of the nation's largest advertising agencies, believes that his management style was influenced by the mentor's insistence on the establishment of team cohesion and the mentor's tendency to instill "spirit" in the team.

"He did everything, as a leader, by the hard work, the excitement, the intellect, congratulating people, supporting people, as our market share was turning around. He just built a totally supportive, cohesive unit."

John's mentor also taught him to secure people he could believe in and then to give new recruits complete support.

Most of the respondents demonstrate quite clearly that the mentoring experience has increased their awareness that their success depends on the level of loyalty they receive from the supporting staff. In a way, the mentor relationship becomes a model for relationships that the protege eventually develops within his own support group. In that sense, mentoring generates a whole series of support chains.

For the last five years Nick Ford, a commercial general manager at the Goodbrands Corporation, has been the mentor of Christine Webster, who is now a logistics manager. In listening to the two of them, I could see the similarities in their managerial styles. Nick constantly emphasized the necessity of the "team approach" in management, and when I interviewed his protege a few weeks later, her comments sharply reflected his belief that building team cohesion was a proven method for getting the job done.

"Let the staff members establish their own turf, give them room to breathe, and make them responsible for what they've done."

I am not sure that Nick Ford ever explained his views on team building to Christine, but it is obvious that her management style has evolved into one that reflects his approach.

Close tutoring in people management skills is especially important for proteges who obtain powerful positions early in their careers. Through the intervention of her mentor, Doreen Tokama was made an officer of the Bank of the East Orient at a relatively young age. She was placed at the head of a staff consisting of older middle managers. Doreen's mentor told her that these managers were bound to be resentful toward her. He suggested that in order to avoid conflicts she run her new department "democratically," soliciting suggestions from the old-timers and thus convincing them that she valued their years of experience.

Faced with uncooperative older subordinates, many young managers become panicky and adopt management techniques that border on coercion. But Doreen was able to fill a powerful position comfortably without alienating her older subordinates. Fortunately, she had a mentor who counseled her through a difficult period.

Many of the proteges I interviewed also felt that their mentors had instilled in them an appreciation of the value of the clerical staff and an understanding of how power was brokered through it. One of the keys to executive success is the secretary—the manager's own secretary and the secretaries of colleagues. An executive who does not comprehend early the power that secretaries wield over the flow of information and general office activity is courting professional disaster.

From a purely functional point of view, having a cooperative and happy secretary means that work will get out on time, letters will be typed, and callers will be handled courteously. But secretaries also have a wide range of informal power. They serve as the executive's gatekeeper, preselecting who gets appointments, who can have lunch with him. They regulate the flow of information to the executive, deciding what will or will not filter into his office. In some cases, they even handle aspects of the executive's personal life. As one protege informed me:

"Secretaries are secretaries for someone, and they know other secretaries for other people. And they probably very often know about things much before other people."

In other words, secretarial networks serve as informational systems. Early on, this protege's mentor had taught him the necessity of treating secretaries and other clerical people with respect, a matter that had certainly not been a primary concern of the protege when he embarked on his business career.

One woman manager, an assistant to the vice president of a large bank, did not know how to deal with a secretary who was spending a good part of the workday talking on the telephone. She considered dragging the secretary into her office and demanding that the secretary do her job. But before reading the riot act to the secretary, she wisely approached her mentor with the problem. The mentor suggested that she ask the secretary why she spent so much time on the phone, implying that family problems might be the reason. He believed that a compromise could be reached. The protege discussed the matter with the secretary and discovered that family problems were indeed the cause of the phone calls. The difficulty was resolved when the two of them agreed that the secretary would delay her personal calls until the heaviest part of the workday was over.

From the many examples of coaching in the human relations area disclosed by proteges, it becomes obvious that without a mentor many of them would have committed errors in personnel matters that could have hindered their career advancement. But these examples make it equally obvious that through direct advice leadership skills can indeed be taught and that this transfer of managerial wisdom occurs optimally within a close mentor-protege relationship.

A Matter of Technique There exists no instructional manual explaining to the mentor the most effective methods for imparting knowledge regarding technical skills and management style. Yet most mentors seem to have developed effective methods for transferring technique (see Table 2–2).

One goal of the mentoring process seems to be the development of the protege's capacity to think through a problem independently. When Christine Webster first moved into her logistics position, she often approached her mentor with problems, demanding hard-and-

TABLE 2–2
Techniques Utilized in Teaching Protege Job

1. Nondirective pedagogic methods that give protege a sense of non-dependence, efficacy.
2. Socratic questioning.
3. Encouraging protege to "learn by doing" under close supervision.
4. Role participation—involving protege in decision-making process. This allows protege to adopt a "freeze frame" approach to stop mentor's actions and question their rationale.

fast solutions. But in typical mentor style Nick Ford threw the challenges back to her, exclaiming, "You tell me what you think, and I'll fill in the holes." In this way, the protege was forced to think her way through problems. The rationale behind this technique is that the protege learns more about people and the job when forced to mull through all the steps in the management process than when he or she merely receives prepackaged guidance.

In a sense, what emerges from the data is the mentor's utilization of the Socratic method.

> *"I felt that my mentor took the responsibility to teach me how to do the job. If I had a question about what decision was to be made, instead of answering the question, he would question me. I actually came out with the solution myself. Then he would tell me, 'See, I knew you knew the answer.' Eventually, you would start asking the questions yourself."*

What becomes evident is that the mentor is attempting to instill a sense of self-reliance in the protege. The mentor wants the protege to acquire a feel for issues and problems instead of mere knowledge about how to carry out a particular assignment. What is really at issue is not what to do in a specific instance but how to think as a manager.

The learning process is not without its difficulties. For instance, the mentor must always be aware of the protege's tendency to depend on the mentor for the right answer, the correct explanation. One mentor overcame this difficulty by adopting a middle-ground stance when the protege had problems or questions.

> *"She gives me enough rope so that I can give it a shot myself but not so much that I'll end up hanging myself."*

In other words, the mentor, while realizing the drawbacks of "learning by doing," knows that this technique is an effective means for giving the protege a feel for the organization and the job.

This nondirective technique is reported by many respondents. Geraldine Links, a business manager at the Steel Corporation, indicates that it has been especially effective in her development as a manager. Her mentor, wanting her to have equal input into her own learning process, will suggest three or four approaches to a given problem and encourage her to choose among them while helping her understand the implications of the alternatives.

Most important, mentors make certain that the learning experience is a challenging one. They structure the learning environment so that what could be a rote ingestion of skills becomes transformed into a richly challenging and varied experience. This method is so effective that proteges absorb it into their own teaching style.

What most differentiates the teaching experience of the mentor-protege relationship from that of the mere supervisor-subordinate interface is the extent to which the mentor involves the protege in the decision-making process. Andrea Feders, Nan McKendrick's mentor at the Womangoods Corporation, says that one way in which she is grooming Nan for a higher position is to include Nan in the more responsible policy formation activities. In key situations she will ask Nan, "What should I do?" Another way is to allow Nan to observe her going through the motions of exercising power.

In the management and social science literature this approach is often designated as role modeling, but in the mentor-protege relationship that designation understates the power of the one-to-one interaction. A subordinate without a mentor may adopt an admired superior as a role model and attempt to fashion his technique and style after that of the superior. But in the mentor-protege relationship, the teaching activity transcends mere observation to include actual participation, so instead of role modeling what we have is *role participation.* As the protege observes the mentor making personnel decisions, launching a new advertising campaign, lending money to Mexico, or closing a plant in New Jersey, he can "stop the action," utilizing a "freeze frame" approach to question the mentor about the rationale behind the decision, suggest ways to improve the decision, and receive the mentor's feedback on his suggestions.

At this point, the mentor often breaks down into understandable parts the separate aspects of "what he is trying to do." Role participation is as different from role modeling as on-the-job training is from textbook learning. Participation is one of the most potent forms of learning.

Often during the role participation process, when the protege confronts the mentor with an idea for a new product, marketing strategy, or organizational plan, the mentor neither accepts nor rejects the approach but forces the protege to convince him of its validity. Andrea Feders favors this technique.

> "It forces the proteges into the role of selling me on why I ought to spend my money, or else it forces them to think more clearly as to how more money ought to be spent."

As will be discussed at length in Chapter 4, the mentor slowly incorporates the protege into the policy and planning process and hence must make the protege aware of the limits and capabilities of the manager within the corporate environment.

A Sense of Efficacy The teaching techniques used in the mentor relationship commonly serve to enhance the protege's confidence in his own ability as a manager. The free interchange of informa-

tion between the mentor and the protege not only teaches the protege job and managerial skills, it also imbues him with a sense of
effectiveness.

The techniques of forcing the protege to sell the mentor on ideas
are mentioned again and again. Gabe Randolph, a divisional manager
at the Goodbrands Corporation, claims:

> *"I could go in and say, 'Here's what I think; what do you think?' To be able
> to bounce ideas off him, to have the ear of somebody who was a good
> marketer, who was very good at the sort of things we were doing, was
> important."*

Exchanging ideas with a mentor enables the protege to attain a
greater understanding of the workings of the processes involved in
management than would be possible otherwise. Communication between peers has a more academic quality than communication between a mentor and a protege. In the mentor-protege exchange the
protege can envision the possibility that some of his ideas will be
implemented by the mentor. Thus the protege's concept formation
and presentation become more intense and more focused than they
would be in peer interchanges.

> *"Many people can't do that with their bosses. They end up bouncing their
> ideas off peers or subordinates who sit there and say, 'Gee, that was nice',
> but don't have the experience to help you build upon it or the power to put
> those ideas into effect. It becomes a way of preselling. If I want to do
> something next month, I could plant the seed this month."*

Even if the protege does not convince the mentor of the validity
of all his ideas, the possibility that those ideas will be put into operation increases the protege's sense of efficacy. Nan McKendrick, the
general manager of merchandising at the Womangoods Corporation,
claims that interchanges with her mentor about business planning
occur quite frequently.

> *"I could go in and argue with her about a business thing, if our perspectives
> were different, and rarely win. She knew where my mind was and how it
> worked."*

The fact that Nan feels good even when she loses an argument
shows that she is being given solid mentoring. When the protege
walks out of the mentor's office feeling that she has had the opportunity to debate the "great policy issues" with a corporate power, the
actual outcome of the discussion is less important than the fact that
it took place.

In addition to heightening the protege's sense of efficacy, these interchanges train the protege in the art of formulating convincing arguments in various business confrontations. Most important, the protege comes to believe in his own capabilities because his increasing capacity to make acceptable and coherent judgments and position statements in the mentor-protege interchange suggests to him that he is in fact becoming a better manager.

Drawing the Organizational Road Map

The mentor's teaching function goes beyond the transfer of information about managerial techinques. In order to transform the protege from a novice into a real manager, the mentor must teach him about the less visible aspects of the organization's life—its structure, politics, and personalities—and about the rudiments of survival in a bureaucracy.

On Politics and Personality Mentors continually provide their proteges with sketches of both the organization and its members, providing information that the proteges would ordinarily not be privy to or be able to discover on their own.

The issue of how to approach organizational members looms large in mentors' concerns about the political savvy of proteges. One mentor explains it in this way:

> "There are approaches to how you talk to people in management levels above you. There are kinds of what I would call positive attitudes versus negative attitudes. Not necessarily going to them and saying this is the way you're going to have to say this and this is the way you're going to say that. It's looking at the things they do that are going to cause a problem and telling them phrases that would be positive."

This mentor tries to instill in his proteges, especially the type that he labels "the young MBA with all the answers," a modicum of respect for the judgment and knowledge of senior management, and he hopes that this respect is reflected in the proteges' behavior at business meetings. He advises his proteges not to try to appear more knowledgeable than they really are at presentations and not to try to overimpress senior people who know the company and its operations well enough to realize when a junior manager is disguising ignorance.

In short, a junior person would do well to maintain some flexibility in his dealings with senior management. The mentor of Arlene Mattola, an assistant to the vice president at Northeast Federal Bank, gave her a valuable lesson on interaction with senior management. Once she and her mentor attended a business luncheon whose purpose was to straighten out certain issues between their department and a closely affiliated department. Her mentor and the vice president of the other department were of equal rank within the bank, and the methods that the mentor employed to communicate displeasure over certain issues required a great amount of tact. Afterward, the mentor explained the whys and wherefores of the many actions taken during the meeting and even decoded the body language of the participants. In the course of their relationship, he has taught Arlene how actions are perceived in the organization, how to deal with seniors, what persons tend to get irritated, and what persons are obsessed with small details.

A mentor took the time to teach Lawrence Garibaldi, a financial analyst at Magnum Enterprises, a large Fortune 500 manufacturing conglomerate, which people made the decisions that would affect him over the course of his career. And the mentor also took the time to inform him about quirks of the higher level personnel and about how to adapt his behavior to those quirks.

> *"If the division president is in a meeting, and if he feels that the meeting is starting to go astray, or he feels disinterested, he will take out his nail clipper and he will start to clip his nails. If that happens, that's an indirect cue that you should change the subject, move to the next topic, tell a joke, or change the atmosphere."*

This is information that the protege might never have picked up on his own and thus must be transmitted from mentor to protege. Proper behavior at meetings, presentation of key information, and not stepping on the wrong toes all enter into the final equation when promotions are considered.

John Levine, the management consultant, is mentored by an outsider to his accounting firm, an academic who serves as chief adviser to two of the five top principals of the firm. Because the mentor has been an adviser to these two partners since an early stage in the firm's history, he is able to give Levine a great deal of pertinent personal information about them. For instance, one of the partners is very risk averse and conservative, whereas the other is more prone to radical business maneuvers. Knowledge of the dramatic personality differences behind their identical titles is important for the young manager who must deal with these seniors on a regular basis and make business proposals to them.

Mentors are very useful to women managers in advising on their interactions with old-line managers. Nan McKendrick was informed by her mentor that she should be aware that the top management at the Womangoods Corporation consisted of men whose views of women were shaped by their own familial experiences. Since the wives of these managers had chosen life paths that excluded market employment, the managers were less than comfortable with female executives.

Nick Ford's relationship with Christine Webster actually began when she approached him about a political problem she was having with a male chauvinist engineer who believed that engineers, and specifically male engineers, were the only managers with the intelligence, background, and conceptual clarity needed to introduce and implement new products. Since Christine's job description required her to be directly involved with the introduction of new products and the development of new business, she would not advance in her career until she could deal effectively with this engineer.

At a new products meeting the engineer had dealt with her rather cruelly, and she had no idea whether she had really come across as unknowledgeable, as he had publicly claimed, or whether there had been a hidden reason for his unbridled attack. Nick Ford, who had attended the meeting, first complimented her on her professional response to what was actually an unwarranted attack, her coolness under pressure, and then proceeded to sensitize her to the territorial imperative among the engineers in her division. Ford advised her to present herself more as a product manager than as a scientist, thus reducing the threat to his job that the engineer perceived, and to discuss product innovations with the engineer only in private so that he would not be prompted to engage in such "face-saving" public attacks. The engineer's chauvinism ceased to be a problem once Christine followed this advice.

The importance for the protege of learning how to maneuver and negotiate through the subtleties of corporate politics and personalities is quite obvious. In order to ensure survival on the corporate battlefield, the protege must learn who are the best persons to approach to get something done, who are the key people in the decision-making process, which of them to talk to first, and how to make sure that other participants in the decision-making process do not feel slighted. One protege describes this process as very much behind the scenes, very low key, with as few people as possible aware of the maneuvering that takes place.

Often the quickest method that a manager can use to enhance his career is to expand the size, responsibility, or organizational position of his department. Politics can have an enormous effect on a manager's efforts to enlarge his departmental scope, and the sooner he learns the role of politics in that undertaking, the sooner he will be able to effectively develop as a manager. This process is exemplified by the case of Carl Valente, currently director of personnel development for a medium-sized services corporation. He had been mentored for several years by the staff vice president of personnel and development at a large textile rental firm, and during that period he had learned invaluable lessons about the politics of self-protection and the expansion of departmental function. His mentor had imparted not only personnel skills but also practical knowledge of several techniques for establishing and expanding the personnel function within the organization.

The role, and legitimacy, of personnel varies from organization to organization, especially because of personnel's claim to a key function within the organization, that of selecting and developing the people working within it. In Valente's company the primary battle had been between the individual departments, which desired control over the training of their own managers, and the mentor's personnel department, which wanted to perform various "gatekeeper" functions with respect to entry into the organization in general and into the departments in particular. Similar conflicts can be found in many corporations: often a particular department claims as its own prerogative the selection and training of its managers. But in this case Valente's mentor, desirous of expanding his own power, fought to establish personnel's control over the selection process. His first step was to institute a system-wide "managerial inventory" that periodically took stock of the current and prospective vacancies in various departments, a process that he coordinated with senior management. The mentor's aim was to have his department provide initial training for all employees. But conflicts were inevitable since some of the individual operating divisions had training staffs of their own.

One handicap in the mentor's quest for power was his title. In the early stages of his battle for control, the mentor's title had been director of personnel. But through various political maneuvers, he had managed to acquire the title of staff vice president of personnel and development. The creation of the staff vice president position had given the mentor a title that outstripped those of the department directors who were involved in this power play, overruled their authority, and provided the mentor with immediate nominal control over the training process.

This mentor relationship taught Valente techniques for expanding the power of the personnel function at his present company. Though Valente expresses no interest in power for its own sake, he does believe that the role of the personnel department is misunderstood by many managers, and he is now aware of the political problems involved in establishing the personnel department's credibility as an integral part of the hiring and training process.

The lessons that the mentor taught him, which he is now applying, are, first, that there is in fact a struggle for control of the hiring and training functions between personnel and the individual departments; second, that these functions must be combined into one department; and third, that personnel can establish its control over them by negotiating directly with top management, setting up uniform corporate-wide training programs, and equipping its director with a title that outranks those of the directors of individual departments.

At last contact, Carl Valente had managed to upgrade his own title, had hired a person to deal separately with the traditional personnel functions of benefits and records, and had become actively involved in the outside recruiting efforts of the various departments. His mentor had obviously been a very good teacher.

The best lesson a mentor can give the protege is that though talent and intelligence are important, the ability to grow as a manager depends largely on learning how things really work, a process that involves such issues as the quirks of senior management and the political idiosyncrasies of the organization's culture. As one respondent declares:

> *"If you don't know the rules, you can't operate. The only way to know the rules is to be invited by an insider to participate."*

Presentation of Self To operate successfully within the corporate political framework, it is necessary to establish a presentation of self that is consistent with the corporate culture. Corporate political savvy comprises a wide range of things, including personal attire and small talk at parties. One senior executive informs his proteges that the so-called fun-in-the-sun three-day business meetings are where careers are often made or lost. Consequently, he has coached them on what to say and what not to say at parties, how to approach certain people on the golf links, whom to sit with at dinner, and how much to drink.

> *"I've seen a few people's careers come to an end, they were doing very well, but their careers came to an absolute end because they overindulged and became obnoxious, overbearing. They got a lot of laughs, but I could see the guy at the top kind of cringe. He chuckled while it was going on, but within two weeks the individual was gone."*

Social gatherings seem to be a testing ground for interpersonal relationships, and this mentor directly confronts his proteges with rules about how to present themselves on such occasions.

"Don't try to overimpress somebody, try to corner them at a bar or dinner table and monopolize their conversation and tell them how great you are. A little lower key than that. . . . That one contact can make or break you from then on . . . that one impression . . . the person doesn't know you at all, and what you say at that dinner conversation can make or break you because you just don't get the exposure to those people. Their calendars are filled 12 hours a day, five days a week."

A vice president at a large company says that though "presentation of self" advice is rarely sought by the protege, she volunteers her opinion when she considers it crucial to a protege's success. If she sees that a protege is prejudicing his case by his manner of dress or if she thinks that a protege's appearance is impeding his career or that his speech habits are weak, she will offer him tips on how to improve his image.

At times, her advice is very personal, and I wondered how welcome it was when it bordered on personal criticism. She claims that the more ambitious the protege, the less he will object to advice that he perceives as a potential contribution to his managerial advancement.

"Sometimes it is very easy. If your protege is truly ambitious, you just say, 'If you want to play with the big guys, you just have to play by the rules. If they say you have to wear a necktie, you wear one.' "

She often deals with people from the creative side of her company, including art directors, advertising personnel, and copywriters, whose dress codes are quite different from those of the rest of the corporation. She has had to take some of these people aside, especially supervisors and directors, and say, "You may have noticed that no one at our staff meeting was wearing jeans." A mentor can point out to the protege that although certain self-presentations are tolerated, a young manager who does not meet image requirements, while not getting fired, may languish in middle management forever. Without a mentor, he will forever wonder why his career is lingering in limbo.

The mentor can be of great assistance when the protege is unaware of the weak image he projects. How, for instance, is a young manager to know that demonstrating an overconcern with business, especially during after-hours, can be detrimental to his career? A mentor informed a surprised protege that if he had any intention of reaching the heights of senior management, he would have to develop certain social graces and expand his conversational horizons beyond business subjects into the domains of culture and art. The senior person attempted to convey to the protege that business proficiency and knowledge are not the only components of business acumen, that one must be a well-rounded individual to communicate with clients. There is a social aspect to business, and unless the manager can develop an image in keeping with the social requirements of the corporation, he will never progress.

State Secrets Allowing the protege access to inside information, by "teaching about the organization," requires the transmission of details about organizational politics and personalities, corporate finances, and other "classified" data. In fact, for the protege's training to be complete, it must include such access.

At some point, the mentor must make available to the protege facts about the organization that would not be revealed to an ordinary subordinate. The tension between the need to reveal "state secrets" to the protege and hesitancy about doing so is often evident. In many situations, the mentor is uncertain about how much organizational information he should reveal to the protege. But most mentor relationships follow a pattern in which the mentor gradually reveals information about organizational plans, top-management personnel moves, and other matters that he was initially hesitant to transmit.

In addition to being functionally important, the divulging of organizational inside information to the protege has symbolic overtones. The transfer of organizational intelligence signals the beginning of the protege's transition into a higher management strata. Giving such information to the protege is intended to involve him in the planning and policy process and implies that he will eventually be promoted into the upper ranks. It also implies that the mentor already thinks of the protege as a functional colleague and perhaps as his successor.

However, the mentor's trust in the protege can sometimes backfire. The mentor's peers may resent the transfer of state secrets, and there is always the possibility that the protege may violate the mentor's confidence. But such possibilities are what makes these information transfers so significant, since they show that the mentor believes in the protege's trustworthiness.

Career Guidance

The last area of learning benefits that the protege derives from the mentor relationship is career guidance, both within and outside the organization. The mentor can be particularly helpful in this area since he usually has a clearer picture of the career paths available to the protege than does the protege himself.

Because of his knowledge of the organization the mentor can direct the protege into the department that represents the quickest route to success. Steve Garret, currently a vice president of international lending at the American Enterprise Bank, began his career as an accountant. His mentor informed him that the Auditing Department was not the "bread and butter" area of the bank and eventually persuaded him to enter a loan management training program within the bank. Because Steve had been directed into a growth area, his career improved dramatically from that point on.

Nick Ford of the Goodbrands Corporation feels that it is too easy for a young executive, once having achieved some success, to settle comfortably into a position.

> "I constantly tell my protege, 'I know you're comfortable over here doing what you're doing. But if you're going to move up, you're going to have to have a broadening of experience here.' "

And many young executives are unknowledgeable about the timing of their careers—about the best point at which to begin an upward move in the organization. For instance, many young managers are under the impression that they must achieve complete mastery over a position before seeking promotion to a higher rank, but a number of mentors advise their proteges against remaining in a position too long. As one senior executive explains,

> "There is a decrease in the learning curve, so don't stay on the job until you learn the whole thing, or it will be too late."

At some points, it is concentration on the issue of career options itself that benefits the protege the most. Nan McKendrick's mentor initiated "constant discussions of where am I going, what am I doing with myself which forced me to think about my career in a way I had not."

Expanding Horizons John O'Hanlon, our senior vice president at Smith & Pitts, represents a particularly dramatic case in which a mentor opened up career vistas for the protege.

O'Hanlon received his MBA from the University of California. An Englishman, he participated in the early 60s in a foreign exchange program in which the students, drawn from several countries, were required to take some of their MBA courses at a business school situated in a country other than their own. Wharton was his choice. His undergraduate degree is in economics and accounting; his MBA is in finance; and he is a CPA.

John's career represents a transformation from an organizationally based finance/accounting orientation to an entrepreneurial marketing orientation, a change that can be understood only in the context of the mentoring experience. When John graduated from the MBA program, he naturally desired to use his finance background, so he applied for a position at a large New York management consulting firm. The recruiters felt that he was as yet too "fresh" for a high-level consulting position and suggested that he seek employment with a company that they themselves were in charge of reorganizing, the Soup Corporation, which in the early 60s was undergoing a severe financial crisis. The position was largely unrelated to his educational background or career ambitions, but the consulting company implied that if he succeeded at the Soup Corporation, his application for the management consultant position would be reviewed.

John would be part of a group implanted inside the Soup Corporation for the purpose of totally redirecting its marketing in any way that the group considered necessary to reestablish the company's previously healthy market position. Heading the group was a person handpicked by the consulting company, the general manager of a large conglomerate's international operations, a hard worker with a proven track record in the corporate rescue area.

Paul, the leader of the project and O'Hanlon's future mentor, while not overly impressed with O'Hanlon's financial background, hired him because of his leadership and work capabilities. In school John had been the captain of some sports teams and editor of the paper, and obviously he had demonstrated a high enough level of intelligence to win an international fellowship over stiff competition.

Faced with effecting a massive reorganization of the Soup Corporation's marketing strategy, the group had to undergo work conditions very much like those of the Manhattan Project. Its members started their daily assignments at 8 A.M., ate a quick dinner at 6 or 7 P.M., returned to work at 8 P.M., and continued until midnight.

Exposure to Paul's management style began to change the way O'Hanlon perceived his own future. Suddenly, he began to see business as an enterprise akin to the sports in which he had participated at college rather than a series of debits and credits.

"My mentor always wanted to win. And particularly when you're dealing with a conglomerate background, you always have your market share. Every two months, there was always a tool to measure where you were."

The mentor began to convince the protege that his career lay, not in accounting, the measurement of business, but in marketing, the distribution of the products of business.

"This is when I started to realize that I wasn't an accountant, a financial person, that I needed more excitement, more challenge, things happening more quickly, more unexpectedly. I began to realize that he was almost an entrepreneur, and was given the freedom of being an entrepreneur within a corporation as being the best means of turning the corporation around."

O'Hanlon's mentor communicated the joys and satisfaction of this type of activity.

"What I was beginning to enjoy was the challenge of the unknown. His entrepreneurial spirit I realized afterwards was the thing that was showing up."

The mentor relationship was evoking a trait within John that he later came to identify as entrepreneurship. The mentor, building around John a team atmosphere of entrepreneurship, taught him how to think creatively and act independently.

As applied to the mentoring process, the term *career guidance* usually refers to the mentor's advice to the protege regarding what jobs to take and at what point to take them. But in O'Hanlon's case the mentor's career guidance encompassed a much broader trans-formation, a reorientation in overall career direction and self-image. After his years with the mentor, John remained with the Soup Corporation—not as an accountant, however, but as general manager of the New Products and Diversification Division. At age 30, he was offered a board membership but backed off because "I would have been tying myself to the company." Two bright young men whom he had appointed to head the new products operation were leaving the Soup Corporation to build their own advertising company in New Zealand. They offered him a partnership in the business, which he accepted in lieu of the board membership. The agency grew rapidly to become the largest new agency in New Zealand, and within a few years it was bought by Smith & Pitts, his current employer. John stayed on as general manager in the new subsidiary agency under a five-year contract, at the end of which he was offered the opportunity to administer the more lucrative accounts at Smith & Pitts. In addi-tion, he became a group senior vice president in a policy-oriented position concerned with corporate marketing strategy for the entire agency.

John's job is really that of adviser to the agency president. He spends most of his day reading books on the future of society and the economy, an exercise whose purpose is to develop a broad sociological forecast that can guide the company into the next century.

Though John is less independent than he would be as president of his own company, his position allows him the independence of thought and action that his mentor instilled in him at the earliest stage of his career. At this point in his career, John is quite satisfied to play the entrepreneur within the confines of the corporation.

LEVEL II—PERSONAL SUPPORT

The protege's transition from junior manager to executive often involves a great amount of stress and strain. Many managers get stuck at the lower corporate rungs because while they were able to acquire the technical and organizational skills necessary to perform at higher positions, certain psychological and personal shortcomings prevented them from successfully dealing with the stresses associated with the upper-management levels. Lack of self-confidence, conflicts between family and work requirements, and inability to handle stress have undermined many otherwise promising executive careers.

The second level of mentoring, personal support, entails an array of activities and services, including confidence building, psychological help, and advice about and intervention into the protege's personal life, that are designed to help the protege confront and conquer the strains of executive life (see Table 2–3).

At this level, the mentor interacts with the protege on a more personal basis than he did at the teaching level. Whereas the teaching level was primarily informational, Level II is essentially motivational and directive. It is assumed that the protege has learned what goals to pursue and that he must now be motivated to pursue those goals while being given the necessary emotional support.

TABLE 2–3
Level II—The Personal Support Function

Psychological support	Mentor helps protege overcome pressures and strains accompanying transition to positions of greater responsibility. Accentuates positive factors of new position. Imparts a sense of perspective.
Confidence building	Through various attitudinal and behavioral mechanisms, mentor builds protege's sense of confidence. If in a position to do so, allows protege to assume greater responsibility.
Assistance with personal life	Mentor helps protege deal with family pressures, personal dilemmas, and conflicts that interfere with job performance.

Psychological Support

There is always a hesitation about exposing weaknesses in one's personality, about revealing fears and trepidations that only a psychiatrist or priest is usually privy to. But since the mentor is probably the person best able to resolve on-the-job insecurities, proteges often overcome this hesitation and interact more candidly with the mentor than they ordinarily would in the organizational setting.

The respondents often refer to the pressures on proteges who are in transition to positions of greater responsibility. David Borowski is a vice president at the corporate headquarters of a multibillion-dollar health products conglomerate, the West Coast Pharmaceutical Corporation. Though being the general manager of a division is reason enough to experience strain, the pressures to succeed are doubly stressful in this case because the division he heads, home health care kits, is one that he convinced senior management to create. Failure would not be defined merely in terms of his inability to oversee the manufacturing, marketing, and sales of this line of products; it would be a grand failure arising from the fact that he convinced the corporation to sink millions of dollars into a new line of products and hand him a division to produce them. Under this kind of pressure, the protege typically experiences fear and self-doubt that can be positively resolved with the help of a mentor. Borowski speaks of a few instances where his mentor, a corporate senior manager, kept him from flying off the handle and perhaps even quitting.

> "Problems pop up every day. There's literally a crisis a day. Somebody calls up and you get a phone message: Urgent, need this by three, must be done, let's hurry this up, what's the status on this—. Production falls apart, a truckload of this was stolen, what do we do for this promotion?"

Since the failure of this project would be attributed to Borowski, the psychological stress can be overwhelming. In this situation, the mentor forces him to stop all work, momentarily withdraw from the activity at hand, and quietly examine his feelings of panic.

> "Usually, when I am ready to explode, literally so annoyed with what is going on, I talk to my mentor and my mentor says, 'Take your ego out of it. You as a business person are having a problem. Why are you having this problem? What can you do to resolve it? You can resolve it by changing or by leaving. If you leave, this is what you're giving up; if you stay, you're going to have to learn to deal with your problems.'"

The mentor in effect reminds the protege that pressures are unavoidable in positions of responsibility, and that if he desires upward mobility, he will have to learn to suppress the urge to escape them.

Most of Suzanne Barclay's product management crises at the Photography Corporation occur just before the semiannual sales figures arrive, when pressures are coming from all sides—from suppliers, the press, and the public—and her cool presence is essential at sales meetings. At this time, her schedule stretches from 7:30 A.M. to 10 P.M. and includes part of the weekend.

> *"There are many times when I will tell my mentor, 'I can't take this anymore; I'm going crazy.' Or he will realize I'm having difficulty with things and call me in and give me a little pep talk, tell me I can do it."*

One mentor, an advertising senior executive, believes that the support function is essential if the protege is to survive in the highly competitive agency environment where deadlines are so important. He quipped that when he worked at one agency, executives could order Gelusil from the mail room, since it was stored along with memo pads, typing papers, and ball-point pens.

> *"You may be making $200K per year as a manager of the International Foods account, and the next week the chairman of International Foods doesn't like your stuff, you're talking about taking your kids out of Harvard and putting them to work in Burger King."*

The mentor's role is to assist the protege in weighing the benefits of the position against its risks, utilizing the positive features of the job as a motivational force to counteract the sense of anxiety with which the protege approaches stressful situations.

Placing the small day-to-day defeats into the perspective of the entire "campaign" also falls within the mentor's role as counselor. Charles Clancy, a vice president of the Eastern Investment Bank, occasionally has unpleasant interactions with representatives of the large institutions that are his main customers, but his mentor points out to him that in the investment business some interactions with clients are simply not as pleasurable as others. This mentor acts as a psychological buffer between the harsh reality of the world of investment banking and the protege's ego. Clancy and his mentor sometimes compare notes about their disastrous meetings with clients. A technique that the mentor utilizes is to make light of unpleasant encounters, convincing the protege that some interactions with clients are not to be taken seriously and that a few negative interfaces are in fact par for the course.

> *"Even to this day we probably go out once every two weeks for a drink after work and just shoot the breeze about what we're working on, joke about people that we've worked with, clients that we've had in the past, compare notes about politics."*

A sense of perspective is invaluable for remaining calm under pressure. Through her mentor's help, Suzanne Barclay has learned to take her work performance less personally. And he has attempted to lessen her extreme reactions to minor mistakes in production schedules. Suzanne admits that her perfectionism, which she developed in the earliest years of school and which followed her into her working life, is a fault that can stifle the creativity needed in a marketing-oriented corporation.

Finally, the mere act of taking the time to personally interact with the protege serves as a source of psychological support. One respondent mentioned that there were not many executives with whom one could discuss stress-related issues, that one could talk to in a personal way. Knowing that there is a sympathetic ear can in itself prevent negative reactions to stress. One protege uses her mentor for personal support only occasionally, but the fact that her mentor has told her, "If you need a place to bitch or a shoulder to cry on, come to me," provides adequate relief for much managerial insecurity. Clearly, the protege's performance level is improved by the feeling of security derived from this relationship.

> *"To know that you have someone within your scope that knows more than you do, whether you're on a baseball team or in a company, or even in your family, is a great help in getting through the day. Just to know there's a grown-up there, in a sense. Somebody who's been around longer than you, knows more than you do, knows more people than you do, who you know is on your side."*

Confidence Building

A young executive faces hurdles, natural and manufactured, and is expected to surmount them. Through various attitudinal and behavioral reinforcements, a mentor can help establish the strong sense of self-confidence that is needed to overcome such career obstructions. But the building of self-confidence is often a slow and difficult process, and self-confidence must often be reinforced and rebuilt at various stages in the protege's career.

Andrew Clark, a senior general manager at the Insurance Corporation feels that his protege, whose work was well respected by senior management, was not getting sufficient praise from her direct supervisor for the excellent work she was doing, to the point where she was beginning to wonder whether the company even knew she existed. Her confidence waned, and she began to consider quitting. But mentors have information about senior management's positive evaluations that may never reach the protege unless an insider decides to transmit the information to her. He feels that by communicating positive feedback about her performance from the senior levels, he prevented her departure.

Michael Madison will someday advance to the top management at the Chemical Corporation, a Fortune 200 conglomerate, but because of the highly vertical structure of his company, he may have to remain at a level just below senior management for several years. This might erode his sense of self-confidence. He is now in his third year at this level, and, according to Madison, his mentor has considerably increased the "back-patting" to rejuvenate his interest in performing the same job. The mentor also points out that what seems like stagnation is actually progress, that Madison is viewed positively within the corporation and must remember that he is only one rung away from senior management.

From this example it can be seen that the protege's self-confidence may be eroded by what he mistakenly thinks are negative career occurrences. David Dorwin, our vice president at the Crandall Advertising Agency, tells how at a time when he felt that he was not communicating well with a client, his mentor rebuilt his confidence by explaining that in advertising relationships with clients had both crests and troughs and that although the troughs could be devastating to the ego, good account executives survived them.

The mere fact that the mentor demonstrates faith in the protege may be sufficient to build confidence. The mentor can first let the subordinate assume responsibility and make decisions and then encourage him to stand by the decisions once they have been made. Even if the mentor does not think the protege's decisions are the very best ones, as long as they are not disastrous, it is important that he let the protege implement them. In this manner, the mentor helps the protege develop the capacity to take risks. Since that capacity is often a necessary prerequisite to career advancement, acquiring it will assist the protege immeasurably.

Mentors who are good judges of character will know how to build the protege's confidence without seeming to be patronizing. One female mentor did not engage in day-to-day personal counseling with her protege but knew the exact time to interject the behavior that would build the protege's self-confidence. The protege had recently been promoted to a position immediately below vice president and on the recommendation of the mentor had decided to smooth her transition into the new assignment by arranging a private meeting with her new vice president. Unknown to her, the mentor was in conference with the vice president while the protege waited in the reception area. When the meeting was over, the mentor walked into the reception area and shouted to the vice president, "Bob, she's very special, and I want you to be very good to her!"

The two seniors had obviously been discussing the protege, and in a very positive light, a fact communicated to the protege by the mentor's public exclamation of support. No amount of private counseling could have equaled this public accolade as a method of building the protege's self-image.

Assistance with Personal Life

Life outside the organization can affect performance inside it. Though mentors vary in the extent of their extraorganizational relationships with the protege (see Chapter 7), they will all give advice on the protege's "real life" problems and conflicts if they think that this will improve his job performance.

One of the crucial adjustments for the protege is learning how to balance commitment to career against commitment to family, to manage this standard conflict between public and private obligations. One protege faced pressures from his family to devote more time to home duties, a situation for which the mentor, a high-level vice president, demonstrated much understanding and sympathy. He made various suggestions for lessening the antagonism of the wife and children toward a situation that severely limited his full commitment to the family. He encouraged the protege to start family discussions on the issue in the hope that everyone affected would develop an understanding of the strong time pressures inherent in an executive career.

Personal problems have an annoying way of intruding on the most well planned career paths. Barbara Sikorsky, the product manager at the Goodbrands Corporation, had surgery that would curtail her activities for a short time. She was hospitalized for two weeks, during which time the mentor called daily to inquire about her health. This show of interest not only served as an emotional support but assured Barbara that her absence from the office was noticed and felt.

The mentor's personal assistance extended beyond Barbara's hospitalization. After Barbara's return, the mentor made an effort to keep her workload manageable and gave her time off as needed during her recovery.

"She did it covertly. And I liked that. She didn't make a big deal out of it, like she was making some supreme sacrifice for my well-being. She saw it as a better way to work with me, a better way to work her organization."

Mentors generally demonstrate a sincere desire to help proteges keep their personal house in order. One mentor supplied a wide array of personal services ranging from advice on abortion to investment counseling and once even subsidized a protege's operation.

Financial counseling by the mentor is quite common. In the 1950s, Thomas Smith, now a senior vice president of finance at the Trading Corporation, was counseled by his mentor to buy into real estate even if this required going into debt. Considering the return on real estate investments over the last 30 years, it is not surprising that he found this "a piece of advice which turned out to be quite beneficial."

Mentors help proteges through separations, deaths, births, financial crises, and other occurrences that are not directly related to the job but can have a disturbing or catastrophic effect on the performance and career of the young manager. In fact, many personal crises, especially adjustments to marriage and family responsibility often occur just when proteges are approaching crucial junctures in their careers and are beginning to encounter greater job demands. The mentor's assistance here can be invaluable. The data suggest that careers can be adversely affected by a manager's inability to coordinate private and public responsibilities.

The Thin Line

Since Level II activities involve confidence building, psychological support, and assistance with personal problems, the mentor who engages in them is embarking on a precarious and perhaps irreversible route in the direction of personal commitment. His criticism becomes more pointed, his advice more personal, his relationship with the protege more emotionally based. But since this relationship is still confined to organizational parameters, when in fact does the mentor overstep his bounds? One executive claims that most mentors are wary of stepping on the protege's toes because they are fearful both of invading his privacy and of overcommitting themselves.

Felice Stolz, a senior product manager at the Womangoods Corporation, believes that there must be a sharp dividing line between mentor and "mother." ("I already have one, thank you.") When her mentor's psychological support begins to involve parental overtures, Felice shoves her back into the mentor role because "I need her to be more objective than a parent."

Clearly, the mentor and the protege must decide how much support is needed for the protege to make the adjustment to senior management, but the respondents emphasize that some personal counseling, however subtle, is an important component of the transitional period. However, most mentors seem sensitive to the possibility that the protege may resent personal assistance and basic psychological support.

LEVEL III—ORGANIZATIONAL INTERVENTION

The Mentor Goes Public

Thus far, we have been discussing mentoring as a set of interpersonal, almost private, exchanges between the mentor and the protege. The mentor teaches skills, provides advice on corporate comportment, modifies the protege's self-image, builds his confidence, and outlines the more important political characteristics of the organization, but all of these activities, however relevant to the protege's career, involve "unpublicized" interactions between the mentor and the protege.

In these situations, the mentor makes a relatively low-risk, almost guarded, investment in the protege. Spending after-hours, lunch, and work time in coaching and advising cuts into the time that the mentor could be performing his own job, so we can say that the mentor's Level I activities entail an investment in time. And at Level II, in which the mentor's psychological support and confidence building involve a more personal commitment, the mentor invests emotion.

But at Level III, both the activities that the mentor performs on behalf of the protege and the accompanying risks increase, since the mentor now assumes a much more active public role in the protege's career, attempting to influence the organization in the protege's favor. In essence, the mentor attempts both to protect the protege and to serve as his advocate, as a marketing agent for the protege in the organization (see Table 2–4). The mentor's degree of commitment is greater, because he is publicly committing himself to the protege, making his connection with the protege known within the organization. This increases the risk to the mentor's career, since intervening on behalf of the wrong junior manager will reflect poorly on his judgment as an executive.

Protection

A person's career can be sabotaged in dozens of ways, and this threat is particularly great during the embryonic career stage of the junior manager. The competition for upward movement in the mod-

TABLE 2–4
Level III—Organizational Intervention

Protection	Mentor provides support environment around protege by intervening in conflicts and situations that endanger protege's organizational advancement. Proteges' careers are often negatively affected by weak or threatened supervisors, requiring mentor intervention. Mentor can also mitigate negative career effects of merger, reorganizations.
Marketing the candidate	Mentor advertises protege's good qualities to senior management. Helps protege gain visibility at in-house interfaces and outside meetings. Protege does not seem self-aggrandizing or self-promoting.
Access to resources	Mentor utilizes his position to make available to protege money, resources, and supply and communication lines that would ordinarily be unavailable to a junior member.

ern corporation, especially with the recent contraction in the ranks of middle management, often resembles the competition for entrance into medical school. In these circumstances, the manager seeking advancement can do without the organizational pressures that could undermine his upward mobility. And the presence of a mentor can help reduce such pressures.

Dan Garner, our senior vice president at the Communications Corporation, did not enjoy a totally smooth rise to the top. He once made a personnel decision that he thought would hasten his ascent to senior management but in fact almost slowed his career to a halt. About four years ago, Garner, in a move that he thought would enhance his managerial capability, hired into an advisory position a person with more experience than his own. But in order to acquire that person, it was necessary to promise him an undefined advancement opportunity. As luck would have it, the new employee soon attempted to utilize his advisory position to leapfrog past Garner in the organizational hierarchy. He was on the verge of accomplishing this unexpected coup when the president, Garner's mentor, intervened in order to restrain his attempts to oversee and overrule Garner's decisions. Through the president's intervention, the new manager was prevented from moving into a position over Garner, who was subsequently given that position.

The mentor's intervention seems most necessary when the protege is making his first major career moves in the organization. Strong support is needed when the protege assumes new roles, and if that support is not forthcoming from the protege's direct supervisor, the mentor must supply it. The transition of Womangoods' Nan McKendrick from her "creative" position in advertising into the merchandising manager spot was particularly troublesome because the new position had an entirely novel emphasis—it was more "budget oriented," and it entailed more decision-making responsibilities. Unfortunately, at a time when Nan needed firm direction from her supervisor, she was saddled with a totally disorganized new boss who needed guidance himself and was drowning in his own department. After several agonizing months in this position, when Nan announced to her mentor that she was ready to quit, the mentor realized that she would have to assume the protective role. She alleviated Nan's immediate fears by saying, "You have to trust me—you trusted me enough to come here, trust me enough to go to your boss's vice president. It won't get back to your supervisor." Nan had approached her mentor to express dissatisfaction, not to request direct intervention, but the mentor convinced her that she would deal with the other vice president discreetly, without bruising anyone's ego.

Nan's dissatisfaction was communicated from her mentor to the supervisor's vice president to the supervisor himself. After the mentor's intervention, Nan's boss became more communicative and "directive," giving her the information and feedback necessary for a successful transition into her new position. He responded to the prodding from his own vice president, never realizing that it originated with Andrea Feders, Nan's mentor.

While the inadequacies of supervisors may account for their neglect of younger managers, such neglect often has more pernicious origins. When at a fairly young age Doreen Tokama first became an officer of the Bank of the East Orient, higher level vice presidents would ignore her when policies had to be implemented or questions answered, sometimes in flagrant violation of established procedures. They would also go over her head to the executive vice president. Since he was her mentor, in almost every instance he would remind them that she was now an officer of the bank and that what they were presenting to him were actually her projects. Doreen feels that these reminders, which forced the other executives to deal with her as project leader, established her credibility and reinforced her position of authority.

The experiences of my respondents demonstrate that the political motivations and machinations of peers and seniors can make it extremely difficult for the young manager to advance in his career, regardless of his talent or business acumen. Though most companies will base promotion on talent to some extent, politics cannot be discounted as an influencial career factor. This condition makes it necessary to have an "activist" mentor.

Thomas Smith, our senior vice president at the Trading Corporation, says that he can recall several instances in which his mentor had to intercede to save his career. The mentor's intervention was required mostly when Smith, as a young manager, tried to serve as an "instrument of change" and "stepped on the wrong toes" when attempting to introduce new policies.

The most serious incident occurred when Thomas was sent to turn around an overseas operation that was the weak link in an otherwise prosperous organization. The person running the operation clearly did not desire outside participation in the decision making and immediately perceived Thomas as a threat to his authority and position.

"As soon as I tried to do anything more than act as a channel of communications, as soon as he perceived it as an effort to correct his activities, he got on his high horse in a hurry. We had to fight that one."

Through a balanced menu of tact and coercion, Thomas's mentor, a senior executive, helped him establish his authority, the end result being that Thomas was enabled to act as an independent policy originator.

The act of organizational intervention into the protege's career often appears to be a watershed in the mentor-protege relationship. Public advocacy, the statement that "this is my protege," while carrying risks for the mentor, seems to be the strongest bonding agent in the relationship.

The respondents provided numerous examples regarding the variety of situations that require a mentor's intervention. Some of the respondents say that they were about to be transferred out of the mentor's division when the move was suddenly overridden by a directive from the mentor. Others recount situations in which layoffs, mergers, and reorganizations might have stifled their mobility, terminated their employment, or separated them from mentor if the mentor had not intervened on their behalf behind the scenes.

Barbara Sikorsky, who for several years in a different corporation had languished without a mentor and been overlooked for promotion, compares her present working environment to her earlier situation.

"For the first time in my professional life, I feel insulated. I feel that if there's trouble down the pike, I'll either hear about it first so I'm prepared, or if it should sneak up on me, I won't be alone to fight it. Perhaps if I had not had such an experience before, this wouldn't be as great a boon to me as it is now. But it's the counterpoint between the two experiences that makes this so unbelievably terrific. I mean, I'd cut off my right arm for this woman."

Of course, intervention requires tact on the part of the mentor. The mentor cannot sweep down into the lower ranks whenever the protege has a problem. Nor would he want to, since part of the protege's learning experience is discovering how to survive on the corporate battlefield. But certain situations, especially those threatening the protege's position, require direct assistance, however tactful.

Marketing the Candidate

Up to this point I have been describing organizational intervention as a method by which the mentor protects the protege from an overbearing and competitive organizational environment. However, the mentor's intervention can take another direction. The mentor's advocacy can assume the form of marketing or advertising the protege within the department or the organization.

After reviewing the career patterns of the managers interviewed, I felt that the term *marketing*, though customarily applied to activities related to products rather than persons, was quite accurate. Mentors do actively market their proteges.

The analogy to marketing is inescapable. There are numerous quality products to choose from, but the products with the best "recall" will be the most successful. This is described quite succinctly by one of the respondents.

> *"One of the critical elements in continuing to move through the corporation is to be talked about. If someone says 'Do you know somebody who might be qualified for this job?' if you don't have top-of-mind awareness, your name doesn't come up."*

One way of helping the protege to achieve such awareness is to give him visibility. An excellent marketing technique that mentors have employed is to bring the protege to business meetings attended by upper-level executives. This gets great exposure for the protege. Of course, once the junior member gains entrée to the meeting, he has to live up to his advance billing. A number of mentors use an interesting technique to ensure that the protege makes a good impression at such meetings: they cue the protege on the subjects that will probably be discussed and then allow him to field questions aimed at the mentor. Thus the protege appears to be "expert" in particular areas.

In addition, mentors are quite proficient at exposing their proteges to various segments of the business community. Proteges recount how their mentors have smoothed the way for their encounters with the sales force, key people in the industry, competitors, and the press. One mentor recently engineered his protege's appearance on a televised series of product-related public service announcements. While appearing to be a selfless contribution by the protege, these announcements established him as an official spokesperson of the company, a liaison between the public and the company. Another mentor allows his product manager protege to deal with the chairman of the board on issues relating to her product line.

> *"For a product manager to be dealing with the chairman of the board of the corporation is a unique situation. It's nice to know that he knows me by my first name."*

Michael Madison's mentor gets him invited to as many official functions as possible. The banking luncheon is a semiannual affair in which the Chemical Corporation fairly informally breaks bread with its lenders, attempting to present as coherent and accommodating a front as possible in order to attract fresh investments. In short, the corporation is trying to establish an image of trustworthiness in the minds of representatives of large investors. Because attracting investments is one of the most critical activities of the corporate world, Michael's mentor made sure not to expose him until he felt that Michael was adequately prepared. As it turned out, Madison was the lowest-ranking member at the luncheon, which was attended by the chairman, the vice chairman, and high-ranking representatives of the bank.

A key function that the mentor fulfills at the intervention level is the establishment of the protege's *legitimacy* and *credibility*. These various business meetings and extraorganizational conclaves are a natural stage for the demonstration of expertise, as one protege indicates.

> *"What my mentor has done in the last year and a half is essentially showcase me with the chairman and the key members of the board as up and coming. For instance, last year's budget and operating plan, which is a once yearly presentation to the executive committee, a four- or five-hour presentation — he had me give it instead of giving it himself."*

The executive committee had a chance to question the protege, to see how he handled that kind of situation—"defending a business," as it were. The presentation was a smashing success, and all of the attending managers felt comfortable during the meeting.

This example illustrates the two dimensions upon which the success of meetings is judged: correct presentation of material (convincing arguments, etc.) and favorable presentation of self. The fact that senior executives felt comfortable with this protege seems as important as the factual presentation, since he was being judged not only in terms of his skill in processing and implementing information but in terms of his ability to fit into the dynamics of the small group at the top.

A latent benefit of being marketed by the mentor is that the protege does not seem overly self-promoting or self-aggrandizing. He or she gets "presented" without seeming forward. The impression created is that he not only has talent but that he also has humility and that he is certainly a good team player!

> *"One of the things you learn if you have half a brain is that doing a good job alone is going to get you no place. It's telling people that you're doing a good job that gets you somewhere. And if you have help in doing that, you don't come across as obnoxious and egotistical; you come across as a comer— someone's blowing your horn for you."*

What emerges from these managers' stories is the enormous impact of Level III mentoring on the protege's career. Such mentoring operates in the underlying strata of personal influence based on indirect suggestion and subtle marketing. If the protege has a skill, can get things done, knows how to find and utilize information, and demonstrates a capacity to motivate peers and subordinates, the mentor can help him establish a justly deserved reputation for excellence. Many mentors, not wishing to wait for people in the organization to discover the protege's managerial ability, sell the protege by letting key people in the organization know that this person has something to contribute to its growth.

Access to Resources

A third form of mentor intervention is required when the protege, in order to perform optimally in his position, needs certain resources and services within the company that for one reason or another are inaccessible. Since one of the sources of organizational power is access to supplies, the inability to obtain needed supplies can undermine the protege's position.

That inability can have several causes. The protege, because of his lower rank, may not be given first priority to certain resources (especially information, computer access, communications apparatus). Or the protege, though accorded nominal access to resources, may not know how to get to them. For instance, a marketing manager may be able to get a truckload of something delivered by calling a regional sales manager, but he must know that he has to call the sales manager.

Most often, access to supplies is interrupted or preempted during periods of corporate turmoil, such as reorganizations, mergers, changes in top management, and slowdowns. One respondent says that when she first started in a product management position (which her mentor helped her get), the company was on the verge of a merger and hence an organizational shake-up. The corporation was in a state of panic. Everyone was scared, fearful of being fired, and, as so often happens in such circumstances, the main activity became, not the work itself, but rumor mongering and office gossip. Complicating the situation was the fact that procedural change muddied the chains of command and thus the lines of supply.

But this respondent's mentor, whose position was stable, was able to commandeer certain corporate facilities and open enough doors so that she could do her job. Because of his direct intervention on her behalf, she was able to get market and sales figures and the supplies she needed for presentations, and to communicate with and continue to motivate the sales force. Through her mentor's intercession, she was able to maintain a cohesive department and to regain some equilibrium in the management of her product line. When the posttakeover dust finally settled, the efficiency she developed during that turbulent period became the foundation upon which her next promotion was based.

3

Promoting the Protege

When all is said and done, from the protege's point of view the ultimate rationale for entering a mentoring relationship seems to be its ability to ease his ascent to higher organizational positions. While teaching and psychological support are invaluable in developing the protege's career, the ultimate measure of a mentor's worth is the promotion of the protege. This chapter deals with this Level IV function.

In addition, the chapter looks at how the organizational culture and structure affect the potential protege's ability to make the "mentor connection" to obtain a promotion. I have found that certain types of organizations seem to foster mentoring, while others make it more difficult for a mentor to advance the protege up the corporate ladder.

One way of assessing the importance of mentoring as a career tool is to compare the mentored group with respondents who have pursued their careers without the help of a mentor. Thus this chapter also looks at the ways that "life without a mentor" can affect the unsponsored manager's promotional opportunities and the quality of his work life.

LEVEL IV—PROMOTIONS DIRECT AND INDIRECT

Level IV, the mentor's advancement of the protege from one organizational position to another, requires a deeper commitment from the mentor than do the earlier levels and affords a greater benefit to the protege.

At Level IV, the mentor either promotes the candidate (if in a position to do so) or recommends the candidate for promotion. Here the mentor's own job, chances for advancement, and the like may be at stake since the mentor has convinced the organization that the protege can be trusted to handle resources, spend money, and make decisions affecting the organization's future.

This section will deal with the numerous direct and indirect methods that mentors use to promote their proteges (see Table 3–1).

TABLE 3–1
Level IV—Promotion Techniques

Direct
1. Increase of title.
2. Expansion of function.
3. Manipulation of political factors.

Indirect
1. Getting protege admission into in-house training programs.
2. Helping protege gain admission into key management programs.
3. Helping protege obtain prestige appointments on trade periodicals, professional journals, boards.

Direct Promotion

It would seem to be a simple matter for a powerful mentor to merely advance his protege into a higher position when a vacancy becomes available, but such factors as organizational structure, organizational growth, and social psychological conditions can affect what would appear to be a fairly straightforward process. Hence, mentors have developed several methods for legitimately advancing their proteges.

Increase of Title A mentor can help the protege by seeing that he gets recognition for a "job well done," and the quickest route to recognition is an appropriate title. In other words, the mentor can legitimately promote a protege by awarding him a title for functions that the protege is already performing. In this connection, it should be remembered that a major complaint of the average manager is that he is doing a job that has not been given a proper title. By promoting the protege into a title appropriate to his functions, the mentor rectifies an injustice. But without the mentor, the protege might assume ever-increasing responsibilities with no change in title, receiving no official recognition for these additional duties. It should also be indicated that the protege who owes his new title to the intervention of a widely respected mentor is often more strongly established in that title than he would be otherwise. Because the recommendation of a trusted senior person helped the protege rise to his new position, the organization will have more faith in the protege's ability to succeed in it.

Expansion of Function Michael Madison, the assistant treasurer of the Chemical Corporation, has received numerous promotions through his mentor, the treasurer, who is one of 28 senior managers reporting directly to the president. But none of these senior managers seems ready to retire. Although the mentor has assured Madison that he will ultimately acquire a senior position, both of them are concerned with the question of what his activities will be between now and the time that he does.

The mentor has an excellent method of seeing that the protege remains a "hot item" within the organization while his position stays essentially the same. On an annual basis the mentor simply expands the responsibilities, budget, and staff of the protege, increasing the protege's area of control and enlarging his job description.

The mentor has also established the necessary preconditions for Madison's accession to the treasurer position by demonstrating Madison's ability to do the job and by informing the other seniors of his intentions. As Madison says, "He's informed me that if he ever retired quickly, he has already left a will, and I'm in it."

Mentoring and the Politics of Promotion How important is a mentor in the promotion process? In Lawrence Garibaldi's corporation, Magnum Enterprises, each financial analyst at his level has an MBA in finance from a good school, several years of work experience, and an undergraduate degree in engineering. So just getting into Garibaldi's department means meeting rigorous qualifications. Thus the benefit of having a mentor's help in moving up in the department is quite obvious.

"Adequate work is not what is expected. Above-average work is expected, and therefore in order to be differentiated, you have to have someone speaking for you and helping others make that differentiation."

Quite simply, mentors work overtly and covertly to make sure that their proteges move up into positions as these become available. Dirk Landers, a vice president at the Canadian Bank, claims that his mentor saw that he would be one of the 10 selected among the 25 applicants for a position in the metropolitan division of the bank. But this was preceded by months of advertising the protege and marketing his skills so that when the position became available, it would seem more "natural" to consider Landers a leading candidate.

Many proteges are mentored by individuals who are two or more levels above them. If a direct supervisor attempts to block the upward movement of a subordinate mentored by a senior person, the mentor can approach the problem from a variety of angles. Kellen McDaniels, director of financial analysis at a Fortune 500 manufacturing corporation, felt that his mobility was being slowed by his direct supervisor and complained to his mentor. Consequently, the mentor decided to have Kellen promoted out of the supervisor's department. Since supervisors usually have input into the decision to promote a subordinate, Kellen's supervisor could have slowed his promotion considerably. However, the mentor, who had some influence on the timing of the interview schedule, simply set up Kellen's interview with the target department when the supervisor was on vacation. When the supervisor returned, she was presented with Kellen's promotion as an accomplished fact. Of course, this was no way for the mentor to make friends among middle managment, but in the short term the method proved very effective.

The mentor can not only promote the protege but also help smooth many problems associated with peer and senior reaction to the promotion. A case in point is Gabe Randolph, the divisional manager at the Goodbrands Corporation, whose actions should have not only precluded promotion but ended his career at Goodbrands completely. Randolph's career path at Goodbrands included both advertising and product management, and he developed a relationship with the mentor when the mentor was a product manager and Randolph was an associate product manager. After several successful years within the corporation, Randolph decided to leave the Goodbrands Corporation and start his own business. The mentor, while not happy about losing a star protege, left the door open for Randolph's return.

Although Randolph did fairly well in his own business, he realized that he felt more at home in the corporate environment, and he decided to return to Goodbrands. But the corporate culture at Goodbrands, like that of many other large companies, regards loyalty to the company highly, so his effort to return generated substantial objections among middle and senior management. After all, he had violated a cardinal principle of the corporate ethos by leaving.

However, during Randolph's absence his mentor had been promoted to divisional president, and the mentor was more concerned with developing a good staff than with honoring the shibboleths of corporate culture. By virtue of his increased power and influence, he was able to overrule criticism and bring Randolph back into the corporation. He gave Randolph the title of group product manager and finally promoted him to product development manager for one of the corporation's major brands.

While the mentor's power and influence helped overcome the political tensions surrounding Randolph's return, more crucial to the smooth reentry was the fact that his mentor's mentor, the former president of the division that had hired Randolph three or four years earlier, remembered Randolph's work and saw him as a welcome addition to the enterprise. As Randolph says, "He was someone with whom I got along well, and someone who appreciated what I could do." It must be emphasized that the objections to Randolph's return to Goodbrands did not center on the issues of competence, worthiness, or other factors related to favoritism. As we will see in Chapter 6, if favoritism had been suspected, the organization might have rejected the mentor-protege relationship, either through lowered productivity due to morale problems or through the expulsion of either or both members. Actually, the source of the objections, the unwritten norms of the corporation, did not seriously threaten to establish a permanent resistance among the objectors.

Sequential Mentoring Since I am primarily concerned with the dynamics of mentor-protege relationships, most of this book focuses on the one-to-one interactions between the mentor and the protege. However, some of the respondents have had more than one mentor during their careers. In fact, once a person has been involved in a mentor relationship, his perception of how the corporate world works is transformed, so that he will attempt to replicate such a relationship whenever possible.

Thomas Smith's career is a good example of sequential mentoring. Smith serves as the senior vice president of finance of the Trading Corporation, and after a long career he has reached a position right below the president. He is one of an inner circle of four who control this huge conglomerate. The other three are the senior vice president of sales, the senior vice president of marketing, and the senior vice president of merchandising.

Though now fairly limited in its operational scope, the Trading Corporation at one time owned banks, insurance firms, and travel companies. It underwent a transition from a family-owned company to a family-controlled corporation, but the actual operating management no longer consists of family members. Though Smith has had several mentors in his career, the first, a member of the founding family, was the most important, and as we shall see, Smith's early identification with the family has persisted to this day, even though his later mentors were nonfamily directors. He was promoted, protected, and otherwise helped in his career development because of this identification.

In the early 50s Smith was working in an automobile dealership run by a younger member of the family that controlled the Trading

Corporation. When the dealership folded, this person brought Smith into the Trading Corporation. He served as Smith's mentor, and since the company, along with the U.S. economy, was undergoing massive expansion, the promotion process was relatively easy.

The mentor's influence within the company was so strong that Smith's career was helped even in his absence. As mentioned, in the early 70s Smith was asked to go overseas and help sort out an operation there. While Smith was successfully completing his assignment, his mentor, now president of the corporation, died.

At this point several factors existed that should have destroyed Thomas Smith's career. The new president of the Trading Corporation, who was brought in from the outside, knew nothing about Smith's expertise and was unaware of his relationship with the former president. At the same time the Arab oil embargo suddenly struck. For years, the service stations around the United States had utilized the Trading Corporation's premiums to induce customers to buy gas. Overnight, for the first time since World War II, the petroleum industry was transformed into a seller's market, and with this change the need for the Trading Corporation's premiums disappeared. The company, losing millions, saw its net worth decline by 20 percent.

While staff reductions swept through the corporation, the mentor relationship posthumously protected Smith's position. The "powers that be" insisted that the president maintain Smith on the company payroll, and even though there was then no real position for him, upon his return from overseas he was given make-work assignments.

The power circle around the new president insisted that the organization bide its time until something appropriate emerged for Smith to do. The halo effect of the mentor had outlived its source, a not uncommon event if the mentor has been a particularly strong figure within the organization. As mentioned earlier, part of the mentor's function is to establish the reputation and credibility of the protege; if this has been done well enough, the mentor's absence should have less bearing on the protege's later career. If the mentor was respected, his stamp of approval is indelible.

A series of mentor relationships followed that period, and today Thomas Smith is mentored by the chairman of the board. He may never become president, but he will never lose his position of power within the Trading Corporation. Because of the original mentor relationship, he was designated early on as an invaluable employee who should be retained indefinitely and given reasonable promotions. Hence, he attracted a series of mentors who eventually promoted him into senior management.

Mentoring as a Corporate Trait Mentoring as a method of promotion often becomes a part of the corporate culture. In some organizations it becomes customary for managers to advance through the direct help of a mentor. Most of the senior managers in such organizations have received guidance and direct sponsorship throughout their careers.

At the Eastern Investment Bank the competition for promotion is brutal and the stakes are high. The bank provides a wide array of financial services. These services include locating suitable investment media—money markets, stocks, bonds, etc.—for the funds of institutions, pension organizations, and other large investors. The daily flow of money handled by the bank runs in the multimillions.

The Eastern Investment Bank is a partnership. The people who run the bank own it, and the partners are people who through salesmanship and organizational skills were able to reach the top. I interviewed several managers there and soon saw how powerful mentoring was as a mechanism for promotion.

Merely to get to a nonpartnership trading level, an MBA from a good school and several years of experience in financial trading are needed. The high pressure of the Eastern Investment Bank trading floor can crush even the most knowledgeable manager, so the recruitment process is aimed at acquiring even-tempered managers who can remain calm and polite while attempting to locate in a few minutes a profitable resting place for $50 million.

The new manager enters the organization as an associate, and after four years he can proceed to the next level, vice president. It is rare for anyone to be made a vice president the first time he becomes eligible, but if he does attain that status quickly, this indicates that partnership is a good possibility, though that possibility may not be realized for 12–20 years. It is worth the wait, however, since a new partner's salary averages about $1 million a year. But perhaps only 1 percent of the 200 or so associates will ever become partners.

The organization provides one of the clearest examples of "mentoring chains." Partners mentor vice presidents, and vice presidents mentor associates. As one vice president told me:

> "Mentoring is definitely encouraged in this organization. At the ultimate level, the partnership level, you couldn't become a partner unless you had some kind of sponsorship, because by definition you have to have a partner or a group of partners who are really sponsoring your advance."

Charles Clancy, our vice president in the municipal bonds department, started off in the mail room of the Eastern Investment Bank while he was an undergraduate. He continued his summer employment at the bank all the way through his MBA, and each year he "just kept getting a slightly better summer job." After earning his MBA, since he had acquired experience and exposure within the organization, he became an associate, even though newly minted MBAs without full-time experience were rarely offered such positions.

Clancy met the person who was to become his mentor on the day he began working full time. The relationship was initiated and developed by this vice president, who quickly maneuvered to get Clancy assigned to many projects where he was the immediate supervisor. Because the mentor and Clancy worked together, the mentor could spin off projects. This put Clancy in the unique position of having a number of accounts for which he was the prime supervisor and freed the mentor to pursue other and probably bigger accounts.

The relationship became so valuable to the mentor that he began to visibly promote his protege. Since the vice president had influence with the partners, he made certain that Clancy was handsomely rewarded for any accomplishments.

> *"Every year, every nickel, every bonus that I got was only because he clubbed them over the head."*

Due to its size, its clientele base, and the general frenzy surrounding its trading division, a young MBA can easily slip into obscurity at the Eastern Investment Bank. But the mentor can help the young manager escape from the organizational shadows.

> *"He was the guy who really pushed to make sure that I was vice president the first time I was up. I subsequently found out that he went around to other people at his level and made sure they told the powers that be that I should be promoted."*

Charles Clancy alluded to the fact that if the mentor did not become a partner, the protege's chances of becoming one were greatly diminished. In that case, the protege might have to attain partnership through a series of mentors, since the partners themselves, as a group or as individuals, approve admission into the club.

The mentor-protege relationship often affects the careers of both the mentor and the protege. The experience of Jim Mulcahy, a vice president in the International Investment Banking Division, exemplifies the interdependent quality of the relationship at the Eastern Investment Bank. He met his mentor, a vice president who is now on the verge of becoming a partner, during his initial interview. Like most of the upper-level managers, Mulcahy had acquired his financial training on the outside before obtaining employment at the Eastern

Investment Bank. The mentor-protege relationship developed quickly during the early months of his employment.

The mentor fought hard for Jim's promotion into the vice presidential ranks, and after he becomes a partner, he is expected to vote for Jim's partnership. The interdependent nature of the mentor-protege relationship is illustrated by Jim's statement.

> *"What he did get from it was someone he could always depend on, always get the work done. He respected how much time and trouble it took. And he had somebody he liked. But I think the most important thing to him was that I was someone he could depend on. If there were any difficult accounts that came in, I would usually get them."*

The mentor's accession to the partnership was obviously dependent on Mulcahy's performance as the junior member of the relationship. Though Mulcahy and the mentor like each other, that is secondary to their ability to advance each other's careers. In fact, the vice president had been mentoring someone who he liked more, but the relationship had stagnated because the protege could not meet his expectations.

The mentor relationship at the Eastern Investment Bank becomes career oriented because mentoring from the top down is part of the corporate culture. Most of the partners are themselves mentoring vice presidents, so the success of a vice president's sponsorship of a given subordinate is often contingent on the political position and strength of his own mentor. What prevents these alliances and cross-loyalties from becoming dangerous to the organization's health is the fact that a manager's survival in the organization is not dependent on promotion. He can remain with the firm at the same level and still be paid handsomely. (The low-to-middle six-figure salary is a minimum at the vice presidential level.) In fact, since mentor-protege alliances increase the efficiency of both members of the relationship, the organization is rather well served by the "healthy competition" of mentor-protege pairs.

The Subtle Approach

There are reasons for advancing proteges in subtler ways than direct promotion. First, the mentor may feel that intervening directly in the promotional picture will upset the department or threaten egos in the chain of command. Second, the mentor may feel that he does not have enough power within the organization to directly intervene in the promotional process. Third, he may have power in the organization in general, but the protege's particular department may be sufficiently insulated from the rest of the organization to withstand external pressure from the mentor or anyone else regarding departmental policy. And fourth, there may simply be a corporate tradition of nonintervention into departmental promotional processes.

Regardless of their reasons for avoiding direct promotion, mentors have developed numerous techniques for subtly advancing their proteges.

In-House Training Programs Steve Garret made the transition from auditing into commercial banking because his mentor saw that he was enrolled in a one-year training program with the bank, a program that served as a sure path to higher key positions within the organization. Though the program was strictly designed for MBAs recruited directly from graduate school, the mentor was able to work behind the scenes to help Garret get into it.

Many organizations have developed management training programs that are intended not only to upgrade the skills of their employees but to establish an elite corps of executives. Since participants in these programs are earmarked as possessors of "executive potential," getting the protege into them serves as a relatively innocuous method of promotion by the mentor.

Outside Training Certain candidates for key positions within the organization are often sent to long-term management programs outside the organization, business "West Points" where the lower-level manager returns a full-fledged executive. The Womangoods Corporation has such an "academy" in the University Program on Women and Management, a college-based program designed specifically for the woman manager. The three-month MBA-type curriculum seems to specialize as much in honing the participants' people-management skills as in improving their ability to administer a budget. And since all of the attendees are preselected by the organization because of their management potential, the program also serves as a seedbed for future high-level executives.

Andrea Feders furthered Nan McKendrick's career by helping Nan obtain entrance into the program. Nan had been at the Womangoods Corporation for six years, moving slowly from copywriter to marketing coordinator, before she first encountered her mentor. Feders, impressed by Nan's ability as a writer for some of her projects, helped Nan obtain her first managerial job, manager of the commercial department. Knowing from experience that power resides in control over dollars and cents, she eventually began suggesting that Nan move from the creative end into a budgetary role.

The indirect method of promotion is well illustrated by the way Feders moved McKendrick into her current position, manager of the merchandising department. The Womangoods Corporation offers only two women per year the opportunity to attend the University Program, and the competition is keen, since entrance into the program signifies that the attendee is regarded as a candidate for senior management. Feders formally submitted McKendrick's name and then went to the president of the corporation to ensure her choice. In doing this, Feders in effect opened the doors of the corporation to Nan. Before entering the program, Nan had been an unknown quantity to the president, whereas upon her return from the program she was offered the promotion to merchandising manager.

As far as most of the organization was concerned, Andrea Feders had no direct influence on McKendrick's career, and in fact she never directly promoted McKendrick. Interestingly, in her interview McKendrick herself exhibited an ignorance of the behind-the-scenes influence that had surrounded her promotion and showed no awareness of the fact that Feders was at that time already grooming McKendrick as her successor.

Prestige Appointments One way of indirectly promoting the protege is to help him acquire prestige by developing a professional reputation in the field. The mentor of John Levine, the management consultant, has placed him on the advisory board of a large professional organization and gained him a position on the editorial staff of a related business journal. Such appointments reinforce the protege's credibility and perceived suitability for a higher position within the organization, since his association with a prestigious outside organization implies a high regard by key members of the business community. There is also the implication that the appointments will generate business connections that will benefit the employing organization.

The mentor also attempts to place articles and short opinion pieces by the protege in such publications as the periodicals of the American Marketing Association, because the more accepted the protege becomes within the corporate community, the more valuable he is to the employing organization. Moreover, his corporate affiliation is usually mentioned in these articles, which increases his company's reputation and credibility. Of course, these activities may be translated into organizational advancement for the protege.

Position of Mentor

Obviously, the mentor's position in the organization can be an important determinant of the extent of his influence on the protege's career. The protege's career is often unmistakably connected to the career of the mentor, politics playing a very important role in the ultimate progress of both members' careers.

Dan Garner's mentor, though president of domestic operations, is not assured of the CEO spot, since two factions, the international and the domestic, are currently fighting for control of the company. Garner realizes that if his mentor does not become the CEO, his career will be slowed somewhat and he will be forced to build bridges elsewhere. As will be evident in this section, the mentor's title does not always indicate the extent of his power.

Official Power versus Influence The example of Nick Ford clearly demonstrates just how deceptive a title is as an indicator of power. Ford's title after 18 years at the Goodbrands Corporation is commercialization manager, several rungs below senior management. Yet he has mentored a number of people during those years, and in fact he began to mentor younger managers when he managed the corporation's "Wisconsin Plant." During the summer four or five students from a local technical college worked at the plant. A particularly bright student caught Ford's eye, was recruited by him for permanent employment, and after several years in various positions was brought over to corporate headquarters.

Though Ford's official position could at best be described as high-level middle management, his influence within the organization is unquestionably dominant. And ironically, most of that influence is based on his standing with former proteges like that student who worked for and were promoted by him and now form a network of cross-loyalties that gives him power greater than that of many vice presidents. Ford's power stems from influence, loyalty, ready access to information, and "expert" authority.

The point is that the sponsorship of a mentor possessing unofficial power can assist a young protege as much as can the sponsorship of a vice president. Christine Webster's meteoric rise to logistics manager was due in great part to Ford's indirect promoting, and she knows that his "planting a bug in someone's ear" regarding her next advance, which incidentally will elevate her beyond him on the organization chart, will probably lead to a further upward climb to the senior levels of the organizational hierarchy.

And Ford is conscious of his power and its effect throughout the organization, as witnessed by his comments on the career of one of the old Wisconsin Plant proteges.

> *"I think all the help I've given him has really assisted him in moving up. I don't think there's any question. Unless you pick a person like that out of a plant or organization and give him the exposure and a chance to move up—he probably would have been, oh, about a half a level of salary now if I hadn't taken him under my wing and moved him along."*

Another form of unofficial power, the mentor's reputation outside the organization, can exert an awesome influence on the career of the protege. Felice Stolz, now a senior product manager at the Womangoods Corporation, met her mentor eight years ago at the Clothier Corporation, where the mentor was vice president of customer services.

As the relationship developed, the mentor eventually guided Stolz into a senior position at their company. Before actively promoting her, she made sure that Felice acquired the appropriate trappings of legitimacy for the senior position: she was instrumental in getting Felice into graduate school; she made time available for the schooling during the workday, and she even juggled the schedule of business trips so that Felice could attend class. Thus, when a senior position came available, Felice Stolz, properly equipped with an MBA, was "worthy" of promotion into the position, which incidentally had never been filled by a woman.

One factor that made the mentor so powerful, and hence able to assist proteges inside the organization, was her industry-wide reputation. Long active in professional organizations and trade groups in the clothing field, she had become an expert in certain trade matters and had acquired professional credibility outside the corporation. She was a name in the industry, a power to be reckoned with. This was evidenced by the fact that when she left the Clothier Corporation several years later, the company, in order to make clear that her departure was not the result of a falling out with senior management, took out a large advertisement in a major trade daily stating that it was extremely sorry that she was terminating their "long and happy" association. The unofficial power that the mentor possessed within the company reflected her reputation and standing within the industry.

The Outside Mentor An interesting aspect of the mentoring phenomenon is that the most influential mentors are often not even members of the protege's organization. Usually outside mentors are thought to play mostly a teaching or coaching role, since it is assumed that a nonmember could have only minor influence in the protege's employing organization. But my findings demonstrate that outsiders can play a crucial role in the organization and the careers of its employees.

John Levine's mentor, as mentioned, has a long-standing relationship with two of the partners in his accounting firm. This gives Levine an edge in the company, from both an informational and a promotional perspective. Even more striking is the example of a psychologist who serves as a human resources/personnel adviser to several companies. The psychologist, who owns a management testing company, has expanded the scope of his firm, which originally confined itself to testing and evaluation, to include management selection functions in the corporations it serves. This gives him a hand in the selection of personnel, and he has successfully placed his own proteges, originally employees in his management testing firm, in executive positions in the human resources departments of his firm's corporate clients. Hence, if one evaluates his role as mentor to a placed protege, the fact that he has no official position in the corporation is of secondary importance. His role in the executive selection process puts him in a strategic position to pass inside information to the protege and to influence his promotion.

Mentor-protege interaction across organizational boundaries often occurs in the course of the relationship between advertising agencies and their clients. One marketing executive was the mentor of his product manager, who later left their company to become an account executive of its advertising agency. Now the two of them maintain a cross-organizational working relationship, and the marketing executive is able to generate a good press in both camps for her work on projects.

"After a project was completed, I would mention to her boss, or write a letter, stating that without her efforts the project would not have been completed."

Thus the mentor's official position within an organization is only one indicator of his ability to affect the protege's career. Though title in the organization is important, so too are political position, informal influence, and functional relationship to others in power.

MENTORING AS TRANSFORMATION

Mentoring is a powerful tool in creating managers. The teaching, support, and promotion of the protege effect a change in the protege from one stage of competence to another. But for many proteges the result of mentoring is more than a change in skills and position—the mentoring experience effects a fundamental transformation in the way they perceive themselves, their careers, their relationship to the organization, their very potential as people. The case of John Chakiris, the head of internal auditing at a major U.S. communications concern, is an example of such a transformation.

Chakiris met his mentor several years ago at his first major position, in a major management consulting firm. He had just received an MBA in public accounting from a small state college, where he had specialized in the application of computers to business problems, and written a research thesis on minicomputers and their impact on the small manufacturing environment. He was unexpectedly recruited into this consulting firm by his eventual mentor, a manager who was in the process of establishing a computer-based data processing center within the firm and needed a "shirt-sleeve type" to run the operation. His recruitment was unusual for this firm, which ordinarily hired MBAs who had graduated from the top 10 business schools and possessed several years of consulting experience.

Right after John came on board, the funding for the computer facility was withdrawn. Suddenly, he found himself without a specific job and surrounded by people with several years of business experience in major corporations and with degrees from MIT, Wharton, and Harvard. Ed, the person who hired John, was at first uncertain about what to do with him. For the next six months, he assigned John to administrative assignments related to data processing functions, but this antagonized the employees who did the actual consulting. John had to be either fired or integrated into the consulting framework, and Ed chose the latter course.

"I had to be redirected into the mainstream of the consulting practice, and I really had no idea what was expected. They had no real training program in the consulting area."

Chakiris understood data processing, but had little expertise in data system consulting, which entails working closely with a client in such areas as data security, computer auditing, financial analysis, and MIS functions. The transition into a management consulting position necessitated an upgrading of his skills and organizational acumen, a process that the mentor could facilitate. Ed's decision to help him make this transition was motivated by both altruism and self-interest. On the one hand, Ed had a genuine desire to help Chakiris in his career. On the other hand, the cancellation of the computer center had been a defeat for Ed and the subsequent dismissal of the person he had brought in to run the center would have been viewed as further evidence of his lack of political clout. Moreover, Chakiris' retention as a permanent member of the organization, especially as Ed's protege, would represent an expansion of Ed's power within the consulting area of the organization.

But the transition had to be fashioned.

The Firm's Corporate Culture The first problem faced by John was the fact that his education, work, and social background made his adjustment to the corporate culture difficult. (The best definition of corporate culture, offered by Deal and Kennedy in a recent book on the subject, is simply "the way we do things around here.")[1]

"I was of a personality and work ethic that conflicted with my peers. They more or less assumed that they were among the chosen."

That assumption derived largely from Ivy League credentials. The other management consultants displayed little subtlety on this score, openly expressing their belief that John's educational credentials did not meet the standards of this major consulting firm.

Because of his lack of experience and proper credentials, John felt it necessary to work harder than his peers. But his resulting work style offended them.

"I was a go-getter. Move ahead. I didn't think because of my past experience I would deserve a special fast-track position. I worked hard, and I was very aggressive."

The corporate culture also mandated a certain type of behavior that John found difficult to adopt, a low-key interpersonal style that could camouflage the actual competitiveness of the firm's environment. While the young consultant was expected to succeed, he had to do so in a particular way.

"They were aggressive in a subtle way. I was more of your open, forward person. If I was displeased or angered about something it was written on my face. I didn't know how to disguise it."

John also had no concept of how to "dress the part." He wore sport jackets in a three-piece suit organization, a habit quickly corrected by his mentor. As Chakiris recounts, "He gave me information I had to know to get along."

As John was assigned to more and more cases, he proved able to fulfill the mechanical requirements of the consulting role, but the personality and style differences remained. The resentment of his fellow consultants manifested itself in various ways. Originally, it had stemmed from the belief that Chakiris could not possibly perform well in his position, but after he had demonstrated his capabilities, the resentment over his lack of credentials was replaced by jealousy over his high performance. John's aggressiveness and creativity were interpreted as "pushiness."

The mentor told John that it would be a shame for him to fail for political and social reasons while performing so well in the client-oriented and "detail" aspects of his position, and attempted to convince him of the importance of adapting to the social climate of the corporation. Eventually, through the mentor's coaching and teaching, John learned to interact with his peers and adopt their code of behavior. Due in part to his own ability and in part to the influence and increasing power of the mentor (who became a partner during this period), he moved up to a senior consultant level.

Career Mentoring But though Chakiris enjoyed the consulting field, he felt that he was not utilizing his knowledge of data processing. He felt that a position in which he could direct, oversee, and develop a computer system was more desirable, and announced to his mentor that he had decided to leave the field. With the mentor's help and advice, he moved into a brokerage firm with a substantial increase in salary and a substantial improvement in title.

Throughout Chakiris' career, the mentor has retained his advisory function, whether in the area of office politics, computer systems, or career strategies. Because the mentor has wide experience in the field, he is able to cue Chakiris on which aspects of his background to emphasize when seeking either promotions within an organization or movement into higher positions. The mentor has indicated to John that his years at the management consulting firm should be highlighted during any job interview. The mentor also keeps him advised on the currently hot fields within data processing, such as data security and control.

Thus, even though John has left the mentor's organization, the mentor continues to fulfill many of the functions discussed in this chapter. For instance, the mentor's teaching of data system skills is continuing through a series of brainstorming sessions on ways to run an MIS system in a large corporation. The mentor, a former McNamara whiz kid with experience in the government and in intelligence, is still contributing to the improvement of Chakiris' computer system know-how.

Chakiris' current position as director of internal audit involves leadership and management, but lacks the innovation/system development perspective. He is being encouraged by the mentor to find a position that utilizes all of his strengths in managing and running a computer system.

But Chakiris' current firm, hurt by changing conditions in the entertainment industry, cannot provide him with the general manager position for which he and the mentor feel that he is ready. Equally frustrating is the fact that the firm does not seem amenable to the changes in its computer system that John perceives as necessary for its survival: fourth-generation computers, personal computers, word processing, and data communication.

The mentor thinks that Chakiris should take the next step into a general management, policy-oriented position. He has even suggested that Chakiris become the manager of a medium-sized data processing firm first, then move into a general manager position in a large corporation.

Resocialization The mentor relationship, in helping transform Chakiris' behavior, his attitudes toward a career in business, and his concept of his own potential, has effected a veritable resocialization.

"With the help of my mentor, I realized that you can't just go pell-mell, willy-nilly and announce to the world that what you see is what you get. You just don't do that in life."

The mentor's input resulted in a transformation of self-concept that had profound effects on John's faith in his ability as a manager. Perhaps the resocialization was necessary because, unlike his management consultant peers from Ivy League schools who had already internalized a "corporate mentality," John had been led by his education and social background to think in terms of a more limited career track.

"My father, though in computer operations, never had this type of job. He's been in a small company for 50 years."

John feels that without a mentor his perception of himself, the business environment, and his place in it would have been extremely circumscribed.

"I'd probably be stuck doing some computer operations work, not knowing the potential out there, not being able to link my capabilities and my strength and rectify my weaknesses, to reach goals and grander things out there. He has introduced me to a level that I was not at all aware of. And I'm aware that once I get to that level, which I will get to in five years, I will see another level."

It is apparent that the term *level* here refers both to his position in the corporate hierarchy and to his degree of self awareness. As I have mentioned, in this case the self-concept of the protege was definitely transformed.

"I never thought of myself as an executive. I thought of myself most, if anything, as a manager type, and that's it. I didn't even know what vice presidents did. Though I had dealings with it in college, I never thought of it or had the ambition for it. The man opened my eyes to it and told me I had potential and skills to be better than them."

The process that took place in this instance transcended the normal confidence building or psychological support usually manifested at Level II and required that the mentor be organizationally situated so as to be able to effect the necessary changes. The mentor had to know what was required to succeed in the organization and had to have sufficient control over its reward system (e.g., promotions) to move the protege through that system and expose him to the proper learning experiences.

Not all respondents need such a transformation of self. Many of the respondents, because of either family background or the "right" business school, have no problem imagining themselves as senior executives, and in those cases the mentor serves as teacher and protector of an already established "executive self." For John Chakiris, however, a reorientation of self-concept seemed a necessary precondition for advancement, and his mentor recognized this.

> "The things I am getting into now I always had in me, but I needed someone to plant the seed, because I had fertile ground for it to grow in."

The Future of the Relationship Recently an executive recruiter contacted John regarding a position as director of a Computer Auditing Department at a fairly large bank. John would be a vice president, and 17 middle managers would report directly to him.

> "I feel I can handle it now. Obviously, I will go to my mentor, who would help me set up budgets, teach me how to run a department, manage it, and familiarize me with the politics involved."

Motivated by his strong interest in John, the mentor has explored the bank's requirements for the opening. The mentor has contacts throughout the bank, and he is gathering information about the position to facilitate the interviewing process. For instance, the mentor discovered that the bank had a computer auditing problem that the new vice president would be expected to resolve, and he advised the protege to emphasize his previous experience with and successful handling of a similar problem. Thus, though now an outside mentor, he continues to assist in Chakiris' promotion and transformation.

The fact that the mentor always seems to be lurking in the background, watching, advising, prompted me to suggest to Chakiris that the mentor might want to affiliate himself with Chakiris on a more formal basis.

> "Yes, he's even said that someday we'll work together again. I said, 'I wouldn't mind working for you someday . . . or you working for me.'"

IF THE MENTOR NEVER EXISTED

From the preceding examples, it is obvious that the mentor can help the protege in numerous ways: he can teach, support, protect, promote, and resocialize the protege, and even transform the protege's self-concept. I felt that we could obtain another clear indication of the mentor's influence on the protege's career if we could find out in what ways that career would have been different if the mentor had never existed. Unfortunately, because we are limited in our ability to manipulate time and space, the best technique I could contrive to do this was to ask the respondent to create a scenario of his career without the mentor. Christine Webster, the logistics manager at the Goodbrands Corporation, described her "unmentored" career this way.

> *"I probably wouldn't be here. My aspirations are pretty substantial. Nick Ford has enabled me to move quickly enough to meet my own aspirations to date. Without him, because I was a woman in what is the last bastion of male chauvinism in this company, I do not believe I would be able to make those moves. Without his faith in my ability to move into a general management role, I do not feel I would have been given an opportunity. Without the opportunity to grow, I would have left."*

Most respondents felt that without the mentor their careers would have progressed less quickly or they would never have fulfilled their ultimate ambitions. Thomas Smith believed that he would not have been able to make much progress. Without the many opportunities he received, each of which broadened his experience, gave him insight into the different paths in the organization, and allowed people within the organization to appreciate the fact that he could get the job done, his career progress would have been impossible. Smith was quite specific about how much lower he would have been in the organization without the assistance of a mentor.

> *"It would not be unreasonable to think I would have come in, started in merchandising, moved over to the control area, and then stayed there and succeeded to a variety of jobs. How far I went would depend more on the situation in which the company's needs were and what happened to people in the organization."*

In recounting this hypothetical career path, Smith noted that managers with backgrounds similar to his own, following similar organizational routes (but without supporters), eventually left due to cutbacks, corporate bloodbaths, or lack of interest in the organization.

"I would now be one of the three people who report to the controller who reports to me."

In other words, Smith's career would have peaked a full two levels lower than his present status. And beyond the issue of level, he would have been excluded from the "inner circle" of policy and politics that formed the lifeblood of the corporation.

The point I am trying to make is not that the absence of a mentor spells ruin but that life without a mentor can substantially affect the chances for playing at higher levels for higher stakes. As Felice Stolz says, "I don't think I would be in the file room, but I don't think I'd be up here."

LIFE WITHOUT A MENTOR

Though the benefits of mentoring are varied, it is well to remember that most of the managers in business today proceed through their careers without a mentor and must fend for themselves. In the process of screening respondents, I came into contact with dozens of unmentored managers, and thus had the opportunity to interview them about their careers, their advancement patterns, and the quality of their work life.

The effects of mentoring have usually been described in terms of career advancement, the central issue being whether the unmentored manager is progressing as quickly or attaining the same title or salary as the mentored manager. While these are salient factors in my comparison, I have found that there are numerous additional differences between the two groups (see Table 3–2).

1. Position of Manager Among the ummentored group there are few if any vice presidents, project directors, or supervisors. It should be indicated that for the most part the unmentored group has the same educational qualifications as the mentored, has been in the labor force for about the same amount of time, and seems to have had similar opportunities for promotion.

An important related factor is that unmentored people with positions similar to those of mentored people seem to have less power, less ability to affect the organizational environment. This difference stems from the legitimacy bestowed on the manager who moves into a position accompanied by the halo effect of a mentor. Since a senior person has smoothed the path for the protege, the mentored executive is more likely than the unmentored one to have real power accompanying his title.

2. Awareness of Requirements for Advancement The unmentored also exhibit a lack of knowledge of the factors related to career advancement. It is remarkable how little information is for-

TABLE 3–2

Comparison of Mentored versus Unmentored Groups

Category	Mentored	Unmentored
Position of manager	More likely to have an authority position (vice president, department head) and to be closer to position of centralized control.	Few vice presidents, lack of control over personnel, budget, resources.
Awareness of organization	High recognition of requirements for road to the top.	Mystified about promotion method, rationale behind advancement.
Knowledge of organization	Rich comprehension of organizational structure, environmental dynamics, personalities involved. Better knowledge of business operations beyond department.	Lower awareness of operation of informal organization, of what affects execution of organizational role.
Commitment to organization	Through mentor feels closer to product and organizational goals. More apt to perceive present organization as career site.	Lack of connectedness to organizational culture. High turnover.
Job satisfaction	Mentor enriches protege's work/organization experience. Quicker positive response to quality work makes job more enjoyable.	Low profile leads to a nonreturn on good performance, leading to decreased satisfaction.
Career planning	Clear objectives a product of frequent interchanges on career goals.	No career road map, low comprehension of how to get from here to there. Goals of low specificity.
Optimism	High. Based on firm belief that mentor will succeed and will at the same time elevate protege.	Generally lowered career expectations.

mally distributed throughout organizations about the requirements and mechanics involved in promotion from one level of the hierarchy to another. Because an "insider" is needed to explain the rudiments of upward organizational mobility, the unmentored have difficulty in determining what actions are necessary for their own advancement or the reasons why peers moved ahead other than that these persons must have "paid their dues" or "put in their time."

3. Knowledge of Organization I questioned the un-mentored about the structure, politics and personalities, and general operation of the organizations in which they were employed. Unlike the mentored manager, who through the teaching of the mentor has a rich knowledge and comprehension of the organizational structure, the general dynamics of the environment, and the interplay of personalities, the unmentored manager seems markedly unable to figure out the intricacies of the informal organization. Though the un-mentored managers know how to perform their jobs and seem to be doing so quite well, the relationship of their department to the rest of the organization, the methods for getting broad departmental goals executed, and the "human side of management" seem to be a mystery for this group.

4. Commitment to Organization Since the unmentored manager does not have a senior executive showing him the ropes and explaining how to advance, he often leaves the organization in search of career success. While doing this can be effective as a short-term career strategy, many of the unmentored respondents have made four or five job changes over as short a time as 10 years, yet achieved comparatively little career mobility, possibly because these were lateral moves designed as much to escape one organization as to join another.

The unmentored managers who do stay are more likely to describe their careers as just a job. Alienation from the organization and its goals, a factor that is bound to affect overall organizational performance, is usually expressed more by the unmentored than by the mentored. According to Peters and Waterman in the book *In Search of Excellence,* the most provocative difference between the Japanese and American worker lies in the greater commitment of the former to organizational goals.[2] I will address this subject further in Chapter 4 in the section on the organizational benefits of the mentor relationship.

5. Job Satisfaction Regardless of position in the hierarchy, the unmentored individual reflects a lower enjoyment of his job than the mentored. This is due to a number of factors. First, the mentor can enrich the protege's working experience through the use of various techniques, including making senior people accessible to the protege and opening avenues of information and resources that make the protege's job easier and hence more enjoyable. But second, and more important, the fact that someone in the organization cares about the protege's career success and organizational performance gives the protege a feeling of self-worth that transcends title and salary and figures heavily in the amount of satisfaction he gets from performing his job.

6. Career Planning Individuals in the unmentored group seem less able than individuals in the mentored group to state where they will be 5 or 10 years from now or what their ultimate business career objectives are. Because of the intense nature of the mentor relationship, most proteges have undergone a series of discussions about their career needs and aims. And in settling in his own mind whether the protege in fact desires to succeed him in his position, the mentor forces the protege to think through his own career plans. Of course, the protege can never be certain that his career plans will not be thwarted by the whims of fate, but a definite career road map is far more likely to breed success than the absence of such a long-term strategy.

7. Optimism Related to the process of planning a career is the issue of the manager's concept of the future. In spite of the recent economic downturn and concomitant squeeze on middle management, I found the mentored group more hopeful and optimistic about their business careers than were the nonmentored group. Much of this hope and optimism grew out of the belief that the mentor would succeed. A manager mentored by an executive vice president with a chance to become CEO or by an executive who has just become a partner will naturally view his own career more optimistically than will an unmentored manager. Also, the manager who, with his mentor's help, has become more aware of the intricacies of the promotion process, will feel more in control of his own destiny within the organizational environment and therefore more hopeful about his organizational future.

I asked the unmentored managers about their impressions of the mentoring process and received a variety of responses Most of these managers could point to specific instances in their career, at strategic points of promotion, where having "someone looking out for them" would have helped tremendously. A good proportion felt that their careers would have been substantially different if a senior person had taken some interest in how they were doing.

Most of the unmentored managers observed mentoring going on around them but seemed completely mystified about why one person was chosen over another. The reaction was not so much resentment (though this did manifest itself) as puzzlement. (A few respondents, upon learning about the nature of this study, asked me whether I knew how they could get a mentor.)

If there is one crucial characteristic that separates the mentored from the unmentored, it would seem to be this: those who eventually got mentors knew very early on that politics and personality play an important role in eventual career success. Those who possess this understanding are more open to the possibilities of such a relationship and seem to recognize the often subtle cues indicating that a senior manager is interested in cultivating a junior successor. Such sensitivity seems absent in the unmentored group.

THE EFFECTS OF ORGANIZATIONAL TYPE ON MENTORING

Of course, the chances of acquiring a mentor who can positively affect one's career depend not only on the manager's political savvy but on the structure of the organization. I have found that mentoring is more likely to occur in certain organizations than in others, that some organizational structures work against the development of one-on-one junior-senior relationships.

For instance, a number of my respondents are employed in a Fortune "Top 10" oil company whose characteristics make mentoring less likely to emerge as a promotional tool. For one thing, the company is rigidly bureaucratized in the sense that it not only has an organizational chart (every company can find one somewhere) but rigidly adheres to it. Power actually resides in the places that the chart says it does. There are more than 40 levels ranging from the very lowest function to the chairman of the board, and everyone in the organization, regardless of position, has a designated numerical level.

How is promotion decided? One respondent says that it is merely necessary to perform well, get noticed, and receive word that you are about to be promoted to the next level. The final decision rests with a committee composed of members of the promoting level. But this respondent's statement also indicates that a bureaucratized environment is no guarantee that a meritocracy is in operation.

"Besides performing well, one would be well advised to begin to adopt the habits, attitudes, and appearance of the members of the next level."

But how does a person learn that this hidden agenda is part of the promotion process or learn the methods for adopting top management's style? A mentor would seem to be the most likely candidate for transmitting such information. However, according to some of the respondents, the manager depends on his own observational powers to learn the requirements of the hidden promotional agenda.

Since the committee system rules, mentoring arrangements are subtly discouraged. One respondent said he had seen only one mentor-protege relationship in over 15 years of employment at the Oil Corporation. The mentor was at least three levels above the protege and could continually move the protege in tandem with his own upward mobility. Yet the machinations required to maintain this relationship were complex—asserting covert influence over the entire committee empowered to promote the protege, transmitting favorable impressions of the protege across rigidly stratified ranks, and communicating with and coaching the protege in a hierarchical organization that discouraged such interaction.

Some of the respondents in the Oil Corporation feel that a mentor would be especially helpful now, in light of the reduced mobility in a contracting organization that has been caught in a static energy market. But each feels that the organization has not developed the culture in which the people in senior management could ever begin to act like mentors. "It's very much like the army here."

Has the lack of mentoring hurt the organization? A mid-level manager thinks that the committee system, while established with the intent of developing a completely fair promotional system, has actually evolved into a rather subjective process. However, instead of reflecting the prejudices of a single senior manager, it represented an exercise in shared subjectivity.

It also seems that upper managers will not serve as mentors, even in the management development sense, because they can see no benefit to their own careers from doing so. Since the organization promotes through committee, and operates in general by group consensus, the establishment of individual loyalties would not have the payoff that it would have in a less structured organization or culture.

A major benefit of mentoring to the organization is that mentoring makes it easier for the organization to retain individual entrepreneurs who would become discouraged and turned off by the size, complexity, and rigidity of the large corporation if the mentor did not provide a "protective cocoon," a humanized subenvironment within an often colder overall culture. The Oil Corporation desperately needs to develop and protect entrepreneurial types—in R&D, exploration, and especially in marketing (oil is a mature product)—and the mentoring relationship seems a perfect vehicle for the cultivation and nurturance of such types. However, its corporate culture and structure seem to militate against the development of such relationships essential to the corporation's continued existence and growth.

Some organizations that claim to be rigidly stratified really maintain the committee system only up to a certain level in the organization, at which point (e.g., lower-level vice president and director/department head) a more laissez-faire approach to promotions is allowed to flower. One such company, a major communications corporation, has a rich mentoring culture that will probably spell the difference between success and failure during the difficult deregulation period, when new markets, new products, and novel approaches will be required not only for growth but for survival.

To repeat the message conveyed at the beginning of Chapter 2, the role of the mentor is to invest a certain amount of power in the protege. In a seminal article on organizational effectiveness, Rosabeth Kanter outlined three major sources of management power in the organizational structure: access to supplies (materials, personnel), access to information, and access to support. She also stipulated that such power comes when the manager has close contact with a sponsor, a higher level person who confers approval, prestige, and backing.[3]

The last two chapters demonstrated in depth how the mentor increases the protege's exposure to these lines of power, through teaching, personal support, and organizational intervention and promotional activities, and how their possession (or nonpossession) can affect the protege's career.

The next chapter will show how the mentor-protege relationship can benefit the mentor and the employing organization.

4

The Benefits Are Mutual—The Mentor and the Organization

The two previous chapters took an in-depth look at the benefits that the protege receives from the mentor relationship. I will now explore the positive aspects of the relationship for the other two partners, *the mentor* and *the organization*.

Although most examinations of the mentor relationship view the protege as the only beneficiary of mentoring, my findings show that mentors consciously cultivate such relationships in order to further their own careers. They also show that benefits accrue to the organizations in which mentoring exists. The statements of both mentors and proteges contain a wealth of information on the many positive implications of mentor-protege interaction for the employing organization and on the role that mentoring plays in organizational development.

THE MENTOR

The literature on mentoring usually concentrates on the fact that mentors assume the sponsor role because they are fulfilling some deep-seated need to teach, assume a parental role, or indulge various altruistic yearnings that presumably haunt executives in late career.

Although these impulses undoubtedly come into play, a variety of carreer-oriented factors also serve as motivating forces behind the assumption of the mentor role (see Table 4–1). Among those factors are enhancement of the mentor's own power, protection of the mentor's position, the mentor's need for help with policy decisions, and the mentor's need for organizational intelligence and information.

TABLE 4–1
Summary of Benefits to Mentor

Career enhancement	Protege helps mentor perform job and contributes to the increase in mentor's reputation. Mentor builds empire with protege.
Intelligence/ information	Protege contributes to the stock of knowledge mentor requires to maintain position.
Advisory role	Protege becomes a trusted adviser, part of policy planning inner circle. Protege tests the corporate waters on key issues.
Psychic rewards	Protege's development provides mentor with a feeling of pride, a sense of contributing to organization.

The following section will deal with the meeting of these needs through the mentor relationship and with the dynamic interplay that occurs between the mentor and the protege.

Career Enhancement

The most obvious benefit of having a protege is that this has a positive effect on the mentor's career. Through a variety of methods, the protege may help the mentor perform his job and may help the mentor's upward movement within the organization (see Table 4–2). Thus the symbiotic character of the relationship should be immediately apparent, since this benefit is functionally equivalent to the positive effect that the mentor has on the protege's career.

Assistance in Job Performance A good protege is a good worker, and mentors generally desire to surround themselves with such people. Gabe Randolph, a protege at the Goodbrands Corporation, understands this aspect of his mentor relationship.

"In business, and especially in big business, it has as much to do with wanting to do something about his career as mine. What happens to me is an adjunct to what he cares about, which is his business doing well. He'll be rich and famous if the business does well, so he's looking for people who can make that happen. So he's supportive of me because I'm supportive of his objectives and will come through for him."

TABLE 4-2

Protege's Assistance in Mentor's Job Performance

1. Protege helps implement programs.
2. Protege provides fresh ideas for projects.
3. Protege provides feedback and critiques existing programs and policies.
4. Through delegation of job to protege, mentor is freed to develop organization and business.
5. By balancing mentor's skills, protege contributes to development of a well-oiled managment team.
6. Protege often assumes supervisory, "second lieutenant" responsibilities.
7. Through teaching job skills to protege, mentor can relearn profession, review (and modify) assumptions.

In most mentor relationships both the protege and the mentor recognize that the protege has made the mentor's life in the organization much easier. One mentor states quite frankly that she would be spending more hours on the job and would have a good deal more anxiety if the protege were not handling many of her projects. The protege is fulfilling a basic need, implementing several programs that would have died in their earliest stage if the protege had not been willing to extend her activities beyond the normal work hours.

Andrew Clark, the vice president at the Insurance Company, is well aware of the role that his proteges play in the day-to-day operation of his department.

> "The success of the manager is tied to the people who are working for him because they can make him look good. I can't handle everything that comes by my desk, but if there are competent people I can farm things out to, and I feel confident that I'm going to get a good finished product, then I'm doing my job."

Such working in tandem also serves as a source of learning for the mentor, in spite of the fact that the flow of information and skills seems to be unidirectionally downward. One mentor says that he learns more about marketing by having to review all the steps for the protege, breaking things down into their barest elements so that the protege can understand the process. By requiring the mentor to rethink and reformulate the assumptions underlying his day-to-day actions, this "teaching" process enables the mentor to relearn his job and his profession.

Through establishment of a give-and-take relationship with the protege, the mentor produces a valuable ally who can point out potential weak spots in policy, personnel, or organizational matters. One manager says,

> *"They can find technical glitches, they can enhance some things. They can provide a constant stream of ideas."*

The element of synergy is crucial to the smooth interaction between the mentor and the protege. Actuated by the goal of developing a "well-oiled management team," mentors often choose as proteges individuals who possess abilities that they may lack themselves.

Charles Clancy's mentor at the Eastern Investment Bank is attempting to develop his division into a "profit center" within the bank, a suborganization in which he can delegate his responsibilities to competent people and free himself for broader planning activities. The protege serves as an important part of the profit center, supervising the other members of the division and in effect becoming a "second lieutenant." When the profit center started, its members were the mentor, Clancy, and an assistant. Now there are eight other people in this highly visible suborganization.

A complementarity of skills between the mentor and the protege is the key factor in allowing the mentor to run the profit center effectively. On the one hand, the mentor has very good marketing skills, a genius for ascertaining where the Investment Bank can place its services and what bonds and financial instruments will further the goals of the institutions it serves. On the other hand, Charles Clancy is skillful at paperwork, at packaging and implementing the broad investment strategies created by the mentor.

Michael Madison at the Chemical Corporation comments that he has a better grasp of detail work than has his mentor. But such complementarity can also extend into the area of management style, the mentor acting more coldly analytical, the protege more sensitively. This mesh of perspectives can be employed quite fruitfully by capitalizing on the contrast in styles when making written or oral presentations and recommendations to third parties.

An issue that recurs throughout the interviews is delegation, the transfer of certain areas of responsibility to another person. Movement into this type of activity entails an often difficult transition for the mentor.

David Dorwin, the vice president at the Crandall Advertising Agency, mentions how difficult it is for his mentor to give up certain responsibilities, even though delegating duties is necessary for his own career progress. Mentors are often people who enjoyed a great deal of success by performing well independently but are now in policy planning/decision-making levels that require a distribution of tasks to others. They may be unaccustomed to delegating responsibility. However, from a career point of view, the sheer utility of engaging in acts of delegation usually wins out over the fear of letting go.

> *"Let's call a spade a spade—this is not a selfless involvement. As he moves up the ladder, he needs to have a backup. He needs someone whom he can delegate to. He can't be as involved with all the clients as he used to be. He needs to delegate and be comfortable with whom he's delegating to."*

The most obvious person to be trusted with delegated assignments is the protege, a person whose performance capability is a known commodity. By having a protege, the mentor possesses an instant replacement, a person who can assume control during his absence. Dorwin mentions that until the mentor relationship developed, his mentor never took a vacation, but now he can take a few weeks off without worrying about whether the agency and the product lines are deteriorating during his absence.

In choosing a protege, a senior manager looks not so much for an adequate worker as for a substitute, a counterpart, or even a clone. Two can not only work better than one; they can often work better than two. This is because the protege often provides not only additional energy but skills lacking in the mentor. Since mentor-protege teams often increase total production, not arithmetically, but geometrically, it should not be surprising that the mentor often uses the term indispensable when referring to the junior partner.

Advancing the Mentor's Career Besides helping the mentor perform his job, the protege may serve as a means by which the mentor achieves organizational and career advancement (see Table 4–3). The most obvious way that the protege helps the mentor advance in his career is suggested in the preceding subsection: having proteges who can help perform his job makes the mentor appear to be a highly productive manager who knows how to delegate well while keeping his eye on the big picture. Regardless of the fact that the mentor accomplishes his goals with the indispensable assistance of

---

TABLE 4–3

Mentoring as a Form of Career Advancement

1. Getting job done through protege builds mentor's organizational reputation for task completion.
2. Becoming identified as a starmaker attracts top junior managers to mentor's department or division.
3. Acquiring ambience of power.
4. Building power base.
5. Grooming successor facilitates mentor's movement upward.

a junior manager, in the final analysis the mentor is credited with divisional productivity.

A protege may make numerous contributions to career advancement that are not readily apparent. By acquiring a reputation as a starmaker, the mentor enhances his status and that of his department or division. Other employees begin to perceive his department as a stepping-stone to promotion within the organization and are motivated to join it. From this group of applicants the mentor can choose the best and the brightest junior managers, who then perform well under his "guidance." The higher-ups increasingly recognize the mentor's ability to develop people. And as each candidate succeeds, the mentor increasingly gains organizational credibility that goes beyond his skills as a department chief; he slowly becomes part of the managerial succession program. In many cases, the mentor becomes absorbed into the senior management policy apparatus as a result of his enhanced reputation.

Becoming a starmaker has other positive side effects. As the mentor's reputation as a starmaker increases, he acquires an aura of power, and promotions, demotions, and firings occurring in the immediate organization are assumed to be somehow caused or influenced by him. Regardless of the accuracy of the perception, when people believe that a given executive has power, they begin to act in accordance with that belief. They become more cooperative, more willing to make resources available, and more likely to accept his suggestions and demands.

The mentor can further enhance his reputation throughout the organization if he is occasionally willing to loan out his protege for work in other departments. Often other senior managers will have assignments that the personnel at their disposal cannot handle, and the mentor may suggest his own protege for such assignments. When the protege succeeds, credit goes to the mentor for his ability to develop skills that are useful throughout the organization.

But by far the greatest benefit that mentoring can bring to a senior manager's career is in the area of empire building. The road to success lies open to the manager who realizes that the strongest type of influence network is composed of proteges whom he can place permanently throughout the organization. As a financial director at a Fortune 500 company comments, it is not widely understood that the manager with the best possibilities for career advancement is one who has an "omnidirectional" influence network.

"It works up and down the network. There are people in the organization that think that the only thing important to them is to impress the boss and the guy on top. While it's definitely true, you can always do that better if you develop a strong network below."

Michelle Ross seems quite aware of her position within her mentor's scheme of things, and understands her importance in an ongoing power struggle. There has been a major organizational shake-up at her company, the West Coast Pharmaceutical Corporation, and while the general manager has made clear to her mentor that the mentor's position is stable for the time being, he definitely wants to see an improvement in departmental productivity. According to Michelle, the mentor realizes that she must develop a power base in order to maintain her own position.

"She needs someone who supports her. I think she perceives now that in me she has someone she can trust and get support from in the organization."

John Chakiris commented that among the reasons the senior executive at the management consulting firm mentored him was that doing so fulfilled the mentor's need for a power base from which to perpetuate himself in his position. At this firm there was always an outside chance of being voted out of a partnership, and the obvious way to avert this danger was to mentor junior managers who would later become supporting partners.

Perhaps the least understood aspect of the connection between mentoring and the senior person's career advancement is the role of this process in grooming a successor for the mentor. Most organizations have a tendency toward equilibrium, and one way of maintaining this equilibrium is to keep people in their jobs once they have acquired the ability to perform them. Ironically, some people perform their jobs so well that they become irreplaceable, a factor that allows people of inferior quality to rise above them when higher positions become available. David Feinberg, a vice president of a medium-sized investment firm, has mentored several managers throughout his career because of the career necessity of grooming a successor.

"Every good manager is training someone to replace him. Why? Because every corporation is a pyramid. If you are asked to take a higher position, if you don't have a replacement, they will take someone else."

Andrea Feders of the Womangoods Corporation uses the term *backup* to describe a protege who will facilitate her advancement into a higher position.

"The only way of getting promoted yourself is by identifying your successor. If you are seeking a promotion, which I have always done, then you say, 'I want that job,' and part of the way that you sell yourself into that job is to say, 'And I know that there is someone to take my place.' "

One of the more unusual cases of career advancement through the development of proteges, that of Nick Ford at the Goodbrands Corporation, illustrates the power of the mentor relationship as a promotional mechanism. Because of his sponsorship of numerous proteges over the years, Ford's organizational reach now stretches further than that of most members of senior management. Many of the proteges who have passed him in the organization now provide him with chances for career mobility. His next promotion may very well be engineered by a highly placed protege.

Proteges may be instrumental in advancing their mentors' careers in other ways. For example, once proteges have been distributed throughout the organization, they may serve as a rich source of "good press" for the mentor. One manager even cited several examples of career advances that he had achieved because proteges had put in a good word for him with key people. In this way, the proteges paid back the mentor for his earlier marketing efforts on their behalf.

An Empire of Loyalties A protege's sense of allegiance toward a mentor can be powerful. Again and again the protege and mentor describe situations in which the protege's action is determined by loyalty to the mentor.

At one point in his career, Gabe Randolph desired a change in departments because, among other reasons, his position as development manager was becoming increasingly tedious. However, since his mentor had installed him in this position, he stayed on in order to maintain the mentor's image. Randolph's departure from the department would have demonstrated bad personnel selection by the mentor and thus would have tarnished the mentor's reputation and compromised his organizational position.

One of the reasons that Randolph wanted to leave the position and department was that his mentor who was moving into another area of responsibility had left his direct supervision to a new person, an outsider in whom Randolph had little faith. But loyalty overruled Randolph's inclination to leave.

"To be successful, you have to rely on people, you have to rely on others. Mentoring is one way of doing that. You can bond a relationship. If I am your mentor, and I do something for you, you in a sense will dedicate your life to helping me out. I felt this tremendous obligation that I had to perform. If I screwed up, it was a reflection on his character. I felt I couldn't quit when this new person came in. As badly as I thought about my guy leaving, this guy coming in and being a total incompetent, if I just stood up and left this position I was just put in, people would ask about the guy who put me in there, 'What kind of judgment does that guy have?' "

Many other respondents described their sense of a moral debt owed to the mentor. The loyalty generated by this feeling of obligation is the element that gives mentor-protege relationships their cohesion. As the mentor builds an inner circle, his organizational empire, he seeks out junior managers who are not only competent but trustworthy. Those exhibiting fealty may become part of the "in-group," trusted confidants who are differentiated by their level of commitment to the mentor. One respondent, a former bank vice president who is now president of his own software company, explains the process in this way:

"There is a certain amount of insecurity. Senior executives somehow think they can further themselves in the organization if they select a few key people and let them carry the ball. And at the same time push back those who they can't get along with."

The mentor wants to draw a sharper line between the inner circle and the outside world. Motivated by loyalty, this elite cadre, through good work and good press, advances the mentor's reputation and career.

Intelligence/Information Systems

Senior managers can quickly become powerless, with lofty titles but no authority, if their lines of communication are severed. They have a real need for information from within the department and, more important, from other departments and divisions. Proteges contribute to the mentor's indispensable stock of knowledge regarding different business sectors and strata.

Because power and position can isolate the highly placed individual, his need for open communication and insight regarding organizational politics and policy can often be met best by a well-placed protege. Office gossip about trivialities as well as potential mutinies or sabotage can be effectively monitored by a widespread network of loyal proteges. While the mentor may possess the hard facts regarding such matters as mergers and management reorganizations, the protege is often in closer contact with the corporation's social climate. Suzanne Barclay, a protege at the Photography Corporation, comments that because she deals with people at all levels throughout the organization she gets certain types of information before her mentor does.

"It is my responsibility to my mentor that he hear whatever the news is from me first. By doing that, he is able to respond intelligently when he is asked

by his management on any issue. It preempts a lot of problems, because he doesn't have to defend anything, because he knows about it."

A surprising amount of organizational information passes from the protege to the mentor even after the protege has moved on in the organization or has transferred to other parts of the country. In fact, most proteges seem quite comfortable about passing on to their mentors information that would ordinarily be considered "off limits" to outsiders. However, it must be remembered that from the protege's point of view the mentor is not an outsider but is still part of a functioning management team. A vice president whose proteges are placed throughout the corporation claims that "if I ever need information, they'll drop everything to give me a hand."

Andrew Clark of the Insurance Corporation tells the story of a protege whom he developed over several years and eventually helped acquire a director's position in a California retail branch office. Although they no longer have a formal reporting relationship within their organization, the mentor still obtains information from the protege anytime he wants it.

"I call him up, and we talk, and from that I get a lot of things you don't see on reports."

Clark has mentored a number of such people throughout the organization whose informational services will help him advance into senior management.

"One of the things you really need in order to survive is information. If you're cut off from information sources, you might as well give up, because you're not going to succeed."

Hence, Clark utilizes his proteges to gather information that, though unclassified, would not be readily available to him. The key to this process is the protege's cooperation, his willingness to extend himself in order to make information available to the mentor, to get around official channels that might require days instead of minutes for the transfer of intelligence.

Because of the importance of this function, many mentors look for proteges who not only demonstrate tendencies toward loyalty and effeciency but can also gather information. This requires an aptitude for gaining the trust of the individuals who control information channels, for acquiring entry into different organizational strata, and most important, for forming enduring alliances.

To summarize, the advancement of the mentor's own career depends on the amount of technical and political information that is readily accessible to him, and proteges and protege networks are an important means for making such information accessible. The protege's willingness to share information of this kind is perhaps the strongest indication of his loyalty to the mentor.

The Trusted Adviser

Though the degree to which the mentor allows the protege access to power varies greatly from case to case, it is apparent that greater benefits accrue to the mentor who decides to elevate the protege to his inner circle. This trusted adviser role entails a greater involvement of the protege in the mentor's organizational role, especially in areas such as policy formation and decision implementation.

Dan Garner, already part of senior management, functions as an internal consultant to the president and in a very real sense acts as his alter ego. The president, who does not deal well with large groups of people, utilizes his protege as a gatekeeper between the "presidency" and the rest of the organization. In addition, the president delegates to Garner certain decisions relevant to operations within senior management.

Trust is an important part of the alter ego relationship, and the mentor must perceive that the protege is acting out of concern for the mentor's status and well-being. Barbara Sikorsky has achieved this level of synergy with her mentor at the Goodbrands Corporation. And the woman trusts Barbara's experience on key issues, even if Barbara is not directly involved with these issues.

"She respects my judgment, she respects my opinion and the thinking I could bring to a situation, even if we don't always agree."

Their relationship should continue for several years, and I think Sikorsky can look to a future in which their careers are linked. When she questioned the mentor about this matter, she was told, "Wherever I go, you can go." The mentor's response strongly implies that she now views Barbara as a career and organizational partner. Their relationship has moved to a level in which both members conceive of their careers and occupational destinies as linked.

As a solid component of the policy and planning process, a trusted adviser can serve an additional function. Many times a president or division head must rely on pure chance in ascertaining the support for new ideas. He must often introduce ideas that look good on paper but whose acceptability to the organization is unknown to him. The difficulties presented by such decisions are most apparent when reorganization schemes are introduced in this way. If a proper consensus has not been achieved, subordinates and supervisors alike will feel that their territories are being invaded and their powers restricted. And when a new product is to be introduced, the president often has little idea of the extent to which the accompanying reshufflings of responsibility and related changes in the power structure will undermine organizational commitment to its introduction.

In situations like these the protege can be extremely helpful. He can serve as a trial balloon for the testing of ideas and plans whose acceptability throughout the organization is questionable. The president may desire to test their acceptability, but doing this often signals to the organization that the person at the top is indecisive and hesitant. Such an impression can undermine his authority and hence the success of the new ideas and plans. But if these are first floated through the organization by the trusted adviser, their acceptability can be determined in a painless and fail-safe fashion. The president can use the protege to put out informal feelers on a plan to other parts of the organization as though it were the protege's, not the president's. If the plan is unacceptable and is negatively reviewed, its true source need never be known.

Presidents of countries often utilize vice presidents in this way, introducing their more controversial ideas through their second in command. In short, plans that might prove unacceptable can be market-tested by disseminating them from a lower office. Then, if they are informally rejected by the organization, they can be harmlessly withdrawn. Very few mentors have mastered this technique for making it seem that their poorer concepts have originated elsewhere.

Psychic Rewards

Although I have generally depicted the mentoring process as operating according to an "enlightened self-interest," career advancement is not the mentor's only motivation for supporting the protege. Although the ultimate measure of the mentor-protege relationship is the career opportunities that accrue to both members, a strong altruistic impulse was manifested by the mentors interviewed (see Table 4–4).

TABLE 4–4
Psychic Rewards of Mentoring
1. Sense of pride when protege does well.
2. Personal satisfaction in teaching.
3. Ego gratification at organizational reputation as "starmaker."
4. Satisfaction that protege will benefit from mentor's mistakes.
5. Feeling of continuity of mentor's own work.
6. Sense of worth due to contribution to organization.

These mentors mentioned a variety of personal satisfactions that they derived from the relationship. For instance, one mentor gets what he describes as a "good feeling" when a protege does well.

"I have looked at work from a lot of different perspectives, and you see what you can get out of a job besides a paycheck. You have to get a sense that what you're doing is worthwhile. Then I get a sense of doing something to help other folks."

Andrea Feders discusses the personal satisfactions of being a teacher, of instructing people in her creative departments to be better writers, better art directors. She finds the gratification of mentoring similar to the gratification that comes from giving someone a gift. Such words as *personally rewarding* recur when people describe the emotional rewards of mentoring.

Suzanne Barclay thinks her mentor takes a lot of pride in her development, in the knowledge that he had a major hand in transforming a novice into a full-fledged marketing professional.

"When other people say 'Suzanne is doing fantastically,' or because of our policies our sales levels are higher than the rest of the world, immediately I get a phone call or get called into his office. And he'll sit there with a big grin on his face and ask, 'How the hell are you doing it?' "

Those mentors who were sought out by the brightest junior managers found it tremendously gratifying to be perceived as star-makers. Some of these mentors became aware of their lofty organizational reputations only when juniors with "executive potential" asked to be transferred into their divisions. One executive says that being sought by someone as intelligent as his protege reinforced his sense of his own abilities.

For some mentors, the relationship serves as a justification of all the trials and tribulations of their long careers. In a sense, the fact that a junior benefits from the mentors' own mistakes and failures lends an air of legitimacy and utility to the mentor's more problematic stages because it signifies that the lessons the mentor learned were not in vain.

But the psychic reward that mentors mention most often involves the concept of continuity. For the senior manager to have any lasting effect on organizational culture and policy, he needs juniors who accept the mentor's policies and will maintain them even after the mentor retires. Whether those policies concern product line, a reorganizational plan, a new division, or a new corporate direction, the mentor desires an assurance that they will outlast him. And having a protege is one way to ensure that his contribution will endure.

Lastly, mentors express the belief that they owe something to their organization, that some form of reciprocation is necessary to compensate the organization for the career benefits they have enjoyed. One major way of doing this is to contribute the extra time and energy necessary for the development of skilled managers who will help the organization continue to thrive.

Hence, altruistic impulses coexist with motives of self-interest. But altruism alone is not sufficient to ensure the commitment of the senior member. For the mentor-protege relationship to sustain itself, the mentor must perceive an eventual payoff. When we examine the risks involved in being a mentor, it will become clearer why career-oriented benefits are the only real guarantee of the mentor's support, the ultimate motivation for his commitment to the protege.

The Risks of Mentoring

It would be simplistic to discuss the benefits accruing to the mentor from the mentor-protege relationship while ignoring the risks (see Table 4–5). As the Hierarchy of Mentoring introduced in Chapter 1 indicates, each level of the mentor's commitment to the protege is accompanied by a corresponding increase in the risk to the mentor.

Time The most obvious risk of mentoring, albeit the least costly, is the possibility that the time, energy, and general concern invested in developing the protege will prove fruitless. The fear here is either that the protege will leave the organization before the investment of training can bring a return or that because of reorganization or cutbacks the position for which the mentor thinks he is preparing the protege will simply disappear. It should be stated plainly that mentoring requires a great deal of time. It involves training the junior person during formal work periods, lunchtimes, and often before and

TABLE 4–5
Risks of Mentoring

Time/energy	Mentor expends time and energy in training the protege that could be spent on business instead.
Exposure of self	Mentor sheds protective psychic layers in discussing his own weaknesses and failures with protege. Mentor commits himself emotionally to protege.
Reputation	Protege with whom mentor is identified may reflect poorly on mentor, alienating key managers.
Risk of incompetent protege	Protege can injure mentor's organizational position by performing poorly in job after mentor influences his promotion into it.
Protege's resignation	Mentor loses influence/position.

after work. It can be assumed that the mentor is engaging in this training in lieu of personal activities that would bring him a more immediate return.

Exposure of Self At Level II, personal support, the mentor takes certain risks that are not entirely apparent. In giving the protege psychological support and helping him to clarify his problems, the mentor often exposes his own weaknesses and failures. Attempts at solving the protege's personal problems usually entail exposing his own.

Also, we must not overlook the emotional investment required to help someone solve a personal problem, for instance, a marital-job conflict. This often involves a prolonged interchange not only with the protege but with members of the protege's family. Though such counseling is aimed primarily at improving the protege's work performance, it often results in emotional strain for the mentor.

Reputation The risk most commonly mentioned in connection with mentoring is the risk inherent in any situation in which a person gives his "stamp of approval" to another person. One mentor is very concerned that proteges be worthy representatives of him and does not want them to reflect poorly on his training. This is one of his reasons for spending a good deal of time counseling and advising proteges on correct corporate behavior. For instance, he gives them rules for proper drinking at parties.

> "When somebody sees that [excessive drinking] happening in a situation, they might think, 'What would happen if this kind of person were three or four levels up?' And I've ended up promoting this person, and I have my name associated with him."

And there is always the chance that the protege will not only commit a social faux pas but alienate numerous members of the organization. Jim Mulcahy of the Eastern Investment Bank realizes that one of the reasons his mentor is sponsoring him is his ability to handle himself well with seniors. He can interact at the very senior level, at the partner level, without behaving in a way that could compromise the mentor.

The Risk of Incompetence The respondents report many stories of injuries to mentors' reputations stemming from the selection of unqualified personnel to fill key positions. According to one mentor, the protege must perform well in a decision-making capacity for the mentor to benefit from the protege's advancement.

> "Some have a lot of interest, initiative, and loyalty, and you put them in a supervisory position and suddenly realize that they cannot handle it because they cannot make a decision."

Ironically, the "risk of incompetence" can have positive consequences for the organization. One fear often voiced about mentoring relationships concerns the possibility that because of the personal relationship between the mentor and the protege, the mentor will elevate the protege to a position that he does not deserve. In fact, the term *favoritism* is sometimes applied to such relationships. But the possibility that the mentor's reputation will be weakened by the poor performance of a protege acts as a natural brake on the movement of mediocre proteges into senior management merely because they have powerful mentors. By advancing the career of an incompetent whom he happens to favor, the mentor endangers his reputation, the efficiency of his organization, and the morale of his department. Mentors therefore tend to avoid the obviously incompetent.

As we shall see in Chapter 7, the "risk of incompetence" is reduced by the high standards that senior executives apply to potential proteges. The primary "good quality" mentioned by mentors is competence.

If the Protege Leaves The mentor builds his empire carefully, committing ever-increasing organizational resources to the development of the protege, entrusting to the protege ever-increasing responsibility for the organization's well-being. As a result, not only are the mentor's expectations with regard to the protege raised, but so too are those of senior management.

What happens if the protege then leaves? Kellen McDaniels recounts how one mentor at his Fortune 500 conglomerate "got burned" when the protege he had supported vehemently and visibly received a better offer and left. From then on, because of his inability to retain his recipient of considerable organizational trust, the mentor's influence within the organization declined. The mentor was blamed for wasting the organization's time and resources on this protege, in much the same way as he would have been blamed if he had persuaded the organization to sponsor a new project or marketing plan that subsequently failed.

This discussion of risks demonstrates why the mentor relationship cannot be based on purely altruistic reasons. Any commitment to a junior person, no matter how loose, requires some risk, and unless a senior manager thinks that the benefits are commensurate with the risks, he will not make the commitment. And the benefits in question are obtainable only if the protege is able, skilled, and loyal.

THE ORGANIZATION

One way of viewing the organization is as a large problem-solving machine that has been established to produce, protect, administer, or otherwise meet the needs that confront society. In order to fulfill its functional mandate, the organization must satisfy its members' psychic and material needs, integrate the members into its goal orientation, and at the same time ensure a smooth and orderly succession at the top.

It is apparent that mentoring can help the corporation do these things, and in that sense mentoring can play a key role in organizational development. In fact, as has been implied in the Mutual Benefits Model, mentoring exists not only because it serves the interests of the mentor and protege but because it simultaneously fulfills the needs of the organization.

The following discussion explores the numerous benefits that the organization derives from mentoring (for summary, see Table 4–6). These benefits, which are in a sense "spun off" from the self-interested interactions of the mentor and protege within the context of the mentor relationship, must be seen as adjuncts of a power-based

TABLE 4–6

How Mentoring Benefits the Organization

Integration of the individual	Mentor helps protege feel closer to the organization, more accepting of its mores and goals. Mentor increases protege's sense of belonging.
Reduction in turnover	Because mentor relationships prevent talented proteges from becoming lost in the corporate woodwork and increase the amount of positive feedback to proteges, proteges tend to remain in organization. Thus loyalty toward mentor becomes a major factor in reduced turnover.
Organizational communication	Because protege enjoys multitiered membership status, he can promote communication between various organizational strata by serving as a Likert-style "linking pin."
Management development	Mentor transfers to protege skills and knowledge that would otherwise be denied to him. Mentor is seen here as an important factor in the transformation of a technical worker to a full-fledged executive. Mentor reduces the haphazardness of management development.
Managerial succession	Mentoring facilitates the smooth transfer of the managerial reins from one generation of executives to the next. Mentor transmits corporate values and other key components of the corporate culture to the next generation of leadership.
Productivity	Mentor fosters productivity by enhancing skills of protege. Mentoring serves as an informal mode of corporate reorganization for maximum efficiency.
Socialization to power	Mentoring produces managers who are comfortable with power and possess the motivation and ability to mobilize people and resources.

relationship. Yes, empires are built and the mentor and protege grow in power and status, but the abilities of the organization's members are also enhanced and hence their capacity to produce results for the organization is expanded.

Integrating the Individual

The relationships that employees have with their employing organizations assume a great variety of forms, but these forms can be classified into two broad categories. The most common type of relationship that an employee may have with his employing organization is labeled *exchange.* The employee works for a wage and increases or decreases his contribution to the organization to the extent that the organization compensates him for his contribution. In effect, the employee says, "I do X because you're paying me to do X." His commitment to the organization is governed by the paycheck.

A second, deeper type of relationship occurs when the employee focuses his actions increasingly within the organizational context. Much of his free time, evenings, and holidays is spent doing work for the organization, and more and more of his life activities, including aspects of his social life, become centered on the corporation. This second type of relationship, in which the employee increasingly perceives himself as an "organizational member," is labeled *integration.*

The integration of the individual into the mainstream of corporate life has become a major goal of large corporations, and they have enlisted regiments of sociologists, industrial psychologists, and management specialists in the war against organizational alienation. A central theme of this section is that mentoring facilitates integration.

Some respondents have described the mentoring process as the main factor in their achieving a "sense of belonging" to the organization. Since the mentor, a representative of the corporation's inner structure, completely accepts the protege as a worthy member of the corporation, the protege perceives the corporation itself as accepting him.

One respondent makes a very strong point about the role of the mentor in creating her "sense of community" within her organization. She says that she would never have had that sense of attachment without the "human face" of this organization as represented by the mentor.

> *"I live here. I spend an awful lot of my time here. And many of my thoughts outside the office are in relation to what I do here. My sense of community is not only my friends and family outside this office. There is a certain sense of community here. And I suppose a mentor inside is having someone care for you."*

Having a mentor helps her feel closer to her particular division.

And the protege's positive perception of the mentor encourages the development of a positive perception of the corporation. In this sense, the mentor serves as a mediating agent between the organization and protege. Thus one respondent noticed that her positive image of her organization changed after her mentor left her immediate work environment. This process also suggests that through mentoring the goals, moral precepts, cultural tastes, and proscriptions of the organization become more acceptable to the young manager. He feels that he is being introduced to these concepts and values, not impersonally, but by a "friend."

A protege's feeling that he is becoming one of the family through his relationship with the mentor is particularly strong when the mentor is helping him to make the transition from his peer group into the senior management group that shapes the policies and overall direction of the organization. The mentor allows him an input that makes him feel that he is participating more fully in the inner operations of the organization. This process generates a closer identification with the organization's goals.

Reduction in Turnover

There are indications that mentoring benefits the organization by reducing turnover. The most obvious way that it helps retain employees is through the integration mechanism just discussed. Being more closely interwoven into the organization's cultural fabric, and hence feeling closer to the organization, reduces the likelihood that the protege will leave the organization.

But mentoring helps lower turnover in other ways. For instance, the properly placed mentor can ensure that the protege will not disappear into the corporate woodwork, become frustrated, and leave the organization. Andrew Clark of the Insurance Corporation cites an example that illustrates how mentoring helps retain proteges in this way.

The corporation has a special training program for selected "high potential" new recruits, a formalized fast track that has been established to ensure that the best talent is cultivated and directed to the top positions. But in a manner typical of its bureaucratic tendencies, the corporation has established a rule that restricts entrance into this program to only two points in a given year. This means that a young recruit who enters the Insurance Corporation out of phase with the beginning of the program cannot gain entrance into it. The alternative for such a new employee is a completely separate secondary promotional track.

Clark's protege was a bright, articulate graduate of a Seven Sisters college who had the misfortune to enter the corporation at the wrong time, off cycle for entrance into the program. However, Andrew Clark, recognizing her talent, felt that the organization would be best served if he established an "informal" high-potential program for this woman. In other words, he decided to devote his energies to her development.

It is safe to assume that if this woman had not been taken under Clark's wing, she would have eventually left the organization, frustrated by a lack of challenge and by the fact that the best assignments were going to program participants. With Clark as her mentor, however, her progress has exceeded that of many of the so-called high-potentials. She reached the associate manager level in two years, a process that usually took four to five years.

> *"I realized the type of frustration that people go through, and I've seen so many people leave just because they didn't have anybody who seemed to care whether or not they stayed or made any effort to help them solve their problems. And because I felt that she had something on the ball, I would do what I could to make sure she stayed."*

Often proteges remark that whether they remain in an organization depends on whether they have a sense of being needed. The mentor is certainly in a position to create a working environment in which the protege feels that he is important to the functioning of the organization. Hence, the mentor relationship tends to become an umbrella over the entire job experience. One respondent says that although she could probably make more money elsewhere, she remains in her mentor's organization because her working environment is as important as money in determining where she chooses to pursue her career. In short, the mentor makes the protege's life at work pleasant.

Of comparable significance is the mentor's ability to ensure recognition of the protege's accomplishments. By verbally rewarding the protege for a job well done, the mentor demonstrates to the protege that since the corporation acknowledges and appreciates his organizational achievements, he ought to continue to pursue his career in it.

Since proteges are usually among the most promising and talented employees within the corporate ranks, they are often approached by recruiters from other companies. It is in such instances that the power of the mentor reveals itself. David Dorwin of the Crandall Advertising Agency was offered a highly slotted vice president's position by the president of a competing agency, an offer that seemed particularly attractive since it came at a time when he was undergoing a difficult period in his current job. Although he did not wish to accept the position, it was becoming difficult to say no, especially when the president repeated the offer at a chance meeting at a trade convention.

David talked the offer over with his mentor, not because he wanted to resign, but because he wanted the mentor's opinion. The mentor indicated that although the increase in salary was attractive, from a long-term career perspective the offer should be ignored. He told David that the agency making the offer was so tied to one particular client that it had little identity of its own and hence was not well regarded in the industry. He informed David that he had a bright future in the agency and that it would be worthwhile for him to remain with it. Had the mentor not intervened, the agency would have lost a good worker. As David says, "It was the proverbial offer you can't refuse, and I refused it."

It should be pointed out that the mentor did not make a counteroffer. In fact, his only substantive statement related to unspecified "good things" that would happen at some point in the future. The fact that Dorwin remained at Crandall indicates that the "gut feelings" inherent in the mentor-protege relationship were powerful enough to convince him that remaining at the agency was in his best interest.

The key to such gut feelings is trust. Any senior manager, in order to retain an employee, can make claims to a junior manager that he has a strong future in an organization, but the chances that he will be believed increase dramatically if he is the junior manager's mentor. Also important in keeping the protege in the organization is the mentor's ability to quickly mobilize the organizational resources necessary to deliver rewards to the protege. Dorwin's early promotion was no coincidence: the mentor, realizing the necessity of making good on his promise of a bright future, made certain that a promotion to vice president was quickly bestowed on Dorwin.

The examples disclosed by the respondents illustrate that the connection between mentoring and low turnover derives from several sources. The mentor can reduce the protege's frustration on the job, ensure that the protege is adequately rewarded, and even create a pleasant working environment for the protege. However, a prime motivating force that encourages the protege to stay is a sense of loyalty. Most of the young managers interviewed expressed a loyalty to the mentor that was manifested on a day-to-day basis, a loyalty that stemmed from the realization that this senior executive was risking his organizational reputation by sponsoring the protege for a high position. The organization definitely benefits from a relationship (or a series of relationships) based on loyalty that ensures the retention of the best and brightest junior executives and guarantees continuity in the managerial ranks.

Organizational Communication

The traditional literature on organizational effectiveness stresses that communication is an important ingredient of corporate success. An organization with open lines of communication can be assured that its goals and objectives are transmitted, understood, and accepted up and down the hierarchy and that the different segments of the corporate machine will move in the same direction at the same time. It is my contention here that the intense interchange between mentors and proteges improve the overall level of communication within the organization as a whole.

An understanding of the mentor relationship as a communication mechanism can be facilitated by reviewing some of the organizational theories of social psychologist Rensis Likert. Likert, who performed pioneering work in this field for at least three decades, has formulated some of the most satisfactory analysis of the structure and operation of the organizational environment.

Likert developed unique methods that could involve the entire organization in the decision-making process by opening communication channels between its different levels. One of his suggestions was that adjacent organizational strata have at least one person—a "linking pin"—who was a member of both levels. Likert was quite specific about the function of such a person.

> An essential function of a linking pin is to provide an information flow and to establish reciprocal influence between the two groups of which he or she is a member. . . . The linking pin should function as a channel between the two groups so that they both have before them the same statement of the problem and the same facts, knowledge of situational requirements, awareness of differences and conflicts and other relevant information.[1]

Likert offered several reasons why the linking pin, the person with a foot in both the higher and lower management groups, is able to increase the flow of information and the empathy between the two groups. First, he exerts influence over both groups. Second, he is closer psychologically to each group than anyone else in one group is closer to the other group. Third, his membership in each group is acceptable to both groups. Fourth, his knowledge of the norms, values, needs, goals, and jargon of each group facilitates his ability to communicate effectively with both groups. Fifth, he coordinates problem solving between the two groups, helping them reach solutions acceptable to both.[2]

Though Likert envisioned this system as a formalized, preplanned organizational structure, with linking pins appointed or selected by consensus, I have found that the proteges I interviewed, while in relationships that may have developed haphazardly, often assumed many of the linking pin functions outlined by Likert.

Because the protege's membership in his formally designated peer level coexists with his informal interaction with his mentor's upper stratum, he can be thought of as an organizational linking pin. Proteges often exert influence on at least two groups, and with the help of the mentor they have mastered the jargon and mannerisms of the higher group. (This has been described as learning the "correct presentation of self" in Chapter 2.) More important, when proteges perform their jobs, they have access to the views of both their peer level and their mentor and they can communicate each stratum's views on given corporate projects and programs to the other stratum. Thus the informal mentor relationship provides each stratum with a method of linkage to another stratum that would otherwise be absent.

Because of the nature of the mentor relationship, its use as a permanent method of maintaining communication between the strata of an organization should not be overemphasized. For one thing, the protege is in a state of transition from one group to a higher one, so his position "between groups" is temporary. After all, his purpose in entering the relationship, according to the Mutual Benefits Model, is to achieve upward mobility. The mentor relationship affords him the possibility of serving as a linking pin only while he is still a member of the junior group. However, I would not want to overstate this as a problem, since the transition period may take months or years, and until the protege is promoted into senior management, he can perform this communication function.

Another point that should be made is that mentors are often themselves proteges. It is not uncommon for a middle manager's mentor, a senior vice president for instance, to be mentored by the president, the CEO, or a board member. When this is the case, the open communication provided by proteges who serve as linking pins may be found up and down the organizational hierarchy.

Management Development

One of the most fundamental benefits of the mentor relationship to the organization is that it furthers management development by facilitating the transfer of management skills from the senior to the junior member. According to the respondents, they might never have acquired many of these skills without the relationship.

For instance, as mentioned earlier, Michael Madison of the Chemical Corporation got a special invitation to an important banking luncheon due to his mentor's intervention. The mentor's aim was to familiarize the young manager with the corporation's "external environment." Since in today's business climate an executive is often expected to double as a corporate representative, the protege's early exposure to the world of corporate financing obviously helps the organization. In fact, it is possible that without a strong mentor relationship the organization would be unable to sensitize the young manager to the nuances of that world.

David Dorwin's advertising agency received similar benefits from the mentor relationship. The mentor changed Dorwin's perspective on the essential relationship between the agency and the client, explaining to him that clients do business, not with an agency, but with the account executive.

> "The really good account executive is a step ahead of the client, coming up with ideas and inundating the client with all types of marketing suggestions so that they look at the agency and see more than an agency. They see a person whom they can lean on."

Phyllis Berman, an account executive at Prescott and Ruderman, a top 10 advertising agency, feels that the mentor's ability to motivate the protege, "light a fire" under him, hastens the development of the protege.

> "In a successful positive mentoring relationship, you will actually be in a better position, through knowledge or general enthusiasm, to do a better job. My experience in a broad sense is that certain people are better in terms of motivating others to do their damndest."

To the extent that the mentor can communicate enthusiasm and a sense of purpose, he enhances the protege's performance.

One respondent sought to quantify the extent to which the mentor might accelerate the development process.

> "Mentoring is an important part of business and industry. Having people know more about the profession earlier is important for the betterment of the profession. If the mentor can shortcut the first 10 years of learning to a manageable 5, the organization will be better."

Accelerating the development of a protege into a manager, an almost natural outgrowth of the mentoring process, is a real benefit for the organization.

The following case demonstrates the almost unlimited role that mentoring can play in management development. An increasing amount of entering employees have skills that are primarily technical, especially in fields such as engineering and architecture. But the administrative functions of their employing organizations cannot be easily fulfilled by individuals who are deficient in managerial experience. This creates difficulties for such organizations. For example, engineering firms that wish to fill administrative jobs are constantly confronted with the problem of whether to hire professional managers who lack a technical background or to promote from within engineers who have little experience in people management. Since technical knowledge of the firm's activities is an invaluable asset in management, such companies often attempt to train their technical staff for corporate leadership positions. But this process may entail a difficult transition for the technical employee.

One respondent, John Fareed, now a general manager at a real estate conglomerate, underwent such a transition during an early phase of his career, an intense training provided by a mentor who recognized in Fareed a raw managerial talent that required shaping and modification. John, a native of Kuwait, was mentored by the owner of the first firm that he worked for after getting his architect's degree. During his nine years with the Kuwait-based firm, Fareed rose from a position as junior architect and designer to the second-in-command position, a transition that he believes could not have occurred without a substantial amount of tutoring and conscious development by his employer.

The skills involved in management, such as delegating duties, developing esprit de corps among the work units, and communicating organizational goals, had never been taught in the architectural department of his university. Fareed had innocently assumed that the major function of all architects was to erect such structures as houses, power plants, and dormitories. Under the mentor's guidance he suddenly realized that every activity, including construction, depended on the coherent organization of the numerous skills involved in the activity and that such organization was made possible by a specific type of management proficiency.

The mentor had to teach Fareed how to handle personnel functions, including hiring and firing. It was less difficult to teach him the behavioral aspects of making personnel decisions than to instill in him the ability, desire, and motivation to perform them.

"I hated firing people. The 'God quality,' that I am here to dispense with the lives of people, was initially overwhelming."

Over a period of time the architectural firm's performance was enhanced by the mentor's ability to develop one of his technicians into a manager, since this freed the mentor to devote more time to cultivating new business. And a latent additional benefit accrued to all of the organizations that subsequently employed John Fareed. In his current position he utilizes the same management skills, the same ability to make personnel decisions, and the same organizational techniques that his mentor developed in him years earlier. As in most such cases, the benefits of mentoring extend well beyond the original site of the relationship.

As testimony to the value of the special management development that the mentor afforded Fareed, it should be noted that the other junior managers of that architectural firm, now scattered around the globe, never progressed to his organizational career level and have remained for the most part in the technician/architect ranks.

Managerial Succession

A primary organizational benefit of mentoring is that it facilitates the smooth transfer of the managerial reins from one generation to the next. This involves more than merely teaching the protege the requisite skills. The organization's values and a "sense of history" must be transmitted to the protege for him and the corporate goals must be clarified. Dan Garner maintains that the mentor relationship is the optimum means for transmitting corporate values.

"I believe in a continuum. I have a sense of history which I find missing in a lot of people, and there's something to be said for these senior folks who have such incredible seasoned experience and judgment and also have a sense of humanity and putting it all in perspective, using those talents and trying to grow from them, as we try to diversify things within the company, try to make it more statesmanlike."

His particular company, the Communications Corporation, is undergoing a transition from being merely a producer of telecommunications productions and equipment to being a "leader of the industry" in a more policy-oriented sense.

"We're growing exponentially and will legitimately become one of the top companies in this decade. That demands that we all demonstrate a different outlook to the world in terms of leadership positions within the communications industry—a certain charisma, a certain statesmanlike posture, acceptance of new social responsibility. And we need to have all the sense of history and all this seasoned wisdom and judgment floating around to be able to do that."

Though styles may change, most organizations aspire to a continuity in their underlying philosophy. Mentoring can assist in the transfer of organizational goals, practices, and values.

The mentor presents the protege with a standard of leadership, a business framework, a line of thinking that is in keeping with established principles. In a sense, he is transferring a whole philosophy.

Andrew Clark of the Insurance Corporation talks about the mentor relationship as a mechanism for transmitting the corporate value structure from one generation to another.

> *"I think the philosophy of the company, and the vast management of the company is, 'we want to do the right thing.' We've always called ourselves the white knight. If it's not right, we will not do it, regardless of the advantage. We have a lot of people here who are concerned because of what the company represents. Working in insurance, which is very conservative, people have to be able to trust in the insurance institution, because we're asking people to collect now on an obligation that won't come due in 60 years. So you have to develop in the protege a sense of integrity."*

What the subject of managerial succession really addresses, then, is the transfer of the values, goals, and traditions making up the corporate culture. And there is a growing literature that views the continuity of these strong cultures as the basis for organizational growth and progress. As mentioned in the book *In Search of Excellence*, most of the companies that have maintained their levels of excellence have done so by preserving the high standards established by their founders.

> Associated with almost every excellent company was a strong leader (or two) who seemed to have had a lot to do with making the company excellent in the first place.[3]

According to the authors, these companies took on their basic character under the guidance of a "very special person," at a fairly early period in their history. Each of them assumed the values, goals, and practices of its founder-mentor, and the shared values were maintained well beyond his life span. The present chief executive and senior management must manage and sustain these values, and mentoring serves as an appropriate vehicle for ensuring their continuation.

Productivity

By reducing the insecurity of the protege, by developing him as a manager, and by furthering the communication of ideas, mentoring becomes linked with increased productivity.

The mentor acquaints the protege with the way things really work, with how resources are actually mobilized, dispensed, and optimally utilized. One mentor insists that the only way to work productively is to realize the functional limitations of the organization chart.

"Mentoring exists to make the organization more functional. If the chart insists that one move from A to B to C to D to achieve a given goal, and A to D is the most efficient, the mentor must make the protege aware of this relationship."

In fact, the functional interaction between mentor and protege, which is often an informal exhange that circumvents the hierarchical layers, in itself represents a movement from "A to D." According to this mentor, organizations are guided by informal structures consisting of people who arrange themselves into functional units, often in disregard of organization charts. In order to increase productivity, organization members transcend the organizational road map and attempt to "reorganize" themselves on the basis of such factors as complementarity of skills, goals, and needs. The mentor relationship is a strong example of an informal reorganization that bypasses the formal hierarchy in order to achieve greater functional efficiency.

Productivity is also spurred by the intense nature of the coaching/teaching aspect of the mentor relationship. Nowhere is this more apparent than in sales organizations. In such organizations the mentor often intervenes to develop the protege's ability to sell a product or product line.

Transforming an individual from a novice into an exceptional salesperson requires a great deal of attention and commitment. Ellen Everett entered the Management Training Corporation with no sales background. Her Ivy League MBA was in the area of general management. She found this sales position particularly difficult because she was selling, not a tangible product such as shoes, computers, or CAT scanners, but what was essentially a service, management training programs.

Ellen's mentor provided her with several invaluable lessons in this unfamiliar area. First, she became a role model of the art of selling, allowing Ellen to observe her in action and to learn from her. Second, and more important, she "greased the wheels" of the company so that various resources necessary for successful delivery of the product became instantly available to Ellen. Since the salesperson did not draw a commission until the product was "delivered" (i.e., taught by a small and hard-pressed institutional staff), it was important that she have contacts inside her corporation who could schedule instructional support for her clients. Ellen Everett's mentor had influence with the instructors and was able to painlessly elicit their cooperation.

"If she hadn't greased the wheels and taught me how to grease the wheels, I never would have had anything to put on the sales sheet, because the products wouldn't have been delivered at the right time by the right person."

Ellen also felt that her morale had been sustained by the mentor's encouragement during the early stages of her selling career. According to Ellen, the Management Training Corporation "motivates" the sales force by distributing a weekly newsletter listing the current gross sales and commissions of each salesperson, for the month and the year. But this "motivational" strategy, which had been established to encourage a "healthy competition" among the salespeople, actually did more to erode the novice's self-confidence than to bolster it by reporting his often weak initial sales. In fact, many salespersons who might have developed into solid performers were discouraged by this unwanted publicity. A mentor, on the other hand, can bolster the new employee's confidence and self-image.

The dividends that the mentor relationship has yielded to the Management Training Corporation in this instance are obvious. Ellen Everett is now the corporation's highest producer.

The payoff of mentoring in terms of productivity is also evidenced in the example of William Busch, the national sales manager of a billion-dollar retail shoe chain. According to Busch, the rationale behind mentoring is simply to make the protege more productive, and he outlined for me the steps he employed in developing a particular protege into an extremely successful salesperson.

Busch coached this protege in the bookkeeping aspects of selling and attempted to infuse him with enthusiasm for the product. Whereas many sales people in the corporation underwent a perfunctory training exercise, Busch spent 10 solid days with the protege, role playing, indoctrinating, familiarizing him with the products, and otherwise training him in the art of selling. He gave the protege pointers on how to survive on the road and deal with the boredom of travel, convincing him that eventually the territory would become familiar and that he and the customers would become friends.

The mentoring continued throughout the protege's career. Busch informed the protege that he himself had suffered through lonely nights in strange hotel rooms and let the protege know that he would always be available for pep talks when the protege was on the road.

"Suddenly, he didn't feel that what he was going through was singular, that nobody had gone through this before but him."

According to Busch, selling requires positive thinking. He teaches his current protege how to concentrate on his successes and on the techniques that led to them. He has interceded in the conflicts that arise between the protege and his wife because of the protege's long stretches on the road and feels that he has rescued the protege's marriage.

Another major effect that mentoring has on productivity centers around the survival of the entrepreneurial person in the large corporation. The megacorporation, like the society in general, needs fresh ideas and creative approaches to remain healthy. But since organizations tend toward the maintenance of equilibrium, it is often difficult to encourage innovation.

A major obstacle to corporate innovation is the difficulty of retaining talented individuals who consider the large organization to be regimented and therefore not a particularly suitable environment for creative activity. Many of the managers I interviewed thought that an important role of mentoring was to establish a safe, secure subenvironment in which novel ideas could be developed, nurtured, experimented with, and successfully introduced into the corporate mainstream. The protection function, which I originally described as a protege benefit, has far-reaching positive effects on the organization as a whole when it gives proteges the time and freedom necessary to develop their ideas and innovations into productive marketing or financial programs and strategies.

Socialization to Power

In addition to integrating the individual into the organization, reducing turnover, improving communication, and accelerating management development, the mentor relationship gives the organization the benefits of a process known as *socialization to power*.

Beyond the skills and aptitudes that a young manager brings to or is taught in his position, there is a quality necessary for organizational growth that in a sense cannot be taught, namely, the desire and motivation to *exercise power*. That quality comprises the entrepreneurial, directional, and inspirational elements that are necessary to run a business, an army, a corporate division, or a government.

The son or daughter of an entrepreneur or a senior executive can be weaned on power, can "watch Daddy operate," and can become comfortable with the patterns and nuances of manipulation and mobilization. At age 39, he may not know all there is to know about a business, but he expects to be involved with, and feels comfortable with, the mobilization of resources, be they people or things. We register no surprise when Joe Kennedy's sons assume the reins of government or when Hugh Hefner's daughter takes over the *Playboy* empire.

However, most managers are of middle-class origin and have not been raised from childhood surrounded by the ambience of power. Their schooling has taught them the elements of business, but the courage to make a deal, close a division, or launch a product line is not inbred. Here mentoring can be invaluable. By "witnessing power," by being included in these processes early in their careers, proteges can become comfortable with power and learn how to exercise it.

At the Womangoods Corporation, one protege has learned to act powerfully by witnessing her mentor's tendency to "stick her neck out." "It's good to be around people like that. There's an energy to people like that," the protege remarks.

Even the ability to spend great amounts of corporate money on products is not inbred. When I said to Andrea Feders, the vice president at the Womangoods Corporation, that none of us has ever been taught to spend $2 million, she responded that you cannot actually instruct in this area. "You don't teach them; you take them along on how you do that." In order not to overwhelm the protege, she teaches the protege to think in terms of single units of expenditure and then to extend such small decisions to larger ones. Through this socialization process the mentor gradually weans the protege by teaching the protege to "make the decisions on the little things, keeping in mind what the long-term costs are."

The cavernous expanse between knowing what to do and actually doing it can spell the difference between organizational failure and success. The mentor relationship produces managers who feel comfortable with power and possess the motivation and ability to move the company forward. By witnessing power the proteges internalize a fearless attitude that serves them well when they are faced with major decisions.

Most descriptions of the mentor relationship depict the protege as its major beneficiary. What I have attempted to do in this chapter is examine the various benefits that the mentor and the employing organization receive from the relationship.

The next chapter will look at how mentoring has benefited a particular management group, female executives. It will examine the obstacles encountered by these corporate newcomers and will show how mentoring has assisted them in surmounting these obstacles.

5

The Female Protege

Up to this point, we have not dealt with the element of the respondent's sex as a crucial variable in the mentor relationship. But as we shall see, the woman manager encounters special problems in the corporate environment that require additional attention from the mentor. This chapter will examine the obstacles women executives face and how mentoring can be especially useful in overcoming the barriers that stand between such executives and career success.

The appearance of women in the ranks of management is a relatively recent phenomenon. The estimates on the percentage of women in management range from as high as 14 percent to as low as 5 percent.[1] In his 1982 report on the American corporation, Allan Cox found that women comprised 8 percent of middle managers and 2.5 percent of senior managers.[2] These figures are not overwhelming. However, it is important to note that the number of women in the managerial ranks doubled between 1975 and 1982, to 3.2 million workers.[3]

One of the reasons for this sharp rise has been the surge in the number of female MBA graduates. In 1971, 3.9 percent of the MBA degrees went to women, but by 1977 they represented 11.6 percent of the MBA graduates. By the late 70s, 15 percent of the entering MBA students were women, and the proportion has been steadily increasing since then.[4]

Many of the structural, legal, and educational barriers to the entrance of women into management seem to have weakened or disappeared completely. But the issue of their upward movement through the organization once they have gained entry to management still remains a central concern. Because their mere presence in management does not assure upward mobility, another mechanism is necessary for success.

MENTORING AND THE BARRIERS TO WOMEN

Despite the increase in the number of women managers, there are indications that women still face sex-related barriers that can thwart their upward progression through the organizational hierarchy. The progress of female managers is hampered by the traditional image of women in the workplace, by the feelings of threat among male managers, and by the general perception among already placed managers that women lack the skills needed to perform in a managerial role. As the following section will reveal, mentors can be instrumental in assisting women to overcome these obstacles.

Barbara Sikorsky, the product manager at the Goodbrands Corporation, spent the first years of her career in an advertising company and learned early how the absence of a mentor could hamper a woman manager's career. She was hired into an account group at the advertising agency in 1975 and was the only woman on the staff. Two women who had preceded her in the same position had failed miserably.

> "The group was very old-fashioned, stuffy. And not necessarily elderly by any stretch. It was a relatively young group, but their whole approach to things was extremely stuffy. I walked in with a couple of strikes against me. They were expecting me to fail, and they were kind of doing this because it would be nice to give it another shot, and it's expected today, and my credentials were impeccable, so why not give it another shot."

Barbara quickly discovered why women had been failing in the position. In an advertising account group, interaction with peers, company officials, and clients is the lifeblood of career success, the foundation upon which deals are made.

> "They made it very difficult for me to succeed. I had some male peers who'd be invited out by the boss for a drink after work or a golf game or something like this, and I was always conveniently left out."

She was also excluded from key interactions with clients.

"At one point I was uninvited to a client party because the feeling was that they might want to go out later on and carouse and I wouldn't fit in, rather than let me make the decision that I could peel off after dinner. They didn't even assume that I had the common sense not to go somewhere I would be personally uncomfortable."

It became increasingly difficult for Barbara to penetrate the informal structure of contacts, parties, lunches, and gatherings, and her effectiveness suffered. She finally expressed her misgivings about her situation to her general manager, directly stating that she had been excluded from key interfaces because she was a woman. As she describes it, "all hell broke loose," with disclaimers of top management's prejudiced attitude toward women flying back and forth. But even if top management had admitted that Barbara was being barred from key informal business interactions, she would still have found it difficult to gain access to networks that operated by invitation only. Her problem was that no one would invite her, and no memo, order, or top-management directive would change that condition.

Having failed to change her situation, Barbara gradually became disillusioned. Rather than continuing to express unhappiness with her situation, she decided to bide her time, score her "résumé points," and begin searching for a better job.

During that time she started to notice how the mentoring process was benefiting her male peers.

"I saw peers who had bosses, maybe not even direct bosses but someone at a higher level, take an interest in them and bring them along."

From Barbara's perspective, the development of these links served as further proof of her second-class position in the account group, and after a few years she requested and received a transfer out of the group. But this move slowed her career further since her new position proved less challenging and responsible than her original position.

Throughout the advertising agency, female managers were just not getting the mentoring necessary to fully integrate them into the corporate-client network.

"The smartest women, the really bright, aggressive women, left to go elsewhere. Because they weren't getting the right kind of support, and I don't know if stroking is the right word, but they weren't getting something, and they found it somewhere else."

I questioned Barbara Sikorsky closely about her inability to acquire a steady mentor at the agency. It appears that there was in fact one man who might have made a good mentor and who provided her with the happiest times she spent there.

"The problem was that he wasn't the most aggressive, outspoken person I have ever met. He was one of the most intelligent marketers I have ever worked with, but he had a hard enough time selling himself—such that I really didn't expect anything extra from him."

Barbara sensed that since this person was having so much trouble advancing his own career, he was not in a strong enough political position to act as her protector.

By the time Barbara moved to the Goodbrands Corporation, she had acquired sufficient political savvy to know that a mentor relationship would be beneficial to her both as a manager and as a woman. When interviewed for the position at the Goodbrands Corporation, she met the woman who would soon become her mentor, the group product manager. The woman later took Barbara under her wing, they became friends, and the mentoring relationship developed.

"I was not specifically assigned to her product group, but she took a personal interest. She would check with me every so often to see if I was progressing the way I wanted to progress, give me some suggestions, take my part."

Afterward, the mentor attempted to engineer Barbara into a position from which she would be promoted into the mentor's product group.

"She just basically kept tabs on me, including phoning me up to ask if I'd made a decision yet, trying to convince me it was the right decision to make."

Barbara eventually took the position in the mentor's division. During that period, her mentor was promoted to vice president of marketing, becoming the third or fourth highest-ranking woman in the company. She is now in a position to provide many of the services that will weaken the barriers to Barbara's promotion into senior management.

Even at the Goodbrands Corporation, which prides itself on a strong affirmative action program, barriers to female advancement still exist. The traditional place for female managers at the Goodbrands Corporation is still the Personnel Department (the chief personnel officer is a woman), and one source within the company informed me that although the Marketing and Finance departments were opening up, the director and vice president levels in the Operations Department were nearly unattainable for a woman.

However, because she has a powerful mentor, Barbara can at last see the light at the end of the tunnel and realistically hope to attain a vice president of marketing position somewhere in the company.

Doreen Tokama faced similar barriers at the Bank of the East Orient. These barriers centered on the poor perception of women managers. But Doreen's difficulties were compounded by the fact that the bank's attitude toward women originated in a culture in which the mere presence of women in the work force was considered unusual.

> *"In fact, when I was at the Bank of the East Orient, it was a typically male chauvinist kind of place where they still thought of women as just getting tea. I have to admit they would still do that with the Japanese women who were coming over from Japan. They would come over for the specific purpose of just pouring tea and sharpening pencils."*

What Doreen needed was an opportunity to prove herself, and her mentor made sure that she got that opportunity. While it is questionable whether her mentor, an American vice president at the bank, ever changed the ingrained attitudes of the bank's hierarchy toward women, his influence served her well enough to assure her rapid promotion. During the four years of her mentoring relationship, Doreen moved from the position of financial writer through middle management to officer status, mainly by virtue of a carefully engineered series of high-visibility assignments that allowed her to establish a track record.

Unfortunately, the mentor was eventually transferred to the Far East, leaving Doreen in a position of authority in an organization that was essentially uncomfortable with women in command. Before the mentor left, however, he made certain that his protege's career would be minimally affected by their separation. Realizing that the barriers to women in the organization were too firmly entrenched to be changed, he advised her to consider moving to a new organization. He knew of an opening in a management training program at the First Bank, which until recently had restricted its recruitment to white males, and he advised her to apply for a position in the program. Doreen had misgivings about the move, since it represented at least a temporary reduction in status.

> *"It was a hard decision. I was an officer, my own secretary and the whole bit. To give all that up and start all over again, to be in the same group as the kids just out of college in their first job."*

But the mentor attempted to convince her of the ultimate career benefits of the change. He pointed out that the First Bank was one of the oldest and largest banks in the United States and that it was about to embark on a fairly substantial expansion into international arenas. Moreover, the prestige of serving on the First Bank's management team probably exceeded that of being an officer at the smaller Bank of the East Orient. Emphasizing to Doreen that she would be taking a step backward now in order to take two substantial forward steps later, the mentor finally convinced her to make the switch.

The next stage in the process entailed gaining entry into the First Bank's program. This was no small feat since the bank's recruitment standards were based on social background and contacts as well as skill and experience.

> "It's an echelon society, even in the management program. Out of the 10 women, one has a father who is the director of a major computer corporation and another is from the cream of English society."

But Doreen's mentor had connections inside the First Bank, and during each stage of the interview process he would place "concerned calls" to the people involved in the hiring decision to reinforce the favorable impression she had made.

> "He opened the right doors for me. I'm sure it helped a lot that I had someone telling the interviewers, 'Would you look at this person? I think she's really good.' I'm sure it helped in their process of elimination."

Due to her mentor's intervention, Doreen even had the opportunity to lunch with several influential senior managers during the recruitment selection process. Because of these informal interfaces, she developed some relationships with potential mentors, so that her current mentor not only increased her chances of selection but helped sow the seeds for new work-based cross-hierarchical relationships.

After the training course was completed, Doreen received a choice assignment, a policymaking position in the bank's recently created Domestic Investment Department. In that position she advised smaller banks on their investment opportunities in the United States.

The Image of Women in the Workplace

As can be observed in these cases, mentors assist female managers in overcoming distinctive types of barriers. These barriers are the products of perceptual, behavioral, and cultural factors that impede the female executive to this day.

One source of the problems and obstacles that confront female managers such as Barbara Sikorsky and Doreen Tokama is the traditional image of women in the workplace. Since for decades women have inhabited the lower levels of the corporate hierarchy as secretaries, file clerks, and receptionists, the new female managers are burdened with a preestablished image of woman's role in the business world that excludes any notion of authority or responsibility.

Because of the traditional position of women in the business world, female executives often suffer from an ambiguous status when they show up in uncustomary corporate settings. For instance, when a female manager appears at a board meeting for the first time, she is often taken for a secretary, because until recently the only females present at these conclaves were clerical workers. Male managers suffer from no such confusion. If a male is at a board meeting, it is assumed that he is not only a manager but an upwardly mobile one who possesses a measure of power and responsibility within the organization.

It is possible for male executives to use the ambiguous image of the corporate woman as a means of undermining the status of female executives. Brenda Vallens, a vice president in charge of accounts at a large bank, recounts how earlier in her career, after she had already attained managerial status, she was approached at an elevator by a highly placed officer of the bank. She happened to be standing next to a particularly pretty secretary, and the officer, who knew that Brenda was a middle manager, commented to her, within earshot of the secretary, "I see you have some competition here," obviously referring to and comparing the physical attributes of both women. She had difficulty responding to a remark that was intended to obliterate the difference in organizational rank between Brenda and the secretary by emphasizing their common gender. The officer obviously had sufficient confidence in the corporate culture's poor image of women to make a blatantly sexist remark which informed her that in this company women are at root not secretaries, middle managers, or vice presidents, but sex objects primarily defined, not by their accomplishments, but by their gender.

Since female managers are intentionally and unintentionally confused with women of lower status, many react by avoiding contact with such women. Perhaps because most nonprofessional office personnel, especially clerical workers and secretaries, are women, the female manager has countered such misidentification by disassociating herself from most other corporate females: she attempts to dress "professionally"; she assumes the characteristics and mannerisms of the managerial class; and above all she tries to be seen in the company of men.

The "image" problem of women in management is rooted in both the location of the average woman in the corporation, and the attitude of the corporation toward female managers. The fact that most of the women in the workplace are lower-level clericals keeps alive the stereotype of women as essentially nonmanagerial. The attitudinal cause of the poor female image is the belief among certain sectors of the corporate world that all women in fact should remain lower-level clericals. Of course, the structural and attitudinal causes are interrelated, since the continued absence of women in top management fosters a belief in their unsuitability for such positions. And the perception that they are less than competent in turn decreases their chances of advancement toward top positions.

The mentor can help in both the structural and attitudinal areas. By selecting a woman as a protege, a senior manager bestows de facto legitimacy on her. Since mentoring represents the senior manager's public commitment to the junior member, this brings the organization closer to the acceptance of women as bona fide members of its managerial power structure. And as more women are given the unique opportunity to succeed that mentoring affords, their accomplishments will further establish their right to a place in management. If residual sentiment against the presence of the female decision maker persists, it will have to do so in the face of hard evidence of these new managers' bottom line accomplishments. And the burden of proof of her legitimacy will no longer fall on the female executive.

Are Male Managers Threatened by Female Managers?

While the formal barriers to the advancement of female managers, such as lack of educational credentials, are rapidly disappearing, the "informal" barriers persist, and if not successfully confronted, these can thwart the managerial careers of women. One of these informal barriers is male managers' feelings of threat from female managers.

Suzanne Barclay of the Photography Corporation is particularly sensitive to the feelings of resistance that she generates in some male managers.

> "There are more than a few people around here who are definitely and obviously threatened by women in management. And it goes to the president of the company."

She explains the necessity of being extremely intuitive in order not to threaten the men in the company in interfaces ranging from a simple "good morning" to an important business meeting.

John O'Hanlon, the senior vice president at Smith & Pitts, believes that women at his agency have not yet reached the board of director level and that the only senior woman executive is the director of research ("a traditional female role here") because mentor relationships have not been formed between senior males and junior females. As John explains,

> *"It probably takes a particular personality in the manager to be the first to mentor a woman. I would guess there's a barrier there."*

This social barrier has two components. First, many men have problems dealing with women as equals in the organization. But second, and more important, they feel threatened by the possibility that women will become leaders and decision makers. O'Hanlon states the problem clearly.

> *"At this stage men don't feel comfortable with women in leadership positions. I don't think it's so much a 'management' position itself, but being the 'director of,' the decision making."*

A mentor can be particularly effective in helping the female protege to confront the threat issue. Mentors have helped reduce the threat image in a number of ways, including proclaiming the worth of the female manager and establishing her legitimacy.

The power of the mentor in dealing with the threat image is well illustrated by the situation of Larry Casesse and his protege Helen Birnbaum. Casesse is currently corporate director of marketing at a large food ingredients company. He met his protege while he was a product manager at a large household goods concern. She came on board as an assistant sales coordinator, and entered into a mentor-protege relationship with Casesse early in her tenure there. Since her background was not in business but in education, the mentor relationship originally served to introduce her to the business world, but eventually her mentor was actively promoting her advancement to higher positions.

For various career reasons, both Casesse and Birnbaum left the household goods concern, she to become an account executive for an advertising agency, he to become a product manager at a large dairy goods firm. As luck would have it, Larry Casesse's company was the client of Helen Birnbaum's agency, and through a series of intraorganizational manipulations she became the agency's account executive for Larry's particular product. The product manager and the account executive, though nominally operating separately for the client and the agency respectively, are usually expected to work together in developing plans for advertising, research, and test marketing.

From his position, Larry could continue to promote Helen's career. He bombarded her superiors with written and verbal testimonials about her advertising ability, her innate sense for marketing and packaging products, and her skill at working cooperatively with the client. Through some crafty "advertising" of his own, he contributed to the creation of an atmosphere at her agency that was conducive to her eventual elevation to vice presidential status.

Larry says that one of the problems that had to be confronted and solved along the way was the fact that some male managers felt threatened by the invasion of male territories.

> *"I've seen everything problematic to her sex happen to her. I've seen her forced into the hitherto male domains and situations. I've seen men react and become enlightened. I've seen men clam up. I've seen them react to her sexually, unable to change role patterns that they followed for the last 50 years."*

Helen's major obstacle in this regard was a male product manager at the dairy goods company. As the account executive for his product, she was in an excellent position to quickly discover that he felt threatened by women in business, especially young, attractive women who had attained a position of power. According to Casesse, this product manager sought to sabotage her position at the advertising agency by fostering doubts about Helen's competence among the senior people at the dairy goods firm. Surmising that the product manager would succeed in undermining her career if these attempts were not challenged, he forcefully interceded.

> *"I would take her side at my company. He would tell the general manager that there was a weakness in her approach, and I would take the GM aside and tell him it just wasn't that way. I short-circuited the problem before it could become a major complication."*

Casesse realized that although he could not change this manager's attitude toward female executives he could influence key people in his organization who were in a position to help his female protege's progress. In short, he discovered mechanisms for undercutting the harmful effects of the manager's actions.

Are Women Prepared?

Mentoring has a Catch-22 quality about it. To be chosen as a protege, a person must already appear to be a "rising star" who can enhance the mentor's career. According to Cynthia Fuchs Epstein, whether in the fields of science, law, or politics, a mentor supports a protege because he expects some return on his investment: the scientist wants a protege who can advance his work; the senior law partner wants a junior partner who can expand the firm; and the politician wants a successor who can perpetuate his power base and ideology.[5]

Part of the protege's value is measured in terms of his or her perceived skills in the given field, and if a certain group, in this case women, is perceived as not possessing the skills necessary to perform well and thus provide a good exchange value in the mentoring bargain, that group will be overlooked by prospective mentors. Women are perceived by some to be deficient along a broad spectrum of managerial, leadership, and technical skills.

Some managers link women's perceived leadership deficiencies to their lack of exposure to sports. For example, a female executive at the Womangoods Corporation complains that women do not understand the cooperative nature of managerial behavior because they lack training in sports. "It is very much a team effort, and if you are not used to being part of a team, it is a little difficult to get used to it."

But John O'Hanlon disagrees. While he acknowledges that cooperative activity during the formative years is an important predictor of managerial skill, he thinks that some women have received this training in areas other than sports.

> "There are other outside activities which women have participated in. Assuming that they didn't play sports at all, they might have served as editors on the school paper. They might have joined various organizations, the Girl Scouts and other public activities. They might have been elected president of the class."

Thus he does not see sports as an indispensable training area for management.

> "You're looking for the symbols that say they have an element of aggression in the productive sense, that they have learned to be a manager or organizer."

And O'Hanlon picks his proteges accordingly.

Arlene Mattola's mentor, the vice president in the retail division of the Northeast Federal Bank, realizing that women's preparedness for management was questioned by some senior people, attempted to counteract these doubts by increasing his protege's skills in certain key areas, particularly management information systems.

When the mentor first met Mattola, a recent MBA, she held a supervisory position in the department over which he had just assumed command, the Marketing Services Department of the bank's Retail Services Division. His own future looked reasonably bright, and he was searching for the right person to fill a perceived need within his department, an unofficial second in command to work closely with him in the overall operation of the department. After briefly observing Arlene Mattola's impressive work performance, he convinced the bank to create a title for her, special assistant to the vice president, that would encompass various liaison and operational functions.

Based on their common view of work and the organization, a mentor relationship quickly developed, and now perceiving a functional linkage between their careers, the mentor sees the two of them moving up together in the bank. Specifically, he sees himself, within six years, as a high-level divisional vice president and Mattola as a second vice president.

At this point, however, the bank has no women in that rank. Some planning is necessary to legitimize Arlene's ascent into this organizational stratum. The mentor must ensure that at each strategic juncture of Arlene's career her résumé already includes the skills appropriate for assumption of the new position. He mapped out a strategy for her to gain "résumé points" in a wide area of operations, so that when she was considered for the vice presidential position, the "powers that be" would have to recognize that she had already been involved in a broad range of problem solving. As Arlene explains,

> "That is why I'm attempting to get involved with computer systems. Not that I'm going to become a programmer, but I will learn these systems' use and application. I had one EDP course during the MBA program, and I never thought computers would be this important for advancement."

The mentor realizes that the ability to express management problems in the language of computer programmers, to make those problems comprehensible to the programmers, is a skill that is fast becoming an integral part of the definition of the complete manager and one that would further legitimize Arlene's claim to a vice president's spot.

But in the cases of Arlene Mattola and other female managers, I noticed that the mentors are not just equipping their female proteges with essential skills but are also advertising the fact that those skills are being acquired. It is almost as though they were consciously combating the assumption that their proteges, since they are women, lack the skills necessary at the higher management levels.

MALE MENTORS VERSUS FEMALE MENTORS: DOES IT MAKE A DIFFERENCE?

When a female protege chooses a mentor, she wants her choice to be the person who is best able to help her advance in her career. In light of the special barriers that women face, it is crucial for her to ascertain whether the gender of mentors can influence their overall effectiveness. In fact, a debate over the relative career advantages and disadvantages of having a male or female mentor emerged during the interviews. This section will examine the relevant factors in this issue.

The "Comfort" Factor

Because communication between mentor and protege plays an important role in the ultimate success of the mentor relationship, it is important for the protege to know whether the sex of the mentor can influence the ease of communication between the mentor and the protege. Do women, for instance, naturally communicate better with each other than with males? A group product manager—a female protege—commented:

> "Coming from an environment in which I had a sister, I think it was easier to fall into a mentoring relationship with a woman. And in my work history I've worked with women. And it was very comfortable. And perhaps it allowed for an emotional exchange that I might not have had if my mentor had been a man."

Another female protege believed that there was definitely a feeling of comfort with a woman mentor, an absence of a "first day" type of awkwardness. Her mentor said that it might be that the ability of women to communicate "naturally" generated female-female relationships by default. In many organizations, male managers find it difficult to advise female juniors on certain areas of corporate image and presentation of self, so they informally transfer this responsibility to female executives. Eventually the female managers in these organizations come to view the female senior executives as the sources of information on politics and corporate comportment and enter into mentoring relationships with women rather than men.

Though Suzanne Barclay of the Photography Corporation is mentored by a male vice president, she does see how a woman can benefit another woman by being able to offer advice on areas of behavior about which men are not knowledgeable.

> "Being straight out of school and on a small marketing staff, and being the youngest, and being the first and only female in the company, was not the

most wondrous experience of my life. It was kind of difficult in the beginning. The simple thing of 'what do you wear to a business cocktail party as a female executive'—not wanting to be portrayed as a wife but not wanting to walk in with a tuxedo and look—there's no other way to put it—very butch."

Where she diverges from the others is on the issue of the "comfort factor." In fact, she stands the argument on its head by suggesting that male mentors often find it easier to talk to a woman, and therefore to a woman protege. She and her mentor exchange personal anecdotes, discuss family problems, and seem to enjoy a genuine friendship. This pattern was established early in her career at the Photography Corporation and continues into the present.

I asked one female manager about the comfort factor, and she responded by placing the question in a much broader context.

"I don't think the male-female relationship is going to be as close; it can't be. Women understand women better because they're both in a female body. Men can understand men better for the same reason. But I mean, you marry each other. And there's no closer relationship, really, beyond mother and child than a husband and wife if things work out like they should. Likewise, if you just take what's expected in a business place and take the cast of characters as male and female, it should work out alright."

A factor that impedes the development of comfortable interactions between males and females is the lack of sex-neutral facilities in which male and female managers can interface. For years, male executives excluded women managers from such locales as the athletic club and the private lounge.

But that situation is changing dramatically. Not only are women being admitted into these traditionally male facilities, but as women become more integrated into the corporate structure, increasingly sex-neutral sites of power trysting are developing that are conducive to interchanges regardless of the manager's sex. At a large communications corporation, managers of all ranks join a variety of special interest clubs. Every interest is represented. Integral yoga, war games, softball, science fiction, parapsychology, wine tasting, computers, archery, boating, and a variety of other sports and subjects allow the female and male managers an opportunity to interact "comfortably." As corporations become more familial, the ease of interaction between the sexes increases.

Barbara Sikorsky has found a new site for power trysting at the Goodbrands Corporation.

"We have an executive health club; it's coed. I work out with my associates every week. We just happen to find that's a great place to talk about things we haven't had a chance to talk about. Some like to talk about broad strategic issues, and in the course of my work, there's very little time to sit down and let them talk to me. So we go to the health club and work out, and they talk broad strategy issues, and I'm losing weight, and it's great."

The point here is that although an ingrained comfort factor works in favor of a same-sex mentoring relationship, the social segregation by sex in the workplace that contributes to the unfamiliarity and "discomfort" that exist between male and female managers is diminishing greatly. And more important, sex-neutral activities permit all involved to develop relationships that overcome the feelings of comfort and discomfort produced by earlier socialization.

The Organizational Power of the Mentor

As illustrated in Chapter 3, the position of the mentor can determine how far the protege advances in the organization, and on this point the evidence favors the male manager as the choice of a mentor for a female manager.

Nick Ford, the commercial general manager at the Goodbrands Corporation, considers himself the biggest proponent of bringing females into the operations area. At this time, half of the 16 professionals there are women, but at one point or another many of them had encountered resistance and skepticism from different levels of management.

"I've spent a lot of time with female proteges telling them how to get around certain things. And I've also spent a lot of time with people who have given them problems, by saying, 'You've got to realize that when you pick women out to do only one thing, like personnel, you're making it seem that it's the only thing they can do. You have to treat them like anyone else.'"

In order to advise and cajole senior managers, and manipulate the internal environment in favor of a protege, the mentor must possess a certain amount of power. At present, it is more likely that a man rather than a woman will be in such a position of power.

One female protege, though she was helped considerably by her female mentor, realized that her mentor had less authority than the men in the organization.

"Yes, women often have little or no authority. My mentor was often excluded from policy issues because she was a vice president of an area that had little power or responsibility. And it affected anyone who worked for her."

A female manager identifies our aforementioned barriers as drawbacks of the male mentor: she perceives men as being either threatened by women or uncomfortable about developing a work-based relationship with them. Nevertheless, she prefers to maintain a relationship with a male mentor, because in her company a female mentor would be spending most of her energy trying to advance her own position. In other words, since the male mentor is already in power and has a supposedly more secure position, he can contribute more to the protege's development.

A female vice president at a large bank reflects this sentiment.

"I've never met a woman senior to me who I thought was in a better position than I to make a decision or who could offer me insights into the workings of the corporation."

Geraldine Links, the business manager at the Steel Corporation, has a certain concept of the perfect mentor and feels that at present most women do not fulfill her expectations.

"How many females are going to be smart, successful, human, and a sufficient number of levels above me? The women who have been successful have been through a very rough time."

She implies that most of the women currently in senior management can no longer fulfill her "humanistic" criteria of a mentor because they have been so toughened by their experiences in fighting discrimination to obtain their own positions.

"There are very few who have not toughened up because of their experiences."

I am not suggesting that all female mentors are powerless, hardened to helping others, or clustered at the corporation's lower levels. The fact that women are becoming more integrated into the executive work force implies that over time, perhaps within a generation, women will achieve status equality in many industries and will have an easier time advancing. Ellen Everett, the account executive at the Management Training Corporation, felt that her mentor, a female, had changed the general position of women in the organization. Her mentor was the second woman hired for the sales force, and during the four years she had been there, the proportion of women in the sales force had increased to over 50 percent, largely due to her success. The founders of the corporation, who were all men, began to believe that women could indeed sell.

But anecdotal evidence aside, the fact that only 2 percent of senior managers are women suggests that, while a powerful woman mentor can help, the odds are that the current young female manager is more likely to find an available mentor among male senior managers. One female executive even suggests that a mentor is not only more likely to be located among the male executives but that he is also more likely to remain within the organization for a long time, regardless of corporate conditions.

> *"Being mentored by a man can help in this organization. Women vice presidents quit; male vice presidents accept special project positions."*

What this executive is suggesting is that during recessionary times demotions are more readily accepted by male senior executives than by female senior executives, a fact that she traces to familial constraints on the male executive's freedom of choice and movement. As a recent UCLA study has shown, 97 percent of male senior executives, but only 39 percent of female senior executives, have children. And the differences become even more striking when the statistics on household support are considered: 52 percent of the female executives have only themselves to support, whereas practically all of the male executives are married.[6] Thus it would seem that if a person wants a mentor whose personal circumstances encourage commitment to the organization, the odds favor a male.

Suzanne Barclay perceives differing advantages in male and female mentors.

> *"Definitely, a female as mentor would help as a model, but it's been my experience, if my mentor was female, that person could have sponsored me, guided me, to a point. But if that woman had to deal with our president, she would have had difficulty bringing herself along."*

Her overall opinion is that the position of the company on women in general must be understood in order to evaluate the benefits of having a female mentor.

Will male mentors support a woman as strongly as they would a man? According to one woman, her experience with male mentors indicates that they will, probably because the requirements of the mentoring relationship transcend the gender differences.

> *"If one allows a woman protege to be attacked in terms of ability or whatever, one is also allowing one's own relationship to be attacked. And that undermines one's own position."*

In other words, the requirements of career and power determine the mentor's commitment to the protege. In essence, what determines the success of a mentor relationship is a combination of the protege's ability and the mentor's power and position.

This point is demonstrated by the mentor relationship of Michelle Ross, the director of employee relations at the West Coast Pharmaceutical Corporation. She has had a fairly unusual career. An English major in college, upon graduation she took a personnel position at a department store chain. She went from there to a personnel position at a publishing house, and she finally ended up at West Coast Pharmaceutical Corporation.

Her relationship with her mentor began during her last term of college, while she was on a one-week internship at the Pharmaceutical Corporation. She was supervised in this internship by Noreen Connors, who later became the vice president of personnel. Afterward, Michelle wisely retained an ongoing communication with Noreen, and when a good position opened at the Pharmaceutical Corporation, Noreen contacted Michelle and hired her into the position herself. For some months, she stood guard over Michelle's position within the organization, and she was directly instrumental in Michelle's promotion to director of employee relations.

As Michelle becomes increasingly identified with her mentor, her career success will depend on the political position and fortunes of her mentor, comfort factors and role modeling aside. Political considerations, not sex-related comfort factors, will be the ultimate determinants of success.

And in organizations or departments where there is a preponderance of same-sex mentoring, sex segregation can occur. While Barbara Sikorsky was describing how nicely her career had progressed due to the influence of her female mentor, she made a statement that indicated the existence of sex segregation within the corporation.

> *"In my group, there is one man, my assistant product manager. But our boss is a female, the other product managers are females. Her assistants are all females, and besides Richard, my assistants are all females. But not by design, it just sort of happened. In fact, it's almost a joke in the company. 'Go over to cereals, and it's all women.'"*

Though not by design, the pattern has occurred in numerous fields and professions: English novel writing in the mid-19th century, secretarial work, social work, personnel. Each became a "woman's field," and eventually women's work, the net result being lower pay, less autonomy, less professional power.

I am not suggesting that the solution to this problem is for every woman to get a male mentor. What I am saying is that men inhabit all areas of the power structure and that women as a group will be more easily integrated into all facets, roles, and segments of the corporate world if they are mentored by the holders of power in that world.

The fact of the matter is that the "old boys" network will probably dissolve due to the sheer number of women who are entering the managerial ranks. (According to Sikorsky, most of the qualified candidates for managerial roles at the Goodbrands Corporation are now women.) But the functions of such a network, which include the establishment of trust relationships and business contacts, will not disappear. The "old boys" network will be replaced by what I term an "old friends" network made up of both men and women who form a web of sponsors, mentors, proteges, and contacts—the "known quantities" as it were. But the sooner women acquire mentors within the current network, the more quickly it will be transformed into a sex-neutral entity.

INVOLVEMENT AND INNUENDO

Unavoidable in any discussion of the male-female relationship are the twin issues of innuendo and sexual/romantic involvement. It became apparent that not only were respondents aware of these issues but that many potential male-female mentor relationships did not develop because of the fear of office gossip. One executive explained:

> *"The male-female mentor relationship might be tricky. It could mean being called up at 8, 9, 10, 11 o'clock at night and meeting in a hotel someplace, in a room. Some people might feel it's not quite right and might not be so happy about it."*

A male executive who does mentor females says that "if you go out for dinner, or a movie, people will start asking questions." This is echoed by a protege at the Goodbrands Corporation, who believes that "outside socializing isn't a good thing for female executives to do." She will not socialize with men because "people are just too eager to make up gossip."

This protege recently had lunch with a division manager to discuss a development assignment. She had never met him before, but she is now rumored to be "having an affair" with him. There had been similar rumors when she became friendly with a marketing executive while both were working on a packaging project. Even though she saw the executive only during working hours, the rumors that developed suggested that she was not only having an affair with him but that she had been instrumental in ending his marriage. Eventually, in order to quell the rumors, she stopped having lunch with the executive and would never even leave the building with him.

The problem from the point of view of her social life is that as she spends more time at the corporate site, she has fewer free hours in which to develop nonorganizational relationships. But if she attempts to establish organizational friendships with men, she risks becoming a subject of office gossip. "Consequently, my social life isn't too terrific," she complains.

One female protege, now a vice president at a large New York bank, admits that she was initially very naive about the issue of sexual rumors. At an executive party one night she discovered that the bank tellers thought that she was having an affair with her mentor.

> "It caught me off guard. I was really surprised that the rumors would have gotten around."

Her female colleagues told her that such rumors were to be expected.

> "If they knew either of us well, they would have known that sex was not the source of the attraction."

Interesting, though, is the fact that her career progress was temporarily retarded at one point, even with a mentor in her corner, and she will never be certain whether it was suspicion of an affair that retarded it.

Most of the respondents emphasize that in the male-female mentor relationship it is necessary to "act professionally," but such statements only prove that the parameters of behavior are much more circumscribed in the different-sex mentor relationship than in the same-sex mentor relationship. This is evidenced by the fact that no one seems particularly concerned that males "act professionally" in the male-male mentor relationship. The pressure to constantly act completely "above board" can have a chilling effect on the quality and intensity of interaction. Mentor relationships require a give-and-take that is facilitated by an ease of interaction, a feeling of camaraderie. But the constant self-questioning and double-checking at every interface can become an inhibiting factor in the development of the mentor relationship.

A male mentor says that he and his female protege could never completely escape organizational rumor mongering.

> "The fact that we did travel together, worked well into the night together, sometimes alone, was easy to exploit and sensationalize, as though there was something sub rosa going on, a sexual relationship. It's the kind of thing corporate rumor mills love."

His protege agrees that "people thought there was more to it than business." As she relates, "Nothing more outraged me than those rumors," and she suspects that the rumors may have even affected her career.

"Because of the suspicion of a sexual involvement, as a woman with a male mentor, you walk a tightrope. To that extent, female mentors are safer."

But in spite of the potential for sexual innuendo, male-female mentor relationships do develop and thrive. A variety of responses to this problem have been devised by executives who consider their mentor relationships valuable to their career progress. A female protege, though admitting that sexual innuendo is pervasive, thinks that its importance is often overstated.

"Much conveyance of gossip is merely someone seeking a second opinion. If you react with a big yawn, it will go away."

A male executive at a large corporation has devised various solutions to the gossip problems.

"Acquire more than one female protege, and you will then be perceived as a people developer, not a womanizer."

Realizing that managers are inherently suspicious of male-female mentor relationships, he reverses the tables by not only participating in such relationships, but advertising the fact. In this way, he forces other managers to accept both the relationships and the role of women in management. Because of his actions and similar actions by other male managers, attitudes within the company have changed.

"There was a time when you didn't close the door when talking to a woman."

It might to helpful to place the innuendo issue in the larger context of perceptions of favoritism by peers and senior management. The perception that the mentoring process has worked unfairly, whether because of family ties, social connections, or sexual favors, makes the process appear less rational and egalitarian. Since the protege is handpicked, privy to organizational intelligence, and promoted quicker than peers, it is incumbent upon the protege and the mentor to demonstrate quite clearly that the protege is a worthy candidate for promotion.

Co-workers are quick to judge the competence, or the lack of competence, of a mentored manager. I asked one male respondent whether he thought that anything beyond "competence" was involved in the promotion of a woman in his company who was obviously being brought along by a corporate vice president.

> *"No, I don't think so, not here, because I believe that there are no women here who are not qualified. They wouldn't have gotten in the door, they wouldn't have gotten the promotion if they weren't qualified. Even for a woman here, it just isn't that way. I don't believe it is anyway. The woman was not given that promotion beyond her level of competence. She can do that job."*

Barbara Sikorsky, of the Goodbrands Corporation observes changes in the way that male and female managers approach each other and in the way that other workers perceive male-female mentor relationships.

> *"Over time, I don't think the sex thing is going to be a problem. I think professionals are going to realize that these are just other professionals and not so much females. But it's not here yet."*

But one cannot ignore the possibility that males and females will get involved. In discussing the "sex in the office" issue, consultants Morton Feinberg and Aaron Levenstein state that there are four gradients of sexual and romantic involvement in the organizational context: sexual harassment, legitimate courtship, a sexual relationship between unmarried workers, and an illicit affair (i.e., one or both of the parties are married).[7]

Even assuming that participation in the mentor relationship is voluntary, and hence without the element of harassment, the mentor-protege relationship can still fall into any of the other three categories. One of those categories, the illicit affair, possesses its own source of nasty gossip, whether it occurs inside or outside a mentor relationship and will not be dealt with here as a separate issue.

But what about the courtship between unmarried mentors and proteges? Does a courtship hinder or help the mentor relationship? As Feinberg and Levenstein indicate, many companies openly exhibit pride about the number of marriages occurring among their personnel. It must be remembered, though, that a mentor-protege courtship is not one of distantly placed coequals within the corporation: the mentor and protege are often cofunctioning workers within the same department or division, sharing common information. When the mentor and protege become romantically involved, there are many of the same problems as exist when any mentor relationship becomes deeply personal. Will the mentor remain objective in his evaluation of the protege's performance? Could he, in effect, critique his wife or fiancée? The mentor and protege are now sharing an apartment, an income, a life, far outside the corporate domain. How can what goes on outside the organization be prevented from affecting their functioning at the workplace?

These issues must be dealt with by the mentor, the protege, and the organization. Some organizations deal with them by simply splitting up the mentor-protege team at work, but this action could significantly reduce the benefits accruing to the organization from the onsite interfunctioning of the mentor and protege.

The companies I examined had not developed a specific strategy for dealing with these issues because their male-female mentoring relationships did not normally entail a romantic element. (I cannot speak for the unconscious feelings and desires of the respondents.) And the possibility of marriage between members was severely limited by the fact that most of the mentors and proteges were already married. Nearly all of them entered mentor relationships for career, not personal, benefits.

But the respondents did have to confront the issue of rumors, and controlling those rumors emerged as a major strategic career goal. One interesting sidelight is that most of the mentored respondents, male or female, were not likely to assume a romantic involvement in other male-female work relationships. This was in stark contrast to the views of some unmentored managers whom I interviewed. These managers were far quicker to interpret such relationships as unfair, prone to favoritism, and so on. In other words, a mentored person sees himself or herself as deserving of the attention and is thus less likely to accuse others of using unfair techniques (such as sexual favors) to foster a mentor relationship.

A RIVAL FOR SPOUSE?

Most discussions of the sex-related problems of female proteges refer to the issues we have already dealt with: sexual involvement, rumor, and innuendo. But my respondents' main concern in this area was not so much the corporate perception of the mentor relationship as the corporate wife's suspicion that something beyond the normal business association was going on behind her back. As the following accounts demonstrate, female proteges, and their mentors, have developed strategies for dealing with this problem.

Before Suzanne Barclay became product manager at the Photography Corporation, she spent five years in a consumer glassware company, experiencing a steady but slow career growth. When she was interviewed at the Photography Corporation, she met the vice president who was soon to become her mentor. Through a combination of the mentor's help and her own skills, she rose in three years to her current product manager position, an upward climb that was especially surprising in a company that liked its executives to be elderly and male.

Her mentor has fulfilled all the functional requirements of the mentoring role. As mentioned earlier, they have achieved a comfortable, close working relationship. And the organization, observing how the mentoring process has been helping both of them to become better workers, has bestowed its approval on the relationship.

The only problem was that the mentor had a wife who was originally quite suspicious of the relationship.

"I think it was difficult for her at the beginning. We'd go away on business trips, or there have been occasions where we were in Germany together. That becomes a little difficult to deal with."

Suzanne's early attempts at helping the wife overcome her fears about the relationship often backfired. Once Suzanne attempted to mollify the wife by going out with the mentor and her socially. They went out on a boat, and a fourth person, Christopher, a male marketing manager at the Photography Corporation, was invited to come along. Suzanne and Christopher were "buddies" at the Photography Corporation and had established a fairly loose, easy mode of interaction. The mentor's wife, who was also a friend of Christopher's girfriend, completely misconstrued their friendly behavior and henceforth perceived Suzanne as a double threat.

Suzanne eventually decided to have dinner with just the mentor and his wife, and now she occasionally speaks to the wife on the phone. The strategy of becoming a "familiar quantity" seems to be working in her favor. The wife is no longer apprehensive about the long hours that her husband spends with Suzanne.

"I think she knows me well enough now not to be threatened. There are no longer those kinds of problems with her perception of the relationship."

This strategy of becoming a familiar quantity has also been utilized by Brenda Vallens, our vice president in charge of accounts. While she was climbing the corporate ranks, she met the person who was to become her mentor, then a fairly highly placed vice president. He was very instrumental in her progress from administrative assistant to assistant vice president, and he managed to get her accepted in many of the bank's key training programs. He was obviously overseeing her career, serving as teacher, protector, and promoter.

Her mentor's spouse was home in the suburbs, had her own job as a teacher, and was also saddled with the responsibility of caring for the three children. The mentor's job and daily commute left him with little time for interaction with his wife, and their conversations over dinner did not bring them closer.

"He would go home talking about this woman all the time. Instead of talking about Phil or Jeff, he would start talking about Brenda this and Brenda that."

This was obviously creating questions about the protege in the wife's mind, so the mentor eventually suggested to Brenda that it would be a good idea if she had dinner at his house. The evening went well, and peace was established. Now, whenever the wife visits the office, Brenda manages to find time for a short conversation with her. Brenda also relieves the wife's apprehensions about the mentor relationship by including her in many of the business dinners in which she and her mentor are involved.

Geraldine Links, manager of business planning at the Steel Corporation, mentioned that although she detests parties at the homes of fellow corporate executives, she thinks that her presence at these gatherings is useful in allaying the suspicions that her mentor's wife may have.

"In the case of the woman manager with the male mentor, it is extremely important that you go to these social gatherings, because you are much more fearful to men's wives by reputation only. If they've met you, at least they know what they're dealing with."

She felt it necessary to meet the wife early on, within the first six months of the relationship.

"I found out talking to his wife since that she had heard all sorts of things about me to make her very worried. But we dealt with those."

Among these things that the mentor had told his wife early in the relationship was that Geraldine was one of the smartest women he had ever known, at which point his wife became absolutely unnerved. Like the mentors of Vallens and Links, many mentors just do not realize that informing wives about the extraordinary talents and achievements of a female protege is not the equivalent of giving them the very same information about a male protege.

These examples suggest that the mentor as well as the protege must allay the wife's feelings of jealousy and resentment about the mentor relationship. One male mentor at the West Coast Pharmaceutical Corporation solved many of the domestic problems that arose from his development of a female protege by discussing aspects of the relationship with his wife.

"If you have a suspicious spouse, you have to be careful or you're going to get burned. But if you communicate what you do, if you mention, 'Oh, I saw Diane the other day, and she was in there talking about this,' or 'Judy called me up,' you shouldn't have any problems."

The mentor relationship can also arouse the jealousy of the female protege's husband. It is not uncommon for a mentor and protege to spend hours after work developing marketing strategies and formulating organizational plans. A wife may spend more time with her mentor than with her husband. After all, the woman is an executive, and her position entails certain time commitments. And her role of protege places additional demands on her time.

Many managers mention this problem. One female protege at the Goodbrands Corporation, fearing the her fiancé would become jealous of her relationship with the male mentor, attempted to initiate a friendship between her mentor and her fiancé. Though she is generally averse to socializing with company people, even her mentor, the situation required some interaction outside the organization. As it turned out, her mentor and her fiancé became close friends.

If he feels sufficiently comfortable about doing so, a mentor may discuss with the husband his feelings toward his wife's job in general and the mentor relationship in particular. The mentor often discovers that the husband is troubled by a combination of factors: the time his wife spends on the job, her close relationship with another man, and even the fact that she is outdistancing him.

It should be pointed out that the potential for suspicion regarding the possibility of a sexual or romantic aspect is usually not greater for the mentor relationship, than for any other office or extra-familial male-female interface. Most respondents seem sensitive to the issue and try to utilize the strategy of keeping the lines of communication open among all involved. Of course, if the spouse or fiancé's jealousy is a symptom of an already weak relationship, the mentor-protege relationship can become a convenient target for preexisting suspicions.

In any event, male mentors and their female proteges seem to weather the problems with their respective spouses that arise from the mentor relationship. Openness, candor, and honesty seem to be the best methods for allaying a spouse's doubts. In the long run, marriages seem markedly unaffected by mentor relationships.

THE FUTURE OF THE FEMALE PROTEGE

Women have chosen both men and women as mentors. But the hierarchical realities suggest that although such elements as sexual innuendo and the "comfort factor" may have an adverse affect on the male-female mentor relationship, the young female manager will still be well served by seeking a male mentor. Sex ratios at all levels of management will change dramatically over the next 20 years, and each level will become increasingly sex neutral. At present, however, acquiring a male mentor would seem to be a fruitful route to success for the young female manager. Many of my respondents claim that women communicate better with each other than with men. But since the mentor-protege relationship relates primarily to issues of advancement, skill acquisition, and corporate political strategies, the power, status, and position of the mentor would seem more important than such psychological dimensions as "comfort" in determining the choice of sponsor.

As indicated in this chapter, a major drawback of the male-female mentor relationship is sexual innuendo. But most respondents, while recognizing the existence of this drawback, have learned strategies and behaviors that neutralize its effects.

A point that has been stressed throughout this chapter is that the factor that presents the greatest obstacle to the establishment of male-female mentor relationships is not inherent difficulties in communication between male and female managers but the generally weak position of women in the work force. If women are not perceived as an integral part of the corporate fabric, their chances of being chosen as proteges (and thus rising rapidly in their organizations) are lessened. But there are a number of social trends that presage women's considerably stronger and more "legitimized" position in the workplace.

One such trend is the large number of young male managers who themselves have wives in the work force. Because it is increasingly the case that the male executive has a wife who works to help support the family's lifestyle, the house, the two or three cars, the European vacation, he is more likely to recognize that his female comanagers are fulfilling the same economic role in their families as his wife fulfills in his. In short, the idea of a working woman is quickly becoming a standard part of the executive's own lifestyle.

Another trend that will hasten acceptance of the woman as both worker and protege is indicated by John O'Hanlon. He thinks that the breakthroughs in computers and communications will enhance the position of women in management. He even claims that a major argument against having women in management positions, their supposed lack of skills in the "people management" and "leadership" areas, will completely disappear.

> *"What I'm saying is that 'people management' is going to change to a great extent because there's going to be a computer between manager and subordinate. There's just going to be a lot less face-to-face contact."*

In other words, machines will transform management into a much more sex-neutral activity. And as such arguments against females in general slowly disappear, it will become much more acceptable, and a lot easier, for male-female mentor relationships to develop.

Finally, I think that the position of the woman manager will change because younger executives are learning to function in male-female management teams, first in graduate school and then on the job. Young male executives who have been socialized along these lines will be less likely to reject females as proteges because of their sex. In fact, this trend implies that eventually the sex of the mentor and protege will be a secondary consideration in the formation of mentor-protege dyads. As more women move into senior management, there will be an increased tendency for female senior executives and male juniors to form mentor relationships.

A recent study of Columbia University MBA graduates of 1969–71 revealed that 10 years after graduation the annual salaries of these male and female MBAs differed by $18,000. The difference could not be attributed to educational credentials, social background, job function, length of uninterrupted employment, or other standard variables.

The author of the study, Mary Anne Dervanna, claimed that "a lot of promoting is done not so much for performance as for perceived potential, which is highly subjective." She located the success factor in two areas, political savvy and mentoring, stating that successful women had indicated that these were crucial to their own managerial advancement.[8]

As I have tried to demonstrate in this chapter, women face many barriers, but there is evidence that mentoring is beginning to help women negotiate those barriers and make their way up the organizational hierarchy.

6

The Negative Side
of Mentoring

So far we have been looking at the benefits that accrue to the parties participating in mentor relationships, and even at how the mentoring process can overcome the special problems faced by certain groups, such as female managers. Most mentor relationships progress smoothly—the careers of the participants advance, and their organizations gain positive residual benefits.

However, some mentor relationships turn out badly for their members, and in this chapter I will explore the reasons that seemingly healthy mentor relationships turn sour. In some cases, problems occur between the members of such relationships, often because the mentor and protege fail to correctly assess each other's needs, goals, and intentions. In other cases, problems emerge between the members of the relationship and the employing organization. For instance, the mentor may fall out of favor with the powers that be, and this may have a negative effect on the protege's career. Or the employing organization may undergo changes that separate the mentor from the protege.

It is my contention that the negative effects of some unsuccessful mentor relationships could have been avoided if the mentor and protege had proceeded differently, if they had been more sensitive to their own and each other's needs and more attuned to the subtleties of the organizational environment. It will become apparent how lack of political savvy and poor communication between the mentor and the protege worked against the continued vitality of such mentor relationships.

In addition to analyzing the inherent problems in these mentor relationships, I will offer some retrospective solutions. Though the relationships have all ended, they offer clear opportunities for ascertaining what actions the protege and mentor could have taken to avoid or rectify the difficulties in the relationships.

One of the ironies of the interviews on the negative aspects of mentoring is that in a number of instances the reasons for the deterioration of the mentor relationship were not entirely understood by the participants. Hence, the interviews served more as a "talking through" of the way in which it occurred than as a mere communication of already comprehended facts. In short, these interviews often represented an exploration, on the part of both the researcher and the respondent, of the reasons for the decline in the mentor-protege relationship.

THE BLACK HALO

The negative side of mentoring is often manifested when the mentor falls out of favor in the organization and by association adversely affects the protege's career, a process I label the "black halo" effect.

John Jordan is president of several small companies, including a software consulting organization and a stock analysis firm. His entire work background is in the area of computer programming and systems analysis. In the early 70s, the person who eventually became his mentor brought him into Sherman Brokerage as an assistant vice president to substitute computers for teletype in the handling of stock transactions. The firm had 200 branches throughout the United States. The project entailed changing the central computer system that supported the delivery of trade orders and records among the firm's branches. The transition represented a potentially massive, multimillion-dollar effort that required training, testing, implementation, and the continuance of a backup system.

His mentor, Andrew Weissman, a senior vice president and a member of the board of directors, had developed the plans to implement the new computer system. Jordan quickly discovered that because his assistant vice president title did not carry the power to mobilize resources, he could not develop the computer system without his mentor's support and help.

Jordan also discovered that there was opposition throughout the organization to both Weissman and the system. That opposition stemmed from two sources. First, there was a massive resistance to change of any type within the organization. The introduction of any changes was suspect and required a combination of patience and diplomacy to ensure acceptance. Second, the mentor's political position was at best tenuous. He functioned both as a standing policymaker and as director of operations. But he was excluded from the inner circle of power because he had not come up through the Sherman Brokerage ranks. He had been the president of a smaller company that Sherman had acquired several years earlier, and Sherman had kept him on. Although he had performed productively, he had failed to overcome the political effects of his outsider status. In the years following the takeover of his company, he had done nothing to become a member of the team and establish relationships with the other board members. That failure had been due not only to their resistance but to his inability to accept a coequal leadership position with them. According to the protege, his mentor had been "like God" in his original company and had not yet shed that self-image.

It became apparent that some board members, instead of viewing the new computer system as necessary for Sherman's growth and expansion, regarded it as a means that Jordan's mentor was using to increase his political and organizational power base.

The new data processing system had been sold to senior management through the recommendations of a third party, a large accounting/management consulting firm. To ensure a smooth acceptance of the new system, the mentor would have had to establish ties and loyalties among the board members, and then diplomatically help build a consensus of approval for the system. But his background and former position of authority had not prepared him for the conciliatory role needed here, and when the management consultant's recommendations finally forced the introduction of the new computer system, some board members felt less convinced than coerced.

Slowly Jordan realized that his mentor, the person in whom he had placed complete faith, lacked the power and support that Jordan originally thought he had. By not apprising Jordan of the political maneuvers in the upper corporate environment, Weissman was unwittingly damaging his career.

"Too many of the things I had asked for were not being carried out, and I was not aware of the ferment on the board."

An entire chain of command seemed averse to the mentor's decisions and policies. This was indicated to Jordan when an immediate supervisor told him, "Whenever Weissman tells you to do something, tell us."

"Here I am supporting Andrew Weissman at these meetings, realizing I'm on the losing side. I've got his T-shirt on."

To make matters worse, Jordan's mentor also exhibited at board meetings an abrasiveness usually reserved for messengers and clerks, not senior board members.

Eventually, in order to carry out his assignments, Jordan began to bypass the chain of command, but in the process he alienated peers and supervisors alike.

"I would walk into his office quite freely, bypassing two other levels in between, not making people in my department very happy. In that type of situation, your allegiances are to your man on the board of directors to get things done. He couldn't accomplish this with his staff, and I had to bypass people in between."

As we observed in Chapter 1, mentor relationships thrive to the extent that they benefit the organization, the mentor, and the protege. The planned organizational benefit of this mentor relationship was the development of the computer system. In this case, however, the mentor was involved in a power game, and through his allegiance to the mentor the protege was becoming alienated from the rest of the corporation. The mentor relationship gradually developed into a "we-they" situation.

And Jordan's own entry into the organization did little to allay the fears regarding the introduction of the new system. The lower levels of management viewed Jordan in much the same way that the board viewed Weissman. A computer whiz armed with knowledge of the latest macro data systems, Jordan threatened the power and position of many middle managers. In addition, he had been brought in specifically to introduce a new system that was disturbing to the organization. He needed a mentor who could establish his credibility and legitimacy. Weissman, hampered by his own political problems, could do very little for him.

The Inevitable Suddenly, after years of antagonizing the other board members, the mentor, in a classic palace coup, was forced to resign his position at the brokerage firm. Jordan's existence in the organization suddenly became precarious, and he was demoted into various lackluster duties. A new person was brought in to supervise the project, but he found himself dependent on Jordan's knowledge and expertise. However, in order to avoid offending the former mentor's enemies on the board, he could interact with Jordan only surreptitiously. The "black halo" continued to shine, but eventually Jordan was returned to his former status in order to finish up the project, which now, ironically, was receiving a positive reaction from a recently skeptical senior management.

In spite of the political problems he had encountered, Jordan felt that his expertise gave him an advantage. In fact, when he threatened to leave the firm over a minor dispute, his new immediate boss, completely dependent on his general skill with computers and his specific familiarity with the company's new system, fought to get him a promotion, which was granted by the chairman.

The system was finally developing, and Jordan's relationship with his new director had become a close working one. Suddenly, the brokerage firm merged again, this time with an even larger house, and a shocked John Jordan was summoned to his director's office.

> "I came back from vacation. They announced the merger and made some changes. And I just looked at the director and said, 'Why me?' And he just said, 'Well, that's the way the cookie crumbles.'"

This merger may have provided senior management with a convenient rationale for cashing in Jordan's chips because of his earlier identification with the mentor. The computer system was nearing completion, and Jordan was becoming dispensable. Now mergers have a reputation for being bloody, and even the most innocent are sometimes victimized. But in the jockeying for position between the staffs and boards of the two brokerage houses, the inhabitants of the inner circles of both companies found safe havens. Those who were considered expendable, or outsiders, such as Jordan, were the ones who did not survive the fusion. Jordan was not even offered a special projects position.

Jordan feels that the number two man on the board held a grudge going back perhaps eight years, when Jordan originally criticized him heavily at board meetings in an effort to champion Weissman's data processing plan. Evidently, Jordan had left a lasting impression.

> "At one meeting, when he had made a suggestion about the system, I bluntly told him, 'You take care of financial, and I'll do the data processing.' This guy is not going to come up to you later, give you a pat on the back, tell you that you made him see the error of his ways. The guy's on top, and that's all that counts."

This entire experience, which lasted several years, has left Jordan soured on business.

> "It all comes back to the fact that even if you do your job well, if you back the wrong guy, your performance does not matter much. Perhaps I didn't do a good enough sales job on myself."

Jordan feels that part of the mentor's ouster was attributable to the mentor's inability to support Jordan's role performance. He sees mentoring, and business in general, as based on the even exchange of favors and services. Therefore, he thinks that by securing his position at the brokerage firm early enough, the mentor would have given him sufficient leverage to move the project along quicker and thus to extend a positive halo in the mentor's direction by virtue of his superior performance. Considering the fact that the political walls were already closing in on the mentor by the time Jordan took over the project, it would seem that quick success in the data processing project was called for, an early victory engineered by a well-secured field marshal. The fact that the mentor could not provide Jordan with the necessary stability hastened the mentor's departure and eventually caused Jordan's.

THE FAILURE TO PROTECT

A politically weak mentor is not the only reason for the disintegration of a mentor relationship. Sometimes a strongly positioned sponsor may fail to protect a protege from organizational pressures simply because the mentor is unaware of the protege's problems in the organization and of the organizational changes that are causing those problems.

When I first met Mike Bouton, he informed me that the mentor relationship in which he had been involved had recently ended, with near-disastrous consequences for his career. Though uncertain of the reasons for the decline in the relationship, he suspected that, among other things, his mentor, mistakingly assuming that Mike's career within the organization was thriving, had quite simply "lost contact" with him.

In 1969 Mike had joined an Engineering firm as an accountant, and in 1972 he joined the Employee Services Company, a medium-sized executive services firm. His mentoring experience occurred during a 10-year period of growth for the company, a span in which its business quadrupled, increasing to several hundred million dollars annually. The company, whose clients are Fortune 500 firms, has 1,100 employees headquartered in offices in nine major U.S. cities.

George Evans, the vice president of finance who later became Bouton's mentor, interviewed him, liked his accounting background, and hired him into a mid-level finance position.

"I think we hit if off well right from day one, though I knew nothing about the executive services business."

The mentor relationship quickly developed, affording Bouton the opportunity to gain firsthand exposure to the worlds of finance, marketing, and operations.

Though Bouton had been hired by Evans, his immediate supervisor was the controller. Early on, Bouton sensed the existence of a real antipathy, almost a competitiveness, between the controller and him, but at first he could not figure out the reason for it. Eventually he realized that the controller was favoring another person for organizational advancement, a woman who lacked the necessary credentials for higher positions, and saw Bouton as an obstacle to her promotion. In order to expand his own power base, the controller was serving as her mentor. Since Bouton was her immediate supervisor, what developed was a pattern of crosscutting loyalties in which each mentor-protege pair worked against the other. The situation finally came to a head when the woman attempted to reorganize the accounting department in such a way that "whatever she had been doing to undercut me would have become official." In short, she was attempting to establish herself as Bouton's official supervisor.

Realizing that so blatant a ploy would not have been attempted without the controller's knowledge and support, Bouton went to his own mentor, George Evans, with a copy of the reorganization scheme. Evans immediately allayed his fears, and that night, during a business flight with the controller, he informed the controller that the reorganization plan was unacceptable. The protege had acted correctly: by immediately bringing the plan to his mentor's attention, he had demonstrated that he was looking out for his mentor's position as well as his own. He had done this by conveying organizational information/intelligence to the mentor and thus providing him with one of the primary mentor benefits discussed in Chapter 4. Ironically, the controller, still nominally Bouton's immediate supervisor, angrily accused Bouton of going over his head and not adhering to the chain of command.

The controller subtly continued his campaign to undercut Bouton. The controller perceived the relationship between Bouton and Evans as threatening, and this was betrayed by his activities during Bouton's tenure at the Employee Services Company. At one point, again in an attempt to undermine Bouton's position, he created the position of assistant controller and hired into that position an outsider who would be loyal strictly to him.

Although Bouton's position was protected by his mentor, he did not feel that his career was progressing adequately. Sensing that he was being organizationally outflanked by the controller and his expanding army, he announced to Evans that he had decided to quit. The mentor stepped in immediately, offering him a financial management position at corporate headquarters that would involve a direct reporting relationship between Evans and Bouton. Most important, this position was outside the controller's scope of command.

The mentor's intervention was the turning point in the relationship. Mike had knowingly forced the mentor to make a commitment to his career.

> *"Intuititively I knew I had very good chemistry going between us. He appreciated my sincerity; he knew that I was hardworking, and I had tremendous loyalty to the company, and I was intensely loyal to him, that I would put in a tremendous amount of hours, make any sacrifices. I had the feeling that the guy was going to look out for my interests."*

From that point, the mentor relationship became much more intensive. The learning experiences, from Mike's point of view, were invaluable.

> *"He was a very busy man, but I would always manage to see him between five and six, every day. I would walk by his office about quarter past five, and there would be an uninterrupted period in which I would just sit and chat. I would give him the gist of my projects and problems, and we would discuss them at length."*

During these sessions, the mentor would informally discuss the ramifications of the business and the future of the company and communicate invaluable organizational information to his protege.

Due to the mentor's intercession, Mike received several promotions over a five-year period—from accounting manager to manager of cash control and taxes, to manager of treasury services to a department director position—each promotion representing a growth in salary and an expansion of responsibility. And general knowledge among the corporate powers about his relationship with Evans did nothing to diminish his status.

However, one oversight of the mentor returned to haunt both Evans and Bouton: the mentor had failed to help Bouton acquire a title adequate enough to reinforce the power and authority he was acquiring informally. Although Bouton's director title was considered to be functionally equal to the vice presidential level, that title was not sufficient to prevent his power from being eroded by the actions of "other players" who were arriving on the scene and who made certain that their mentors not only broadened their responsibilities but periodically upgraded their titles.

One of these players was a director of planning, Kevin Jones, who reported to the chief executive officer and was generally considered to be the chief executive officer's protege. Jones was quickly promoted to the position of vice president of finance, an appointment that seemed to come out of the blue. But Bouton should have been informed of this development by his mentor, especially since the position had been vacated when Evans became executive vice president.

The Mentor's Political Position Through this appointment, Jones became Bouton's immediate boss, effectively severing the formal reporting relationship between Bouton and Evans. While Mike protested, his mentor insisted that nothing would change between them: "I'll still be watching out for you." Besides, there was not much Evans could do about Jones's promotion because it was obvious that the chief executive officer favored it and Evans could have weakened his own position in the organization if he had opposed the chief executive officer on this score.

Friction between Jones and Bouton, former peers, was inevitable. Kevin hoped to control the entire financial operation.

"It's hard to report to someone who has been a peer. If you have been buddy-buddy with that person, it becomes difficult. If you have not been on favorable terms, he will be neutral or negative. In my case, it was negative."

The relationship between the mentor and protege inevitably declined. During this period, Mike should have been apprising his mentor of his unhappiness so that he could be helped to move into another area, away from Jones. A position as special assistant to the executive vice president would not have been unreasonable, especially considering that this position would have reestablished the direct reporting relationship. Instead, Bouton allowed his career and his relationship with the mentor to languish, thus permitting Evans to operate under the mistaken assumption that Bouton was generally satisfied with the working arrangement.

Kevin Jones's attitude resembled that of the controller years earlier. Feeling threatened by Bouton's position and his perceived relationship with Evans, he eventually found what he thought would be a legitimate reason for firing Bouton. Several members of Bouton's department had left during the year, an occurrence that Jones decided to officially portray as an example of poor "people management" and managerial incompetence. But to Jones's consternation, he discovered that Bouton was about to turn loss into profit by utilizing the turnover in his department as a convenient occasion to acquire someone whom he could train as his own replacement.

"I wanted someone whom I could groom to replace me so I could move to another area. I felt obligated to hire someone who was strong enough to serve as my replacement."

Bouton did not realize how threatening Jones found his intentions. Jones thought that Bouton with his mentor's help would try to assume a coequal vice president position and segment Jones's control over the corporate financial operation. It was obviously time for Jones to do something, and he activated the corporate mechanisms that would terminate Bouton's employment at Employee Services Company.

What saved Bouton's job was a chain of events completely divorced from any protective action of the mentor. Kevin Jones had been receiving "bad press" throughout his tenure due to his abrasive attitude and personality. Eventually he alienated his mentor. Ironically, Bouton's position, which had been threatened by a slowly deteriorating mentor relationship, was saved because Jones's mentor relationship failed. Jones, whose hard-nosed management style was beginning to severely affect corporate morale, had obviously overstepped his bounds with the chief executive officer. Although the chief executive officer had mentored Jones because of his ability in finance and accounting, the disadvantages of the relationship, namely the potential destruction of organizational cohesion, far overshadowed the advantages. Furthermore, during this period a brokerage house had bought the Employee Services Company. Kevin's brusqueness had alienated the management of the brokerage house, a situation that could have endangered the chief executive officer's position as divisional chairman of Employee Services Company. Moreover, mentor relationships are measured not only in terms of the interplay of mentor and protege but in terms of what they can bring to the organization. Kevin was obviously threatening organizational stability, and on a Friday afternoon he was unceremoniously dismissed.

Bouton soon was again reporting directly to his mentor, but the damage to their mentor relationship had been severe during the Kevin Jones years. The deposed vice president, a master of sabotage, had done much to weaken the relationship. He even moved his office right next to Evans' in order to monitor and intercept communications between mentor and protege.

"I didn't do enough on my own to strengthen my relationship. He had a lot of pressures on his time—it was incumbent on me to take an active role in strengthening the relationship."

The Responsibility of the Protege In hindsight, Bouton realizes that his mentor had to balance the benefits of supporting a skillful protege against the costs of antagonizing a chief executive officer who championed that protege's rival. Given that situation, it would not have been unreasonable for the protege to somehow demonstrate to the mentor that bestowing such support was not a political liability. According to Bouton, if he had acquired independent political strength, his mentor would have been more encouraged to give him visible support.

> "The mentor cannot always by himself pull the protege up the ranks. I think the junior person needs some support among at least two other senior officers in the company. The mentor is mindful of his own interests. He is not going to go out on a limb unless he thinks you have the support of his senior officers."

With Jones out, a clear path for Bouton seemed assured. However, the organizational situation had changed dramatically. The brokerage house that acquired the Employee Services Company gradually began to install its own people on the management staff, and though the mentor's position was solid, his ability to manipulate the organizational environment decreased considerably. If he had moved Mike into a senior management position a few years earlier, Mike would have been less vulnerable. In addition, the company suffered a bad year, and Evans became one of the scapegoats.

Bouton realizes that by not communicating his misgivings and needs, he allowed the mentor relationship to deteriorate. He also realizes that he did not understand the quid pro quo aspect of the relationship.

The unfortunate ending of this story is that during the last reorganization, in a brokerage house decision, Mike Bouton received a demotion, from director to senior financial analyst. His loss of perks, position, and power forced him to resign. The mentor, like the rest of Employee Services Company's old senior management, was in a retrenchment position, and thus could not intercede in Bouton's behalf. Though the brokerage house had made the mentor president of Employee Services Company, his power, such as it was, depended on a faceless committee at the brokerage house. Making Evans' position even shakier was the fact that the brokerage house had originally wanted to fire him and put in its own president. However, some of Evans' recent business gambles as executive vice president had led to substantial profits, so he was safe for the moment. But to resolve any remaining doubts about the location of ultimate power in the division, the brokerage house installed its own representative as senior vice president of finance, with de facto power equal to that of Evans and a direct reporting relationship with the committee at the brokerage house. Evans could have protected Bouton years earlier, but now he had little control over personnel decisions.

This relationship seems to have had the necessary ingredients for success: both members were competent; a chemistry existed between them; and each had something to contribute to the other. Yet several problems led to its deterioriation. Though both members initially understood the ground rules of the relationship, as a result of their failure to communicate their expectations over time, the mentor assumed that Bouton was satisfied with a situation that Bouton in fact found increasingly intolerable. Also, despite the protection that a mentor can provide, the protege must still demonstrate a certain amount of political savvy. This would have helped Bouton overcome Jones's efforts to block his communication with his mentor. If the protege lacks political savvy, even the strongest mentor relationship can be sabotaged.

Bouton's most fundamental error, however, was his incorrect assessment of the mentor's position and power, especially in light of the gradual massive reorganization mandated by the brokerage house. Had Bouton taken earlier notice of the organizational changes, he might have persuaded his mentor that bestowing a senior management title on him would be his only real protection from the eventual erosion of his position.

The failure of the mentor relationship affected both members. Bouton was forced to resign, and Evans, though nominally president, was being challenged by the brokerage house from within and without, his position becoming ever more unstable because he lacked a power base. Proteges make excellent power bases.

And I think the failure also affected the organization, because it lost a good employee in Mike Bouton. It seems a shame to me that he was forced to resign, because it was obvious during the interview that he still possessed a great enthusiasm for the company, the field, and the job.

THE BETRAYED PROTEGE

So far we have seen that various negative aspects of the mentor relationship, including differing career and organizational expectations, a breakdown in communications, and a politically wrong mentor, can all add up to a failed relationship. Up to this point, though, the cases have involved members who exhibited, if not great political acumen, at least a general tendency to bargain in good faith.

In the following case, however, the mentor had a hidden agenda that, though it did not destroy the protege's career, led to a bitter dissolution of the relationship.

Allan Caldwell is director of international sales and marketing development at a large dairy products corporation. He was hired as a technology and product development specialist to work on new dairy products in the company's laboratories. Early in his career, he met his future mentor, Elliot Denny, then head of the company's largest division. Allan had been loaned to that division temporarily to help develop a training program for technical people. Denny was impressed with Caldwell, and what began as a temporary loan from the lab became a permanent position in management.

Early Benefits Though Denny never achieved chief executive officer or chief operating officer status, he eventually became the most powerful person in the company, reaching the level of vice chairman. Hence, he was in a strategic position to benefit Caldwell both as a teacher and as a promoter.

> *"I learned a lot from him, in terms of business and areas like finance that I had no knowledge of. I learned what my weaknesses were from him, and as a result tried to expand through education."*

The mentor helped in the development of Caldwell's career, sponsoring him for various positions within the company. Early in the relationship, one of the jobs for which the mentor sponsored him, assistant to the corporate president, though promising at first, quickly deteriorated to a personal secretary role. This motivated Caldwell, without prior announcement, to resign. It was at this stage that the relationship became solidified, because Denny was immediately forced to intercede and visibly demonstrate support for Caldwell.

> *"Elliot came to me and told me that he couldn't let me leave the company—he refused to allow that to happen—and I could have whatever I'd like just to stay with the corporation. When I asked him what he meant, he said, 'You can name your position, name your title, and name your salary.' "*

Caldwell discussed Denny's proposal with his wife and decided that he would remain with the company.

> *"The next day I told him that I had one position in mind. It wasn't a position that existed but a job that needed to be done, and I told him what that was. Within half an hour it was arranged, and the salary level was satisfactory."*

This incident signaled to Caldwell that Denny possessed an unexpectedly high level of commitment to his career progress. It suddenly became apparent that his progress up to this point must have been more dependent on Denny's intervention than he had guessed and that the mentor was willing to extend himself to retain him as a protege. The incident also signaled to Caldwell that Denny possessed awesome power within the organization. He could not only cajole the organization into instantly bestowing a new salary and title on his protege but force it to create a function hitherto unknown.

As the relationship developed, the mentor also began to give Caldwell psychological help. At one point in Caldwell's career, through his mentor's intercession, he was given the opportunity to go to California and take over the West Coast marketing operation. After spending four to five successful years on the West Coast, Caldwell returned to New York.

> *"My wife and I were having a tremendous amount of difficulty readjusting to living back on the East Coast. He went out of his way to be understanding of that situation, both with myself and my wife."*

Denny actively interjected himself into the family situation. In an effort to ease the relocation difficulties that the Caldwells were experiencing, he wrote a very warm letter to Caldwell's wife and followed it up with phone calls. It was partially due to Denny's personal support that the family effected a successful readjustment.

While the protege received numerous personal and career benefits from participating in the relationship, the mentor also gained advantages.

> *"What I think he got was someone who could play a tremendously supportive role for him, who enabled him to expand his range tremendously in developing and implementing plans that he had for different areas which he was involved with."*

The Break Over a period of years, Caldwell came to expect a certain level of treatment from his mentor, in both career and personal matters. For a few years after his return from California, Caldwell's career progressed with the help of the mentor, and his loyalty was assured due to guarantees made regarding further career advancement. Denny promised Caldwell a position as division general manager in the near future.

But quite inadvertently something happened that irreversibly changed the relationship. One evening at a sales meeting Caldwell discovered, through a private conversation with a regional manager, that the mentor was considering someone else for the divisional general manager position he had been promised.

> *"I will never forget the evening. I thought he was drunk; he frequently drank. But I checked with him the next morning, and I said, 'Do you know what we were talking about last night? Do you remember saying that?' "*

The regional manager replied that the information had been transmitted to him by Denny. Within two hours, Caldwell confronted his mentor with the general manager's statement, which the mentor immediately denied. Caldwell then picked up the phone, placed a call to the regional manager, and in Denny's presence had the manager repeat his statement.

A 15-year relationship seemingly dissolved in a period of two days. Instead of trying to rectify the situation, over the next several months the mentor became outright destructive in his handling of Caldwell.

> "He was actively injuring me rather than actively helping me. And I didn't even learn that directly until probably six to eight months after he started doing it."

From Caldwell's account, there seems to have been no rationale for the mentor's actions. After all, several ways of correcting the situation seem to have been open to the mentor, including then and there promising Caldwell the position, while further denying that he had ever considered anyone else for it.

Power and Authority An analysis of the structure of the organization and of Denny's methods for negotiating his way through it makes it obvious why he could not do that. He had in fact offered the divisional general manager position to another person, and he needed the loyalty of that person as much as he needed Allan Caldwell's. Hence, to have denied that person the position would have meant a loss of organizational power. A deal had been struck and the payoff would have to be made, even if this meant that his 15-year relationship with Denny would have to be severed in the process.

But why had the mentor been involved in such a web of deals, favors, and intrigues in the first place? For an explanation, I reviewed some of Caldwell's descriptions of the mentor's management techniques.

> "Early on, Denny had pointed out that the people who had the supposed titles, that you would normally expect to be there with power and authority, really did not possess the power that he had. And later I verified that Elliot really did have the power."

It has been noted in this book and elsewhere that organization charts do not tell the whole story regarding organizational power. But those who choose to rule without the proper title must rely exclusively on such subtleties as influence, persuasion, and personality to leave their mark on their organization's operations. Elliot Denny, however, attempted to impose his will through coercion, trade-offs, and deals, and as his list of enemies grew and his power diminished, these mechanisms (as in the case of giving the other manager the position promised to Caldwell) became his predominant means for maintaining his organizational position.

If friendships had to be sacrificed, so be it.

Overdependence Throughout his relationship with Denny, Allan Caldwell has received indications regarding negative aspects of Denny's position in the organization. The Machiavellian methods that Denny used to impose his will on the organization, Denny's disruptions of the chain of command, his disregard for fellow managers' feelings, all should have served as warnings that Denny was not the person upon whom Caldwell should base his career.

> *"If someone wouldn't listen to his point of view, he'd go into a tirade— literally into a tirade—and he had developed techniques of disruption of more than one one-on-one session. I got to see the techniques he used, which were absolutely devastating to the growth of the organization and to the growth of the individual."*

Of course, when a protege is under the influence of such a mentor, what is in fact manipulative may appear to be a legitimate exercise of power.

> *"He had techniques that were mainly used in meetings with more than one peer—a technique for disrupting and getting his point home which was absolutely phenomenal. In a meeting that had an agenda developed for it, he would come in, and the first thing he would do was somehow throw open the discussion, change the meeting agenda."*

In the mentor's quest for organizational domination, he would instigate the abandonment of agendas that, in the organization's best interest, really should have been pursued. This technique, while harming the organization, made him the center of attention.

> *"No one else was prepared to discuss what he wanted to discuss in the way he wanted to discuss it. And he succeeded in doing this with some high-level people in our whole organization. Phenomenal! And I've seen him do it with outsiders."*

The changing of agendas by a top manager is a not uncommon phenomenon, but in most cases this is done in order to set the meeting, and the organization, on what the chief perceives as the correct course. Often the chief will allow all present at the board meeting to state their case, and if the agenda he perceives as correct has still not emerged, he will subtly introduce the ideas necessary to move the discussion to the desired plane. This is a techinque that many of

the proteges I interviewed have witnessed and attempted to dupli-
cate. But Denny's method was entirely different. He changed the
agenda, not for organizational growth, but for domination over other
managers!

Why didn't Caldwell perceive the implications of these drawbacks? I think one of the reasons is that Caldwell had developed an
emotional dependence greater than that usually exhibited in the
mentor-protege relationship.

> "It's funny I haven't mentioned this before. The relationship started about the
> time my father passed away. And in some ways Denny and I would talk
> about whether I was viewing him as a father or whether he was viewing me
> as a son. Although he had a son who was about my age, he had a very bad
> relationship with him. So that maybe there were some elements of father-son
> gratification. We talked about it but never reached any conclusions."

This emotional dependence probably interfered with Caldwell's
ability to clearly perceive the implications of the mentor's destructive
bahavior within the organization, and it certainly blinded him to the
"black halo" effects of his association with the mentor.

At various places in this volume, the chemistry between the mentor and the protege is dealt with as a healthy part of the mentoring
process. However, there is a difference between chemistry and emotional dependence. Chemistry furthers interaction arising between
people with similar perceptions, interests, and goals. But when emotional dependence develops, the protege and the mentor begin to see
each other as substitutes for persons normally found outside the
organization: a parent, a spouse, a child, a relative. Each member of
the mentor relationship substitutes emotional satisfaction for the real
goal of the mentoring process—career progress.

Aftermath   After it became apparent that Elliot Denny was no
longer acting in Allan Caldwell's best interests, the mentor relationship went downhill. Without Denny's support, Caldwell's career
stalled, though his income continued to increase. He looked for another position, but he could not locate a suitable alternative.

Ironically, Caldwell's falling out with his mentor over the broken
promise eventually rescued his position within the company. Since
Denny was the focus of widespread hostility, a public break with him
actually strengthened Caldwell's image. "If you've severed your relationship with Denny, you must have something on the ball."

The emerging awareness of Denny's ulterior motives among senior management led to a gradual weakening of his position. And
since his title and position did not provide him with protection from
top management, he was ultimately retired.

At Denny's retirement, Caldwell wisely made an irrevocable public disavowal of his mentor. Since Denny was being ushered out of the organization involuntarily, he wanted his departure to be accompanied by as little fanfare as possible. Unfortunately for him, top management had other plans and gave him an "unsolicited" surprise retirement party.

"The people who were invited were just told to appear at the restaurant at a certain hour, and they were told it was a surprise, not to mention it to him. The party came off, and each person in senior management got up and offered him toasts. The top man in the company at that time, titlewise, made a toast, and then other people started to make toasts."

But each of the toasts had a double meaning. The retirement party became transformed into a "roast," with none of the underpinnings of "fellowship and good cheer" usually associated with such affairs.

The organization, in one evening, reasserted its solidarity against the Rasputin-like qualities of the deposed pretender. But more important for Caldwell, the occasion gave him a platform for publicly asserting his sympathy with this cause. Caldwell, of course, had suffered as much as anyone in the organization from Denny's duplicity.

"My toast to him was I thanked him for teaching me to tell the truth, the whole truth, and nothing but the truth at all times."

The double meaning was immediately appreciated, and Caldwell's career was on its way back to health. He is now part of top management. And after Denny's retirement there was a distinct absence of negative feeling toward Caldwell within the organization, not merely because of his public disavowal, but because the organization had seemingly reached an unspoken agreement not to acknowledge that Denny had ever existed.

"It's almost as though the person's been Stalinized, and by that I mean the Russians are stereotyped as being able to cause someone to disappear from their history books. The statues of people are torn down. It's almost as though the person never existed."

WHEN MENTOR LEAVES

The negative side of mentoring is also manifested in situations in which, through retirement or promotion, the mentor and protege suddenly become separated before the mentor has been able to secure a strong position for the protege.

Bert Gregory received his MBA from Columbia University in the early 60s, and had worked for a number of companies before he came to the Wine and Distillery Company as assistant director of advertising and promotion. The company was one of the smaller divisions of a large conglomerate.

Gregory met his mentor, the president of the division, early in his career at the company. Frequent close contact at meetings and in travel encouraged a familiarity that established the groundwork for their mentor relationship.

In the early stages of the relationship, the president's mentoring technique was extremely blunt and directive, but the protege considered this an encouraging sign.

> *"If I would make a mistake, he was sometimes brutal. He would say, 'That was wrong; you made a mistake; you said the wrong thing; you did the wrong thing.' But it takes somebody with a particular interest in the individual to do this. A person who didn't care would never take the time to correct him."*

Gregory's relationship with the president developed fairly quickly. It even involved an extraorganizational component since outside socializing was basic to the president's management technique.

> *"I was sort of singled out as an individual whom he was interested in. I was identified as someone who was not merely floating through the company. I had an affinity for what he was trying to do, and I was contributing to his growth."*

The Chain of Command   Early in my interview with Gregory, it became apparent that the president used great tact in promoting "his boys," making sure not to threaten other managers in the chain of command. And in order to promote Gregory, he had to allay the fears and jealousies of Gregory's direct boss, a vice president.

> *"The closer the individual was to me in the organizational structure, the more jealous the VP was of his own position and his own growth. This person wasn't about to bring me along that quickly, because I was a threat to him."*

There were just so many next steps in the hierarchy, and the vice president was not about to promote Gregory. Thus his advancement became closely tied to the direct efforts of the president. But the president wisely promoted his boss along with him, so that the vice president was always two or three steps ahead of Gregory in the organizational hierarchy.

Gregory enjoyed his relationship with the president because of the president's particularly personal mentoring style.

> *"You were more than just a face in the crowd. He was more than someone writing a periodic evaluation of you. He took an interest not only in your progress but in you personally."*

But because the mentor's interest was so personal, the mentor relationship was becoming increasingly visible.

Gregory was in agreement with the president's management goals. For instance, he shared the president's enthusiasm for some of the products, and this shared enthusiasm certainly facilitated the maintenance of the mentor relationship and benefited the organization. Gregory's commitment to the corporation's goals was one of the factors in motivating the president to groom him for a higher position.

The mentor relationship protected Gregory from office politics. Battles between office factions left him untouched because the president, after 30 years in the organization, controlled many factions and interests subgroups through various loyalty networks.

A Mentor Deposed As the years passed, the president's allies among the division heads were slowly retiring and he was failing to generate new loyalties within the company. The senior vice presidents of the overseeing conglomerate, who had also been the president's allies, were tending to their own careers. As a result, the president's power was almost imperceptibly eroding. The president, now in his 60s, was looking forward to several more years in his position at the helm. He did not notice that his lateral organizational support, the basis of his power within the conglomerate, was disappearing. This problem was compounded by the fact that certain factions wanted to replace the older presidents of all the subsidiaries with younger ones.

I asked Gregory why the mentor did not attempt to secure his place in the power structure through a higher title or position. Two factors precluded this possibility. First, the president had slowly lost contact with many of those in power, so that toward the end of his career he was unable to move a favorite son into a safe haven. Second, the president's deposition occurred so quickly that he had very little time to act.

> *"He had done as much as he could but felt that his influence at that point in time was nil. 'There isn't much I can do for you anymore, and I hope you can succeed on your own.'"*

After the president left, there was a virtual reversal of corporate marketing and organizational trends. That reversal was accompanied by a transformation of the corporate climate, prompted in large part by the impersonal, "academic" management style of the new president.

Gregory's departure was not immediate. The mentor's second in command, an executive vice president, retained him for several years afterward, more out of need than out of any sense of loyalty, but Gregory never moved beyond middle management. Eventually, the new president replaced the entire management staff, including Bert Gregory, with his own people.

Gregory feels that he allowed himself to be lulled into a false sense of security during the mentorship period. By isolating Gregory from political unpleasantness, the mentor had failed to familiarize him with the hard facts of corporate life—the politics, the personalities, and the factions. In that sense, the mentor performed the promotional function of mentoring without really teaching the protege anything about the realities of management. Not having received the benefit of "learning the organization," the protege had no idea of where to turn in order to progress inside the new corporate structure.

Another factor that affected Gregory's postmentor progress was the mentor's falure to so integrate him into the power structure that the next president would identify him as a "comer" who would make a useful ally. Instead, Gregory was merely perceived as one of the old president's boys, and hence less than useful once the president left. Gregory's experience taught him the difference between having a mentor and not having one.

"To a large measure, keeping your nose to the grindstone, and being sound and industrious and good about the whole thing, plays some role in progress. But if you get your mentor along the line, I wouldn't say your fortune's made, but it certainly is in your best interest. It's an unwritten but indispensable functional role."

Gregory's career has never rebounded from that experience. After being forced out of the Wine and Distillery Company, he went from one company to another. He is still searching for a company with a humanized social climate like that created by his mentor. But he sees most of the corporations he encounters as cold, hierarchical, and computerized. Currently unemployed, he seems to have lost all hope of finding the organization he can live with.

Clearly, losing a mentor can be a traumatic experience. But whereas Bert Gregory lost his mentor due to the mentor's downfall, our next subject, Andy Franklin, became separated from his mentor as a result of positive developments in the mentor's career.

Franklin is the manager of medical regulations at a subsidiary of the West Coast Pharmaceutical Corporation. His job, to serve as a liaison between the corporation and the Food and Drug Administration, requires a thorough knowledge both of the new products that are being developed by the corporation and of the regulations that emanate endlessly from the FDA. The department is run by a director, and Franklin and two other peers are at the manager level, each in charge of a different function.

This is the only place that Franklin has ever worked. His undergraduate degree is in chemistry, and he earned his MBA while working for the Pharmaceutical Corporation. His company experience includes manufacturing supervision, financial/computer functions, and budgeting and forecasting as director of research.

While Franklin was director of research, he met the director of medical affairs, who later became his mentor. Their relationship, built on common values and goals and a mutual respect, developed quickly. Soon the director was exploring career opportunities with Franklin.

The mentor became extremely interested in Franklin's advancement through the organization. In fact, he influenced Franklin's promotion into his current position. Franklin seemed assured of his mentor's continued support and followed his counsel in most matters.

The problem in this relationship developed in a peculiar fashion. The mentor suggested that Franklin participate in a management development program that the Pharmaceutical Corporation had established for its most promising young executives. Each participant was required to spend six months in a position in another department. Franklin was selected and spent this time in the financial area. Upon returning to the medical affairs area, he learned that his mentor had been promoted out of the subsidiary into a position at corporate headquarters. In the interim, outside personnel had been promoted into positions of power within his division. Franklin's career has since suffered in subtle ways.

"My career is not as fast track as it used to be. I used to interface with the top level of the division."

The changes have not been drastic enough to impel Franklin to leave the organization. But this new phase of his career has made him aware of how being suddenly unmentored can hamper chances for organizational advancement.

"Everyone seems to have a mentor somewhere. My new immediate boss has selected a new guy in the department who was a statistician working for him when he was in charge of another department. It's very subtle, not so much in what he's not doing for me as in what he is doing for him."

Franklin is no longer given chances to "visibly succeed," as was the case when the mentor was still on deck.

"Let's say some guest, someone from an outside laboratory, came in from Europe, and my mentor was busy. He would ask me to take him out to lunch. My new immediate boss throws these goodies to his protege—trips, covering meetings, a general exposure."

Franklin mentioned that since his mentor relationship ended, the deferential treatment he once received from peers has disappeared.

"Oftentimes, you knew things they didn't. So they often came to me and asked me questions about the direction of the organization."

After the mentor relationship ended, Franklin noticed that he possessed just a "little less horsepower" than he had had as the director's protege. Consequently, he has become a bit cynical about the relationship of quality to career advancement.

"One of the things I see in business is if a guy likes you, and the circumstances are exactly the same, he can look at the situation and say 'that's fantastic.' And if you're in the same situation, and he doesn't like you, he can perceive your actions negatively. And he will present it to others that way. And once that gets cast in any way, it's hell to get it changed, if it ever can be done."

The projects that were once assigned to Franklin are no longer coming his way. In his division, being "good" depends not so much on the quality of the person's work as on the importance of his project, and important projects can be quietly steered to a young manager by an astute mentor.

Andy Franklin feels that his mentor is still looking out for him, but of course the day-to-day protection and assistance that the mentor could give him through organizational proximity are absent. Franklin and the mentor still communicate, but the mentor's influence cannot stretch from corporate headquarters to the subsidiary. The career of this protege has been less adversely affected by the loss of the mentor than have the careers of other proteges discussed in this chapter, but it is undoubtedly on hold. Fortunately, the separation between the mentor and the protege occurred as a result of positive rather than negative developments in the mentor's career, so no "guilt by association" emerged. The new supervisory staff's attitude toward Franklin is characterized by indifference, not dislike, and though the condition does not strengthen Franklin's prospects, it at least does not prevent him from pursuing alternative routes to organizational success. However, if he does not manage to shine on his own or attract the attention of a new mentor, his career will remain on hold indefinitely.

THE FAILED MENTOR RELATIONSHIP AND ITS EFFECTS ON THE ORGANIZATION

Up to this point, we have confined ourselves to the harmful effects of poor mentor relationships on the individuals directly involved—the mentor and the protege. However, the effects of poor mentor relationships on the overall functioning of the organization are equally harmful.

For instance, when mentoring is perceived as favoritism, the effect on the organization's social climate can be disastrous. One female product manager at a large firm recounted how a mentor's unabashed favoritism nearly destroyed the cohesion of a department. The favoritism in this case included visibly rewarding the protege for services that were unrewarded when performed by the protege's peers.

Eventually the protege's peers came to resent this partiality and tried to curtail her advancement through the most obvious technique: sabotage. Thus the outcome of this mentor relationship based on obvious favoritism was a succession of unanswered memos, unattended staff meetings, and unheeded directives. Clearly, the organization's needs were being badly served by the relationship, as indicated by a decline in morale and a concomitant drop in productivity. Top management interceded to rectify the situation, demanding the resignation first, of the mentor and then of the protege.

However, as the following case demonstrates, not all organizations are so quick to curtail the harmful consequences of certain mentor relationships.

David Baskin is currently manager of business planning in the management consulting division of a large accounting firm, his position one step below that of a partner. His mentoring experience involved two mentors at another major accounting firm. Baskin met Allan Wallace, a vice president of that firm, on his job interview for a financial position there, and Wallace quickly took Baskin under his wing. Their relationship seemed positive from both a professional and personal point of view. In fact, Wallace was himself being mentored by one of the most powerful men in the organization, Martin Robinson, a partner and head of the New York office. Shortly after Baskin was hired, Wallace became a partner.

Since Baskin had allied himself with one of the more powerful factions in the firm, his future, it seemed, could not have been more promising. Unfortunately, however, his mentor, Allan Wallace, had great personal weaknesses, including a drinking problem, that interfered with his functioning as a member of the firm. At one point, Allan's mentor secretly sent him to a clinic to "dry out" because the problem was becoming a public embarrassment. In addition, Wallace, who was married, was so indiscreet about his affairs with women in the office, that it seemed he wanted the world to know about his adulterous relationships.

Why, I asked Baskin, did the New York partner, Wallace's mentor, retain his services, let alone sponsor him for a position of power.

> *"Martin Robinson was cold to a fault, austere, manipulative, the apotheosis of the 'business is business' mentality. Allan Wallace, on the other hand, had affairs, laughed, was great at parties."*

Baskin suggested that in this instance the attraction of opposites took precedence over straight business concerns. While this psychological explanation seemed plausible, further investigation uncovered factors within the firm that encouraged the promotion of unworthy individuals.

Martin Robinson wanted as many proteges as possible so that he could expand his network in an organization that fed on empires.

The partnership system in this firm differed from that of the Eastern Investment Bank. In both firms, a partner mentored people below him with the intention of bringing them into the partnership circle. But at the Eastern Investment Bank, when the protege became a partner and was given a piece of the business in the form of stock, he was permanently assured of a measure of equality with the existing powers. In this accounting firm, however, a partner could be "fired" or involuntarily bought out by a vote of the other partners. Thus the standing of the partners was based on the strength of their coalitions. Even at the exalted level of the partnerships, an informal culture of "senior" and "junior," powerful and weak, developed, so that Martin Robinson, though head of the New York office, was still climbing up the national organizational ladder, still acquiring power, forming coalitions, and protecting his position, with the intention of assuming a commanding position in the company, possibly as chief officer and primary partner. His relationship with Allan Wallace, then, was an outgrowth, not of a desire to vicariously experience the wilder side of life, but of a political opportunism encouraged by an organizational power struggle. Robinson's willingness to promote into partnership a known liability seems to have been motivated by the desire to strengthen his coalition and expand his voting bloc.

Unfortunately, Allan Wallace's ability to function as a partner became more suspect as the years passed, especially since his lifestyle interfered increasingly with his ability to generate new sales, the ultimate foundation of a partner's power. Thus, in spite of Robinson's support, Wallace was eventually voted out of the company.

Oddly enough, Baskin was then suddenly brought to the New York office, where Robinson tried to assume a mentoring role with him. At first, Baskin was flattered by the attention, especially since his career had slowed considerably as his first mentor's political problems got out of control. But soon Baskin found himself in a situation that he found uncomfortable. His first mentor had been amiable but had exhibited a dramatically diminished ability to fulfill the role of the good promoter as his personal problems increased, whereas Martin was as cold personally as he was powerful organizationally.

"Robinson was too manipulative, no warmth. I saw him after work rarely, at his house once. His attitude undermined any chance for loyalty on my part."

Though Baskin's career was advancing, this mentor relationship remained more political than personal. However, in order to advance in the organization, Baskin was willing to overlook the unpleasant aspects of Robinson's personality.

Compounding the difficulty created for Baskin by his uncomfortable relationship with Robinson was the fact that the firm was developing an increasingly factional environment, where partners were jostling for position and using their proteges as pawns on a financial battleground. According to Baskin, who increasingly came to feel like one of those pawns, the organization's social climate assumed hellish qualities. Though Baskin thought that through Robinson's influence he might soon be made a partner, because of the deteriorating financial condition and social psychological environment of the firm, he resigned.

What Was Happening to the Organization? From the vantage point of his position at his current company, Baskin now feels fortunate that he left his previous firm. That firm suffered because its mentor relationships were not directed toward developing either individuals or the organization. According to Baskin, it has shown a loss over the last several quarters and some dramatic action is needed to save it. However, it is so factionalized that no coalition capable of pushing the company in a well-defined position direction has risen to the fore.

After listening to David Baskin's story, I was not surprised at the firm's inability to flourish. Proteges there are picked not so much for their talent as for their willingness to remain loyal during a power struggle among factions. It is therefore only incidental to a mentor whether the protege will be able as a partner to generate new business, the lifeblood of any corporation in the accounting/management consulting field. It is questionable whether David Baskin learned to be a better consultant as a result of his six-year experience with two mentors in that environment, where the development of personnel was secondary to the acquisition of power.

I would have expected David to now perceive mentoring relationships in general extremely negatively. Surprisingly, however, he still sees them as contributing positively to the individual and the organization. But his own experience has changed his views about what these relationships should accomplish. When he was asked about the optimal characteristic of a potential mentor, descriptors such as "bright," "handles himself well," and "long-term commitment to professional development" had replaced such earlier descriptors as "in a position of power" and "knowing the right people."

UNDERLYING FACTORS IN THE DECLINE OF MENTOR RELATIONSHIPS

The decline of a mentor relationship is often a product of a combination of factors, most of which have been illustrated in the cases in this chapter. These factors can be subdivided into two major types: problems that exist in the relationship itself and problems that exist between the members of the relationship and the organization (see Table 6–1).

The Mutual Benefits Model refers to complementary needs that can be satisfied by an exchange between the mentor and the protege. In any exchange, however, each party must be apprised of the other's needs in order to meet them, and thus the mentor can meet the needs of the protege only if they are properly communicated.

TABLE 6–1
Factors in the Decline of Mentor Relationships

Problems in the mentor relationship
1. Failure to communicate needs.
2. Failure to communicate goals.
3. Protege's failure to correctly assess mentor's intentions.
4. Emotional overdependence.

Problems between members of the mentor relationship and the organization
1. Both parties' failure to assess political environment.
2. Mentor's inability to control political environment.
3. Protege's failure to establish other alliances.
4. Mentor's failure to upgrade protege's title, job description, and formal power.

As we observed in some of these cases, the mentor often found it convenient to assume the the protege's progess, organizational relationships, and career in general were moving ahead according to plan. In Mike Bouton's case, this assumption had disastrous consequences.

Some of the problems in a mentor-protege relationship are rooted in the misconceptions that each member has regarding the other's goals. Many of the failed relationships were characterized by a lack of communication regarding goals: the mentors and proteges did not even sit down and talk about where each wanted to be, what each hoped to gain in his career. Such noncommunication inevitably leads to a situation in which the mentor and protege operate at cross-purposes, working toward goals that each mistakenly perceives the other as sharing.

A related problem is the situation in which the protege fails to correctly assess the mentor's intentions regarding his own future. Support, as we have seen, varies greatly in degree and intensity, and the protege's political sensitivity will determine just how accurately he can estimate the mentor's level of commitment. The Allan Cald-well case, in which the mentor's intentions changed completely over time, demonstrates how the protege's faulty perception can damage his career. The Caldwell case also suggests that a caveat against emotional overdependence is in order, especially since emotional over-dependence tends to camouflage any hidden agenda that a mentor may have.

But the data indicate that in most mentor relationships a communication exists between the mentor and the protege that facilitates clear signals regarding goals and needs, that both parties are usually sufficiently mature not to overcommit themselves emotionally, and that each party can trust the intentions and motivations of the other. In fact, where the continued health of the mentor-protege relationship is in doubt, the primary source of concern usually arises, not from the members themselves but from the surrounding organization.

The healthier mentor relationships reflect an awareness on the part of both members of the interaction between the relationship and the organizational environment. The first necessity in this regard is for both parties to be able to assess the political environment. Knowledge of the power structure, general political savvy, and access to information about upcoming mergers and shifts in upper management all help to ward off threats to the relationship. In this regard, the merger issue seems to be of greater importance. Many otherwise healthy mentor relationships die an untimely death when the members of the relationship are unexpectedly caught between the old and new managements. The break up is caused not so much by the actions of either party as by the emerging power structure in the reorganized corporation.

Since the mentor usually has greater organizational power than the protege, it would seem fitting that he assume most of the responsibility for controlling the surrounding political environment. The mentor's inability to control the political environment has various bases, including a lack of ties and cross-loyalties among senior managers and a poor information/intelligence system.

But the protege must assume some responsibility for controlling the political environment. The protege must always see himself as a coequal contributor to the relationship and thus must make an effort to establish alliances that can serve both himself and the mentor. Such alliances will help establish the protege's credibility, a process that the mentor cannot accomplish alone.

It should also be remembered that any dyad representing a cohesive unit, such as a mentor relationship, can appear threatening to the organization. According to the Mutual Benefits Model, the mentor relationship works best when the organization perceives that it also derives benefits from the relationship. The mentor and protege must therefore demonstrate that their relationship is useful to the organization by performing well.

The activities of the higher levels of the Hierarchy of Mentoring, namely intervention and promotion, are of paramount importance here. On the organizational intervention level, the protecting, advertising, and marketing of the protege strengthen the position of the relationship. And Level IV functions are equally critical, because, as we have seen in several of the studies, failure to equip the protege with a more powerful title and job description, and hence formal power, will haunt both the mentor and the protege during times of organizational transition and upheaval.

By working at a high level of competence, by controlling the political environment as completely as possible, and by establishing the legitimacy of both parties through title and formal power, the mentor and protege can increase their chances of corporate survival. Although there are circumstances outside the control of either the mentor or the protege, the decline and termination of many mentor relationships could have been avoided if certain power-base and organizational issues had been addressed at some time during the tenure of both parties. Through the proper application of political acumen, most of these relationships could have been protected.

Mergers, reorganizations, upward and outward movements of managers, and forced retirements occur regularly in all organizations, but most mentors still manage to protect themselves and retain their proteges. The mentors who retain their proteges are usually those who have sufficient control over their own careers due to their political perceptiveness and their establishment of cross-organizational loyalties. (Faced with a reorganization, some of my mentor respondents managed to retain not only their proteges but their entire lower management and secretarial/clerical staff.)

Although the reasons for the decline of mentor relationships vary, it can be stated with some certainty that the career effects on all concerned are usually negative. The protege may be fired, demoted, or left to languish in a corporate limbo; the mentor is often stripped of his power base. Some of the respondents discussed in this chapter stated that they would have been better off without a mentor, especially since their career progress was retarded because of their identification with an unpopular figure. Some of these managers were extremely bitter.

It should be noted that even in the most severely impaired mentor relationships, those with little chance of surviving the winds of corporate change, the mentor can often soften the fate of the protege by ascertaining his own fate early on. One executive told how a senior vice president protected his protege, a general manager whom he had mentored from the time the protege was a newly minted MBA, so that his own departure left the protege relatively unscathed.

> "The mentor saw that he himself was going to get nailed. He took steps to protect his protege by sending him out, making him vice president of marketing of a large division. They didn't need a vice president of marketing. They didn't have an office for a vice president of marketing. Six months later, the mentor was out, but the protege was protected."

The mentor realized that at some point the protege, because of his contacts within the company and the field, would be useful as a resource and reference. Thus he retained a remnant of his power base even after losing his job.

This chapter, while recounting how political snafus and other problems created a negative mentoring experience for some managers, also suggested ways in which the manager might have avoided these problems. Chapter 7 will provide a fuller discussion of the methods that managers and others employ to avert or survive the political dangers that inevitably emerge in corporate life.

7

Establishing the Mentor Connection

The preceding material on the negative aspects of mentoring illustrates how important to career success are such factors as selection of the right mentor or protege and astute assessment of and interaction with the organizational environment. But how the right mentor or protege is chosen and how the partners work at maintaining the mentor relationship are matters yet to be explored.

In this chapter I deal with these issues, examining the strategies used for meeting mentors, the types of qualities that attract mentors to proteges, and the best type of mentor for a protege. I also examine the place of the mentor relationship within the organizational environment as a whole. How does involvment in a mentor relationship affect peer relations, and how to do upper managers perceive the protege? In short, how should the mentor and protege behave to maintain good organizational relations?

Most of the proteges and mentors I interviewed were sensitive to politics, had acquired a semblance of organizational savvy, and were thus able to present techniques for entering the mentor relationship and for surviving in the relationship once it was established. The following material reflects their accumulated wisdom.

MAKING THE CONNECTION

The mentor relationship benefits the protege, the mentor, and the organization, but the talented manager can reap the potential benefits of the relationship only if he finds the appropriate mentor. I asked the respondents a series of questions about the qualities they considered most important in selecting a mentor or protege, about the personal characteristics that made the partner want to initiate a relationship with them, and about the methods they used to initiate a relationship after they had identified the "correct" person. This section is based on detailed responses to these questions.

Factors in the Selection of a Mentor

As most of the respondents emphasized, not all senior managers are created equal. As was evident in the last chapter, the mentor who is moving on, falling out of favor, or caught on the wrong end of a political struggle is a career liability. As Barbara Sikorsky at the Goodbrands Corporation says,

> *"You've got to watch whom you support. You can't afford to just willy-nilly say I like this person's face, or the person has great clothes, or he happens to be good to his mother and writes home every week. That doesn't put bread on the table. The real question is, 'Does the person seem to have a lot on the ball?' "*

Here are some specific concerns that a budding protege should keep in mind during the mentor selection process (see Table 7–1).

TABLE 7–1
Factors in Selecting a Mentor
1. Is the mentor good at what he does?
2. Is the mentor getting support?
3. How does the organization judge the mentor?
4. Is the mentor a good teacher?
5. Is the mentor a good motivator?
6. What are the protege's needs and goals?
7. What are the needs and goals of the prospective mentor?
8. How powerful is the mentor?
9. Is the mentor secure in his own position?

1. Is the Mentor Good at What He Does? As one respondent mentioned, there are many senior managers who are only too willing to expound their knowledge, who are only too quick to serve as champions. Since many young managers find the attention of a senior person flattering, they will immediately accept such a person as a mentor, never asking whether he exhibits competence in his own position. The junior person might assume that a vice president, for instance, had to possess a basic managerial proficiency to attain the position he now holds. But incompetence, though not typical in the modern corporation, sometimes exists. Since the protege will be best served by a relationship in which the mentor can teach job-related skills, it is wise of him to look for someone who possesses expertise in many areas. While many young executives envision the mentoring experience per se as a "road to the top," they must realize that it will serve that purpose only if the mentor helps the protege achieve a high performance level. The mere association of the mentor with the protege will not accomplish this.

At times, the protege can readily discern the mentor's ability to perform his role in an exceptional manner when they first meet. As one respondent claims about his mentor,

> "He is one of the top minds I've ever encountered. He's one of the few people who thinks thoughts on such a consistent basis that I think, 'God, I wished I thought that.' "

Some proteges rely on the manager's position as the sole indicator of his desirability as a mentor. But sometimes in the mentor selection process a veteran executive's years of experience and lofty title must be weighed against the amount of knowledge and skill that a lower-level senior might have. For instance, a skillful manager who is currently in the process of translating his knowledge into power may, at the time of his first encounter with the protege, have less organizational status than the already powerful. Jim Mulcahy of the Eastern Investment Bank compared the prospective mentor with his older colleagues, who in most cases had already achieved partner status. He found that the prospective mentor had a much better feel for negotiating his way through the world of investment banking than did many of his seniors.

> "He had a far superior handle on the market than his senior people. And I'd say after being there about six months I picked that up because I worked more closely with him. There was a point where we started to ask each other questions, and he would listen to my opinions. Then I would get his opinion. And the more I heard him, the more highly I thought of him."

Mulcahy felt that in the long run he would become a better investment banker, and achieve greater career success, by choosing a manager who, while he was not yet on the highest rungs of the corporation, had a deeper understanding of the financial world than those who were.

2.   Is the Mentor Getting Support? A mentor characteristic that seems of paramount importance is the mentor's ability to develop alliances within the organization. A vice president at the Eastern Investment Bank summarizes it as follows:

> *"Let's face it. There are some people out there who could be more helpful than others, and there are some people who seem to be on the fast track or have the chairman's eye or whatever; and in the short run, you could benefit by allying yourself with that person."*

According to the vice president, the young manager has to make a political choice about whom he wants to expend energy impressing.

> *"You have a thousand assignments that come cascading over the desk every day, and all things being equal, it's more important to do a good job for somebody who's on the way up than for somebody who's on the way down."*

Of course, this type of advice assumes that the protege has spent some time assessing the political situation and can ascertain who is "in," who is marked for success.

A female special assistant to a vice president at a large commercial bank believes that an executive who has a passive relationship with others in the organization would make a poor mentor. "I wouldn't want a senior weaker than I was to be my mentor, regardless of position."

3.   How Does the Organization Judge the Mentor? Aside from assessing the direct support that the senior person is receiving and the alliances in which he is involved, the junior manager must evaluate the general impression of the senior person that exists within the corporation. In these terms, proteges think that the crucial characteristic is respect. The person who can command respect through performance, professional stature, or interpersonal abilities is perceived as a good mentor candidate.

Most proteges indicate that the grapevine is a useful source of information about a senior person's reputation. If the senior person commands respect and elicits the admiration of peers and the organization in general, it can be assumed that the protege identified with him will share in that esteem.

4.   Is the Mentor a Good Teacher? According to the Mutual Benefits Model, a primary function of the mentor is to impart knowledge to the protege. In addition to possessing political pull and commanding organizational respect, the senior person must be able to communicate to the young manager his knowledge in the areas of basic job skills, organizational structure, and politics and personalities on the job. The mentor who cannot teach will be of limited usefulness in helping the protege become an achieving manager. One vice president at a large advertising agency suggests that executives who rely on the phone and memos for all organizational interfaces may not be the best candidates for a relationship that requires a large amount of personal communication to be effective.

5. Is the Mentor a Good Motivator? Level II includes an array of confidence building, psychological support, and personal motivation functions that form a foundation for the protege's performance. But many senior people, in spite of their position and status within the organization, make poor mentors because of their inability to motivate on the one-to-one level. The protege would be advised to closely survey the organization to discover who exhibits the best support and leadership abilities.

6. What Are the Protege's Needs and Goals? The prospective protege must be aware of his or her needs. Does the young manager want a teacher, a psychologist, a protector, a promoter? Does he want all of these roles to be fulfilled or just some of them? He can ascertain his present needs by first examining his overall strengths and weaknesses as a manager and then determining his current stage of career development. For example, many managers are at a point in their career where "handholding" parent-child needs have been replaced by promotion and position-oriented needs. If a given senior manager can mentor on the personal support level but has little influence within the corporation, his Level III and IV deficiencies will detract from his ability to benefit such a manager.

Of course, many respondents were mentored early in their careers by senior people who did no more than serve as instructors, teaching the proteges about their profession, their organization, their field. In the process, they helped the proteges make career decisions that paved the way for their professional success. The example of John O'Hanlon, the financial accountant who discovered through the mentor relationship that his professional fulfillment lay in an entrepreneurial direction, suggests that the sponsorship/promotional function is not always the most powerful one in affecting the protege's career. Guidance, not direct sponsorship, emerged as O'Hanlon's fundamental need, and the fulfillment of that need proved crucial to his later achievements.

7. What Are the Needs and Goals of the Prospective Mentor? Similarity between the protege's goals and needs and those of the mentor is of paramount importance to the success of any mentor relationship. The protege will usually have many opportunities to discuss his professional and career goals with the mentor, and these interfaces should be utilized to explore the compatibility of their goals. Does the mentor desire to advance within the division, the corporation, and the field? Does he see this corporation as a permanent home or as a mere stepping-stone to bigger and better things? Does he share the protege's feelings about the direction of the protege's career?

And even if both the mentor and the protege desire to remain in the organization, do they both approve of the policies and programs of the corporation, the division, the department? If they think changes are necessary, does the prospective mentor agree with the protege's assessment of the elements most in need of modification?

Many mentor relationships seem to be preceded by a mutual clarification of the two parties' respective career needs and goals. This process serves to avert conflict and feelings of betrayal and nonsupport at later stages in the mentor relationship. It is important to test the waters, to allow time for a trial period in which each party can judge the other party's capabilities and career goals. As one corporate vice president at the West Coast Pharmaceutical Corporation points out, difficult as it is to initiate a mentor relationship, it can be even more difficult for a protege to get himself out of one without offending the mentor.

8. How Powerful Is the Mentor? As the protege learns more about structure and dynamics of the organization, he comes to understand the difference between position and power. The organization chart is more an "ideal type" than a mirror image of the reality that is Corporation X. As one middle manager came to realize, "Not all vice presidents are the same."

The two factors that a protege ought to consider here are the mentor's power and his closeness in rank to the protege. Many proteges describe a strong mentor as one with a "direct line to the top," an access that can originate at different levels in the organizational hierarchy. The relative ranks of the mentor and protege can affect the mentor's ability to involve himself in the protege's day-to-day activities. Some of the lower-level proteges I interviewed expressed dismay that their mentors, senior vice presidents in large organizations, were more than slightly out of touch with their immediate situation. Though in the long term such a mentor could provide sponsorship and promotion, he was too far above the protege to transmit many of the political and occupational skills that the protege needed in order to become a good manager, accountant, or financial analyst.

In fact, the most fruitful mentor relationships often involve a mentor who is located somewhere in between the top and the protege's level, two to three levels above the protege but relatively close to the divisional leadership. The ideal rank difference will, of course, vary with the structure of each organization. One respondent advised that in selecting a mentor, the young manager ought not to "shoot for the top" but to find someone on the way up.

9. Is the Mentor Secure in His Own Position? Most good mentors have the ability to bask in the protege's achievements. But if the mentor perceives these achievements as a threat to his own position, then he is more a danger than a help to the protege's career. Most mentors consider the protege's progress as a reflection of their own tutoring and intervention. But some mentors see it as an opportunity for the protege to strip them of their position and authority. Such mentors, however unconsciously, will try to stymie the protege's development even while profiting from the career and informational benefits of the mentor relationship.

Before entering a mentor relationship, the junior manager should attempt to determine, through observation or the grapevine, how the prospective mentor reacts to the promotions and accomplishments of peers, subordinates, and seniors throughout the organization. This is a good indication of how he can be expected to react if the junior manager draws closer to him in terms of knowledge, skill, and authority.

I asked each respondent how the mentor would feel if the protege drew even with him. Most thought that if both the mentor and the protege were getting benefits from the relationship, the protege's steady advancement through the organizational ranks would not affect the relationship, especially if the mentor saw the protege's success as a catalyst for his own.

Personality Fit and Chemistry

One of the issues I am concerned with is whether or not a personality fit, a "chemistry," between the mentor and the protege is important for the success of the mentor relationship. In other words, is similarity in personality one of the factors that should be considered in selecting a mentor?

The issue of personality fit and chemistry is quite different from the issue of compatible career needs and goals. It involves a level of complexity that is not present in the goals and needs issue. Can a mentor relationship work if it involves dissimilar personalities? How important are personality fit and chemistry in the formation and continuation of the work-based mentor relationship? Can the mentor and the protege work together, form political alliances, and exhibit mutual support while having only a weak attraction or none at all on a social or personal level?

Because of the way in which the mentor relationship had been written about, I expected to find mentor relationships that were consistently characterized by warmth, smooth interpersonal dynamics, personal friendship, and strong interaction away from the workplace. However, only a few of the relationships that I observed followed this pattern.

The mentor relationship of Dan Garner, the senior vice president at the Communications Corporation, is the kind that has been romanticized in much of the literature on the subject. A strong interpersonal relationship exists between the president and Garner. They frequently socialize; they attend parties together; their wives know each other well; and their personalities mesh perfectly.

"There is a warmth, a chemistry, that seems to work. One of the executives commented that 'if your mentor could adopt you, he would.' "

Part of this "personality mesh" arose from the strong similarity in their backgrounds. Garner's parents were business executives; both the mentor and the protege were raised in affluent Connecticut communities; and they share a love for high culture (opera, concerts, art).

But most of the mentor relationships I examined were not characterized by such a close interpersonal involvement. In most instances, the mentor and the protege did not share common outside interests, did not have the same social background, had not even had the same kind of schooling. Most of the younger managers were MBAs; the older managers had only undergraduate college degrees at most. The mentors and proteges lived in different communities and did not socialize frequently. Yet the relationships worked.

A crucial component of the mentor relationship is the ability to work together. This ability is a multifaceted characteristic that involves the broad elements of mutual trust, respect, and a belief in each other's ability to perform competently. Personality was important but not paramount in the mentor relationships I examined. For every manager whose answer to the question "What qualities attracted you to the mentor?" was "We just happened to hit it off," there were two or three who answered in terms of the work-based qualities of competence, position, power, and organizational support. In other words, participants in mentor relationships perceive personality as important but not sufficient to ensure the success of the relationship.

In fact, the responses seem to indicate that characteristics that make an individual attractive in nonorganizational relationships do not correspond to the characteristics that fire the mentor relationship. Loyalty, trust, cohesiveness of action, competence, and cooperativeness, while of minor or no functional importance in the ordinary friendship, assume a pivotal role in the mentor relationship.

But if chemistry is not an overriding concern at the outset of the mentor relationship, this does not mean that it will not develop in the course of the relationship. Over time, a certain chemistry emerges between two people who are working together toward a common goal. And the mentor-protege chemistry that emerges from the performance of tasks and the pursuit of career goals on a day-to-day basis proves a stronger bonding agent than the mere attraction of personality.

Though the "pleasure of each other's company" does figure in the success of the mentor relationship, it is not uppermost in the minds of managers. It is surprising how infrequently most mentors and proteges interact on weekends, at parties, at nonbusiness social gatherings. Many mentors and proteges see each other only during working hours; others eat lunch together and go out for a quick drink after work; but only a small number interact after office hours. Much of this depends on the norms of the organization. Michael Madison, the assistant treasurer of the Chemical Corporation, mentioned that the corporate culture instilled in all employees the sense that a firm distinction existed between the public and private spheres. In this context, an outside relationship between the mentor and the protege would violate the cultural norms of the company.

But during office hours, the mentor-protege relationship blossoms. The mentor and the protege work together, have a personal rapport, engage in mutual constructive criticism, and participate in a relationship that fulfills all of the functions mentioned earlier. They have lunch together once or twice a week, even discuss things that are not work related, but there is a sharp line between the public and private spheres that excludes weekend socializing from their relationship.

Hence, the protege needs to look beyond chemistry and "comfort" in evaluating the mentor. The point here is that chemistry is often a result, not a cause, of the mentor-protege connection; that mentor relationships develop on a much more functional basis than chemistry; and that the ability to fulfill a work role emerges as a more important determinant of mentor relationships than personality mesh. As a high-level executive at the West Coast Pharmaceutical Corporation explained:

> "I don't think chemistry is as important as the technical fit, the job-related factors. Just getting along together, having the same sense of humor, is secondary. It really has to be based on common perceptions and common judgment."

Gabe Randolph, the divisional manager at the Goodbrands Corporation, agreed.

"Although we hit it off very, very well . . . personally and professionally, in a business relationship it's hard to get along personally unless you have that professional respect. For a boss and subordinate to really get along personally, they have to get along in a business sense first before they gain the kind of respect for each other that would allow them to develop a personal relationship. So it was both a personal and professional respect for each other's work that led to a general liking for each other."

Strategies Employed in Attracting a Mentor

The problems that corporations have in the areas of management development, managerial succession, and general productivity can be alleviated if talented junior people can be identified and somehow connected with mentors. However, except in the formal mentoring programs that some organizations have instituted (see Chapter 8), the "mentor connection" occurs haphazardly, leading to a neglect of potential managerial talent.

In most companies, it is largely up to the members of the mentor relationship to find each other. There are methods that the respondents have used themselves and have observed others using in order to connect with the right mentor. This section will present those methods that seem to increase the likelihood that the protege will attract a mentor (see Table 7–2).

TABLE 7–2
Strategies Employed in Attracting a Mentor
1. Possessing and demonstrating competence.
2. Achieving visibility.
3. Getting key assignments.
4. Showing a desire to learn.
5. Taking advantage of key interfaces.
6. Showing a willingness to help the potential mentor accomplish his goals.
7. Taking the initiative.
8. Making self accessible.

1. Possessing and Demonstrating Competence To attract a mentor, the protege must display a basic competence and perform well. Almost every mentor and protege stated that the junior manager attracted a mentor first and foremost on merit. The proteges I interviewed showed an ability to perform their jobs and understand their organization, and above all, they demonstrated an ability to express themselves clearly and effectively. Proteges can create an advance billing for themselves, through conspicuous hard work and a capacity to learn, so that their solid reputation precedes them when they do seek a mentor. Prior success is an important component of being judged a "comer."

2.   Achieving Visibility Related to the technique of working competently and professionally is the technique of doing so in such a way that the young manager's proficiencies become known to the powerful people in the organization. For the young manager unfamiliar with the organization and unaware of the channels to power and authority, the means for attaining visibility are a mystery. But according to many executives, the young manager is presented with numerous possibilities for "showing off" and must learn to recognize these as they arise. John O'Hanlon describes situations at his advertising agency in which the as yet unsponsored young manager can demonstrate ability.

> *"Even if the person comes in as an assistant account executive, an entry level for an MBA, he would be working with all the account people up to the account supervisor level. He would be dealing with the research people or the head of media. You might be in some meetings with the president, who must keep up to date on what's going on."*

In other words, opportunities to shine are always there. But I think that too often the new manager, because he is not directly requested to contribute at such meetings, misses chances to make his presence known. Many of the unmentored respondents seemed less aware than the mentored respondents of the numerous opportunities for greater visibility that arise during the normal business day.

A senior vice president advises that it is important to adopt an aggressive posture in achieving visibility.

> *"Though you shouldn't take on more than you can handle, volunteer for things that can make you visible. Make presentations, write reports and analyses, and make sure management gets a copy."*

One protege attracted his mentor not only by producing good reports but by delivering them to the senior officer for whom the reports were intended. Since serving as the bearer of good tidings is often as important as being their source, the young manager who supplies a face to accompany his competent report is one step closer to developing a top-of-mind awareness of his capabilities among potential mentors. As one protege describes it,

"If you do a great job, and it is not known who is responsible for the output, it is not going to help get a mentor."

3. Getting Key Assignments The respondents often first attained organizational recognition by becoming involved in new business enterprises, the "hot projects," and from then on began to receive support from a senior person. Too many managers do high-quality work in low-priority projects, a situation that does nothing to advance their careers. As one senior manager says,

"Get a hot project and do a good job on that project, you're going to get rewarded. The guys at the top will notice you."

Unfamiliar with corporate priorities, novice managers cannot distinguish the highly valued projects from the inconsequential. One company labels as "A" projects those that top management has informally designated as the most relevant to its current goals—the most innovative and demanding projects—and automatically considers participants in those projects to have "executive potential." The problem for the young manager is not merely gaining access to participation in such projects but learning the criteria upon which senior management differentiates the "A" projects from the rest of the organization's activities. The criteria are not always self-evident, often reflecting long-term corporate goals that may not be widely known within the organization.

But a grapevine does exist through which the organization's priorities can be decoded for the novice. Many managers have the freedom to choose among a few projects, and if they are aware of organizational priorities, they can further their careers dramatically by selecting the right project.

4. Showing a Desire to Learn Most mentors are at least partially attracted to young managers who display an eagerness to imbibe their knowledge. When the mentor senses that a junior will make a willing pupil, he can see the beginnings of a cooperative interchange.

Jim Mulcahy of the Eastern Investment Bank initiated his mentor relationship by presenting himself in the student role to the vice president who eventually became his mentor.

"I showed a great deal of interest in how he approached the business. I found that not many people go in and actually sit down and say, 'Teach me the business.' I would ask him specifically, 'OK, how would you price this particular transaction? What would you do?' As time went on and I got more responsibility where I could make certain decisions on my own, I'd still come back to him. He was always there; he continued to be there."

By initiating the mentor relationship from the perspective of a teacher-student interaction, the young manager is honestly signaling to the prospective mentor that he feels that he has something to learn from the latter's years of valuable experience. Undoubtedly there is a bit of ego involved in the senior manager's positive response, but the senior's store of knowledge is in fact a valuable corporate asset and will serve the protege well.

The junior, by hinting that he wants to adopt the potential mentor's work as a model and standard for his own work, implies that he considers the senior executive's style and approach to be unique.

> "Probably one of the most effective ways of attracting a mentor is to go in and say, 'I know that you did a really good job on the marketing study. Everybody said that your bakery study is the best thing that ever happened. Would you be willing to look over my draft'—which you think is perfect—'on the dog food industry and give me some suggestions? I really appreciate your taking this time. Maybe we could do it over a drink?' Or 'I'll come in early tomorrow morning because I know you always get here.' You're acknowledging the things the person does that are different."

The Mutual Benefits Model suggests that among the various "carrots" motivating the mentor to enter the relationship are certain "psychic rewards." One of these rewards is the revelation conveyed by the protege's pursuit that his organizational reputation for proficiency is so widespread that even the junior managers at the protege's level are motivated to seek out his advice and counsel.

But the protege must be truly willing to be the mentor's student. According to one product manager, many potential connections between senior and junior managers are aborted by the unwillingness of the latter to accept a temporary student role.

> "Newly minted MBAs love to tell people how it should be done, which is probably the worst thing in attracting a mentor."

5. Taking Advantage of Key Interfaces At times, junior managers are invited to informal gatherings, cocktail parties, and professional gatherings. Such occasions give them opportunities for cross-rank socializing that are otherwise unavailable to them. Some of my respondents first met their mentors at such informal gatherings.

At social gatherings, one manager tries to meet the president and the chairman of the board and to make some memorable comments that will cause these persons to "remember the name."

> "If they're standing there with a drink in their hands, it's OK to go up to them, identify yourself, and try to say something insightful. These parties are occasions in which they're all peers."

Many junior managers do not realize the potential of such interactions for helping them to make a positive impression on top management and perhaps to initiate a more formal relationship.

6.   Showing a Willingness to Help the Potential Mentor Accomplish His Goals As has been emphasized throughout this book, the protege must be sensitive to the ultimate goals of the potential mentor. Ellen Everett of the Management Training Corporation summarizes it this way:

> *"It's basically a question of figuring out what they want and what they need—their need for power, or their need for an audience, or their need to perform, or their need to tell somebody how it is."*

After ascertaining the potential mentor's goals, the junior manager must demonstrate a willingness to work with him in achieving them, must convince him that the relationship will not be a one-way transfer of benefits.

If the potential mentor senses that the junior manager is sincerely interested in helping him improve his own career, there is a greater chance for the mentor relationship to blossom. Most of the respondents claim that facilitating the senior manager's job performance was a crucial step in the development of the relationship. The corporate head of marketing for a medium-sized baking goods company contends that a person cannot attract a mentor unless the senior manager is offered early evidence that his expenditure of time, energy, and reputation will benefit him.

> *"I think the way it can happen is for the young MBA to provide currency to that relationship, by taking on some of the work for him. 'Teach me how to help do your job.' Then, there's a give-and-take."*

By helping the senior person perform his job, the junior person contributes to the furtherance of that person's career. And according to the Mutual Benefits Model, furtherance of his career is one of the senior person's prime motivations for entering into the mentor relationship.

An executive at a Fortune 500 conglomerate stressed how important it was for the junior person to be aware of the requirements of the mentor relationship, to be willing to meet the senior person's job demands, and above all to demonstrate a readiness to work hard with the mentor on joint projects. The junior manager can actualize the potential mentor relationship by making himself available to the senior person when needed and by being flexible in his own demands.

However, as one executive warned, this does not imply becoming a yes-man. One of the greatest benefits that the junior manager can bring to the senior manager is an objective analysis of that person's business decisions. Part of the process of helping the senior person "do his job" is to make an honest, but tactful, appraisal of his work, offered not as criticism but as a solution to a specific problem.

7. Taking the Initiative Time and again, the respondents mentioned that "waiting for a mentor" could prove a frustrating and sometimes fruitless experience but that there were methods for accelerating the process. Michelle Ross, the director of employee relations at the West Coast Pharmaceutical Corporation, suggests that the business student should already be thinking about acquiring a mentor. Her perspective has been influenced by her experience in meeting her future mentor while she was enrolled in a college internship program. It is her contention that some of these one-on-one internship formats serve as surrogate mentoring programs.

> *"If you find someone, or think that you see somebody, you should make yourself known to that person and keep those channels open. I worked at this. I knew that she would be helpful to me, and thus made sure I let her know that whatever I could do to help her, I would."*

I mentioned to my respondents that many young executives felt that either organizational structures or unfortunate physical arrangements made it a formidable task for them to forge a relationship with a senior person, regardless of the willingness of upper-level managers to engage in mentoring. A senior product manager replied that young managers must apply the same creativity to the mentor acquisition process as they would apply to the mastery of any management function.

> *"Figure out who's closest to the division president, and try to get closest to them. Look through a phone directory. Maybe a senior person just happens to live in your town. 'Hi, just noticed you lived in Pleasantville. Isn't that a coincidence?' It starts small, but you have to be a private investigator to get it."*

The opportunities for meeting senior managers are endless. One respondent advises young business school graduates to introduce themselves to senior executives during lunch periods. Though some companies have separate cafeterias for upper management, some of the largest corporations provide only one eating area. According to this respondent, senior executives often eat there alone, perhaps because of their odd schedules or the lack of peers. The young manager is often unaware that although the corporate culture may prohibit the senior manager from boldly sitting down and introducing himself to a junior, it often permits the junior to take the initiative and offer his companionship for a short lunch. In such situations, the senior often welcomes a young manager's company.

One thing that many managers seeking a mentor should keep in mind is that they may have already established contact with members of upper management when they were first interviewed for the job. Most new recruits think this encounter perfunctory in nature, but the senior manager who participates in the interview process obviously has had some imput in the hiring decision and is familiar with the new recruit's qualifications. The new recruit would not be ill-advised to casually seek out that person, perhaps even to write him a note to inform him that he has joined the organization and that he enjoyed the time spent during the interview. In this way, the new recruit is reestablishing contact with the senior person while that person still has top-of-mind awareness of him. The note could be followed up by a phone call.

It might also be incumbent on the senior executive who approved the hiring to then ensure the "rightness" of the decision, perhaps by taking a personal interest in the new manager's development or even by becoming his mentor.

If done tactfully, taking the initiative in the mentor relationship can do no harm to the junior's career. But not taking the initiative, and hence missing the chance to acquire a mentor, can guarantee a less dynamic and successful career path. A vice president at a top management consulting firm put it this way:

> *"You can flounder and take what fate brings to your door, or you can go about your career in a more conscious way."*

8. Making Self Accessible Business is normally conducted from nine to five, Monday through Friday, but those in senior management know that the successful organization demands a dedication beyond the "normal" time requirements. As we shall see in the next section, one of the qualities that mentors consider most desirable in a potential protege is a sense of organizational commitment that compares with their own.

Lawrence Garibaldi is quite explicit in his description of how he emphasized this quality to attract a mentor.

> *"I made myself available. I made it very clear that I was at his beck and call. The time schedules around here often get very cramped, and it's necessary to work for short periods of time very long hours and weekends, and I let him know at the outset, 'Here's my home phone number. If we have to work, if you have any problems, I'm available. Don't hesitate to call.' "*

But commitment is not measured merely in terms of the time spent on organizational tasks. The senior executive will also assess the protege's willingness to transcend job description, departmental scope, and prior training in a specific business discipline.

> "So I was willing to take on any other jobs that were peripheral that he could have given to the marketing department or the sales department. I think once he understood that, he liked it."

In short, the manager gave every indication to the senior executive that he was dedicated to the organization's goals and could meet the demanding requirements needed to be successful.

What Mentors Look for in a Protege

As pointed out earlier, because of the effect that the protege can have on the mentor's career, participation in a mentor-protege relationship is as important to the senior executive as it is to the junior manager. When I asked the respondents what characteristics they would consider decisive in defining a person as an acceptable and valuable protege, their responses clustered into several categories (see Table 7–3).

1. Intelligence Nearly every respondent mentioned intelligence as an essential attribute of the protege. Before a senior executive learns anything about the junior person's credentials, background, work experience, or even organizational position, he will gauge the junior manager's level of intelligence from their initial encounter. The protege's ability to survive in the organization depends on his intelligence, the basic "clay" that the mentor can subsequently mold into full-fledged managerial proficiency,

TABLE 7–3
What Mentors Look for in a Protege
1. Intelligence.
2. Ambition.
3. Desire and ability to accept power and risk.
4. Ability to perform the mentor's job.
5. Loyalty.
6. Similar perceptions of work and organization.
7. Commitment to organization.
8. Organizational savvy.
9. Positive perception of the protege by the organization.
10. Ability to establish alliances.

But this quality is as nebulous as it is important, and unless the senior executive has developed an accurate 10-second IQ test, he will overlook many bright junior managers. Upon further examination, it appears that mentors view as crucial indicators of intelligence, first, the respondent's "quickness," his ability to analyze a problem rapidly, and second, his "alertness," his ability to identify the elements relevant to a problem.

Thus "intelligence," at least the type a senior is sensitive to and can recognize at first glance, is related to the ability to solve problems rapidly.

2.   Ambition Native intelligence must be complemented by the desire to succeed. The junior manager who is not interested in furthering his own career probably has little interest in helping the mentor advance in his. Senior executives mention numerous methods of detecting ambition, including the junior's willingness to extend himself and make unsolicited presentations and his interest in acquiring the qualities and skills necessary to move up in the organization. A director of employee relations agrees that people who look as if they want to get ahead are identified as potential proteges.

> *"They inquire about how I did it, asking some advice about what they should do, including their next educational step and how their career should develop."*

3.   Desire and Ability to Accept Power and Risk

The need and ability to accept responsibility—the innate propensity to lead, direct, and supervise—emerge as a crucial quality of the protege. And a senior manager's mistake in concluding that the protege desires power can prove disastrous, especially when the lack of that desire first becomes obvious during a crucial situation at some high organizational level.

It should be noted that ascertaining personal qualities often involves as much intuition as science, so that the potential for disappointment is inherent in any mentor-protege relationship. An upper-level executive reveals how one protege, carefully groomed through numerous positions, was finally promoted by the mentor to a high-level management position, only to suddenly reveal a lack of imagination and risk propensity, qualities that she was though to possess during the early phases of the mentor relationship.

> *"Some think they want power, and it turns out they don't really want the power, the authority, and the responsibility. What they want is the status and salary, on the 35th floor, making more money than they're making today. But God forbid they should have to make a decision."*

The mentor had to preside over this person's demotion and eventual "resignation." Since then, the mentor has been more aware of the symptoms of either a predisposition or a reluctance to engage in activities related to power and risk. How well does the person handle smaller chores? How willing is the person to estimate and administer a budget? How active is the person in hiring and firing? How much commitment to his or her decisions does the person exhibit early on?

One junior initiated his mentor relationship when he was the internal financial auditor for the department of his future mentor, the treasurer of the company. While many juniors in his position had shied away from writing reports laden with suggestions for improvement, this junior barreled forward with critical, incisive analyses of the department.

> *"I think he respected my perspective in taking an interest, a somewhat strong interest, and he probably did not see some other people's opinions being so strong in these areas as mine. I think he respected some of the very strong reasons I had for suggesting these measures."*

The mentor liked the protege because he was not a "paper tiger." This risk taking suggested the presence of a quality that the mentor found attractive.

4.   Ability to Perform the Mentor's Job   According to most of the respondents, one method for assuring promotion to a higher position is to have a replacement for the position currently held. Ironically, the careers of countless individuals are stalled by their ability to perform their current job better than any potential replacement. One of the ways that managers overcome this "problem" is to develop and nurture their own replacements, and more often than not, the person who replaces the executive on the way up is his protege. For this reason, an often mentioned characteristic of the potential protege is his ability to competently perform the mentor's job.

The senior person can ascertain the potential protege's ability in this area through his performance on joint projects, through reports he might have prepared, even through the grapevine. In addition, as stated in the previous section, the potential protege is at least partially responsible for informing the senior executive of his competence.

I am not sure how important to the protege selection process is the perception that physical appearance implies ability. However, some respondents did refer to elements of appearance as selection criteria. For example, neatness and reasonable weight, attributes indicative of self-control and self-respect, enter into the senior's perception of the young manager's overall desirability as a protege.

5.   Loyalty   The mentor must believe that the potential protege will maintain a strong loyalty to him throughout the relationship. The risks involved in being a mentor, the transmission of "state secrets," and all of the interdependencies characteristic of the relationship require that the protege be loyal.

Mentors use various means to ascertain the strength of the potential protege's tendency to commitment. Some executives see a parallel between relationships in private life (loyalty to wife, mother, children) and performance in business. But most often, the mentor tests the waters by first seeing whether the potential protege demonstrates loyalty in small-scale, low-risk situations.

As mentioned earlier, in the mentor relationship loyalty is the basis of an informal empire that, because it possesses no official mandate, depends entirely on trust among the parties for its continued existence.

6. Similar Perceptions of Work and Organization Mentors indicate that an important characteristic of the potential protege is a basic agreement with the mentor's values regarding goals, operations, and general direction of the organization.

Mentors utilize numerous methods for detecting whether others possess attitudes toward work and the organization similar to their own. The search for this "common point of view" often leads them to test as proteges individuals of the same background, town, or university. Unfortunately, similarity in background is often a poor indicator of a shared perspective on the organization and its goals.

Mentors are often surprised to discover that a variety of people share their values. The success of the male-female relationship described in Chapter 5 demonstrates that people who have undergone supposedly different socialization processes can have similar attitudes within the corporate environment. One male mentor was attracted to a female protege because, like him, she was deadline oriented, stuck to specifics in her reports, got straight to the point, and dealt in a direct way with subordinates.

But as mentioned earlier, the senior manager looks for a protege who, while in basic agreement with the mentor's values and perspective, will be able to "constructively criticize" the mentor when the mentor is straying from agreed policies or is pursuing methods that the protege perceives as potentially disastrous.

> *"I've gotten into much more trouble with people who agreed with exactly my way of doing it. We would go so far down the wrong road you wouldn't believe it."*

A good protege has the ability, and the intrepidity, to effectively play the devil's advocate. One executive at the Goodbrands Corporation mentions that the "knockdown, dragout fight" is funda-

mental to the mentor-protege relationship, a basic part of the policy
and planning process.

*"The people who are the best proteges are the strong-minded people, not the
weak people who cannot develop their own independent thought processes
to be able to bounce their ideas off the mentor."*

The differences between the mentor and the protege usually relate more to means than to goals. The two can share similar objectives
for the department, yet hold differing opinions on how to achieve
those objectives.

   7.   **Commitment to Organization** Many senior executives
desire a protege who not only has a corporate outlook similar to their
own but also exhibits as great a commitment to the organization as
they do. The mentor realizes that such commitment is necessary for
organizational success and has in fact been instrumental in his own
rise. He enters the mentor relationship with the idea of receiving
some benefit, and he will obviously stand to gain more from a young
manager who is willing to put in the extra hours needed to further the
organization's goals and thereby advancing both their careers. A
highly placed executive with the Womangoods Corporation reflects
this sentiment. Her protege "somehow had the spark of concern,
interest, and commitment that made me think she would be terrific.
And she was."

   One mentor knew of a young manager who had remained with
the organization during a particularly depressed economic period in
its history. While most of the other young MBAs quit for safer career
havens, this manager had "stayed the course," demonstrating a commitment that became the basis of their now solid relationship.

   8.   **Organizational Savvy** Though most mentors consider it
their function to teach the protege about the organization's people
and politics, they are still attracted to the young manager who exhibits an innate understanding of the corporate culture and its values,
proprieties, and priorities—in short, a sense of the "right way" of
doing things. Such managers usually exhibit this quality immediately.
As one executive claims about her protege:

*"She always seemed to have a greater grasp of what was going on, not just
in her particular area, but in the whole corporation. And she seemed to have
the ability to take the larger view."*

   9.   **Positive Perception of the Protege by the Organization**
A vice president at a medium-sized advertising agency, while realizing the limitations of the grapevine, depends on it to some extent for

cues as to the people who will move ahead. The upper-level executive tends to ally himself with those whom the organization identifies as "comers."

Small promotions along the way often suggest to the senior executive that the junior person is impressing immediate supervisors. This "look of success" that begins to surround a junior person serves as advance billing that precedes him or her at every level. It can eventually aid in attracting a powerful mentor.

10.   Ability to Establish Alliances One mentor told me that he based his choice of a protege on whether the young manager was able to interact smoothly with fellow workers. This served as a good indicator of whether he would be able to command respect and garner loyalty from peers, subordinates, and superiors in the future.

How cooperative is the new junior person with his peers? How well does he interact with all levels within the organization? How willing is he to do favors when asked? And how sociable is he on a day-to-day basis? The answers to these questions may predict the quality of his interpersonal relations throughout his organizational career, the number of friends he will acquire during his stay at the corporation, and his ability to mobilize the human resources crucial to the operation of the mentor's division or department.

Jim Mulcahy of the Eastern Investment Bank demonstrates this ability to get along with people.

> *"I go in to see people with questions about their areas, and I've subsequently become friends with them. This has made it easier for my mentor to do things, because he knows I get along with people who are senior to him. Without his ever telling me, I make his job a lot easier."*

The potential protege's ability to establish alliances is also indicative of how easy or difficult it will be for the mentor to market him.

> *"He knew when he went out and marketed me that there would be some receptive ears, because I went around myself and marketed myself to those people independently of him. And he caught only a bit of that, but he knew enough that I had a relationship with some senior people."*

Though the mentor did not know how close Mulcahy's relationships were, his confidence in Mulcahy was strengthened by the knowledge that this junior could sit down and relate to senior people on a one-to-one basis and "have a laugh with them." The mentor knew that they perceived Mulcahy as a colleague, not just as another young manager talking to a senior executive.

Thus the attractive protege combines personal skill and organizational savvy. While a junior manager may not possess all of the characteristics listed here, possessing a fair number of them increases his chances of acquiring a mentor.

ONCE THE RELATIONSHIP IS ESTABLISHED

The previous section dealt with the making of the connection between the mentor and the protege, the qualities that each seeks in the other and the extent to which chemistry is involved in the establishment of the mentor relationship. Now we will examine the dynamics of the relationship after this initiation period and we will explore such issues as the health of the relationship itself, the protege's relations with unmentored peers, and his interaction with senior management and nonmentor supervisors.

A Midpoint Appraisal

There are various bases upon which a mentor relationship can be evaluated. For example, each of the parties can examine his own career advancement in order to measure the general health of the relationship.

A major consideration should be whether the goals and needs of the two parties have remained consonant. Originally, each entered into the relationship on the assumption that they held the same views regarding the direction of the organization, their place in the organization, and the methods for attaining their goals—a common vision, as it were. As we observed in Chapter 6, the deterioration of the mentor-protege relationship often results from a breakdown in communication between the members regarding each other's needs and goals.

Many of the respondents make sure to discuss these goals and needs at various points in the mentor relationship. They do not wait for a period of personal or organizational crisis to find out whether they both still want to remain in the division or organization or pursue a given business objective. But aside from the issue of the continued congruence of goals, other factors must be considered in determining the general health of the relationship.

The protege must at some point ask hard questions regarding the benefits he is receiving from the relationship. One executive claims that the relationship is serving the protege well if he is willing and able to reward the protege's performance with a higher title, expanded staff, and additional supervisory responsibility. If the protege's performance is not being rewarded with power, he is not receiving the maximum benefit from the relationship.

Is the mentor including budgeting among the protege's expanded responsibilities? Control over budgets and people is an important indicator of potential power since it allows the protege to expand his scope beyond the power to market, advertise, research, or plan, into a generalized ability to mobilize many different resources outside his speciality. Hence, increases in such control indicate that the mentor is acting in the protege's interest.

The protege should also determine whether information about the organization's politics and plans is being forwarded to him by the mentor. It is the mentor's responsibility to transfer to the protege important information that the protege needs in order to perform well. If such information is not forthcoming, this may be a signal that the mentor relationship is weak and tentative. According to the respondents, the relationship, especially in its early phases, should always be judged in terms of the maintenance of a healthy exchange of benefits.

The mentor must also confront tough issues at some point in the relationship. Is the protege exhibiting all of the positive characteristics suggested by his initial behavior patterns? How does the organization perceive his performance after he has been in it for a number of months or years? How has he handled the increased responsibility of each successive promotion?

Aside from demonstrating his job competence to the mentor, the protege must demonstrate his ability to continue to establish and expand the alliances that are crucial to the mentor's career. Some proteges become overconfident about their place within the organization because they are being mentored by a senior manager and because their careers are progressing quickly. Such overconfidence can seduce the protege into imagining himself to be more secure than he really is, less dependent on organizational allies. He may therefore fail to maintain associations that are crucial to organizational success. If the mentor notices that the protege is developing a cavalier attitude toward the political subtleties of corporate life and allowing strategic corporate alliances to lapse, he ought to examine closely the effects that this is having on his own organizational reputation. As we shall see in the next section, the protege must employ a high degree of political savvy to allay the resentments of peers and the insecurities of direct supervisors. Without that savvy, the protege can cause problems for himself and the mentor.

Another area that the mentor should monitor is the loyalty displayed by the protege over the course of the relationship. As mentioned earlier, the protege's loyalty is an essential ingredent of the mentor-protege interchange. According to the Hierarchy of Mentoring, at each successive level of his commitment to the protege, the mentor's risks increase, and when the protege ascends to the status of trusted adviser, the mentor becomes most vulnerable. He has transferred state secrets to the protege; he has allowed the protege to become part of his policy-making and decision-making process; and he has left himself vulnerable to the protege in numerous other ways. Because of this vulnerability, he must be sure that the protege is not betraying his trust, for example, by forwarding information to an enemy camp or making deals with rival managers.

All of these issues an affect the mentor's ability to move up the corporate ladder, since the protege is generally the person who fills the position that the mentor just vacated. The protege's performance in each position is a direct measure of the mentor's judgment.

The Quality of Interaction But beyond the exchange of benefits that occurs throughout the mentor relationship, the relationship can be judged on another dimension, the quality of interaction. I asked many of the respondents how well they worked with their mentor or protege, what it felt like on a day-to-day basis to interact on a functional and personal level with that person. The quality of interaction is indicative of the general health of the mentor relationship.

Surprisingly, many of the relationships involve a certain amount of tension, "head knocking," tumult, and turbulent meetings of the minds. In a sense, this illustrates the difference between the supervisor-subordinate, boss-worker relationship, in which the person with authority directs and controls the underling, and the mentor-protege relationship, in which the parties bring a commitment to their own and each other's development and career and hence assume a more equal footing in day-to-day interaction. The protege is expected to present independent ideas, help the mentor formulate policy, assist in the planning process, and make a substantial contribution beyond the formal scope of his job title, experience, or organizational tenure.

But this brainstorming, along with the looseness that typifies the mentor-protege relationship, often leads to visible exhibitions of tension otherwise unseen in the large bureaucracy.

The rise of David Dorwin, the vice president at the Crandall Advertising Agency, has been meteoric, helped in large part by his mentor of five years, a senior executive in the coproration. At times, their interactions can be best described as stormy.

> *"My mentor can be very brusque with people, but it's been a good growth process for me. He's viewed as a very difficult person to work with by a lot of people. Frankly, there have been a number of personnel changes of people who couldn't hack it and couldn't advance. He's very strong and very domineering, and if you don't stand up to him, you're in a lot of trouble."*

The mentor seems to invite opposition from the protege. He seems to perceive interpersonal tension as a necessary part of idea creation and task completion.

"I think that he is trying to elicit ideas. There are people who can't push back, and they don't last. But if you do stand up to him and make yourself known to him, he'll back off. He'll get the sense that you know what you're talking about and that you're prepared."

The mentor uses dynamic interfaces to develop an aggressiveness in David that he considers important to success in an advertising career.

"Before this relationship, I did not push back to that extent. . . . In this situation, it's safe to push, behind closed doors, when you're not in a situation that has to be pursued. He pushes with me in order to get a response, so I will do more with the client."

The dynamic interchange in this relationship serves two functions. It leads to the creation and expansion of ideas, and it helps forge in David a sense of self-assurance regarding their validity.

The mentor is trying to develop in David a confidence in himself and his ideas because of the changing nature of the advertising field. He believes that clients are becoming increasingly dependent on the advertising agency's expertise regarding the direction and development of their products, and hence want to know what the account executive specifically thinks about the market, the public's perception of the products, and changes in consumer tastes. Since the account executive must exhibit confidence in his ideas when dealing with the client, the mentor uses one-to-one confrontational methods to force David to develop the strength of his convictions.

Such exchanges, however, are usually carried out in private. "Nobody airs dirty laundry," Dorwin claims. Hence, the organization is unaware of friction, and the mentor and protege are certain to present a united front on issues of policy and performance.

It should be indicated that the mentor "pushes" the protege in those areas where he thinks the protege already knows the answer or can at least make an educated guess. Sometimes such interaction is caused by a mentor's own ambivalence about given policies and practices, and often the confrontation of views represents a real desire of the mentor to "settle" certain issues, in his own mind and in reality. Since the protege thus becomes part of the policy decision process, in effect the mentor is admitting that he is dealing with an intellectual equal. A protege who recognizes that fact will not be overwhelmed by the confrontation of minds, the dynamic interplay of personality, that often typifies the mentor-protege relationship. In fact he will be encouraged by it.

Of course, some people would not survive in such a relationship, and the mentor ought to make sure that the potential protege is a good candidate for such interaction. A weaker personality, mistaking confrontation for conflict, will shrink from it, and possibly from the relationship itself.

Suzanne Barclay of the Photography Corporation describes the friction that occurs between the mentor and herself.

"I am a strong-willed person, and I will not concede. I realize that there are times when my mentor will make a decision I will not agree with, and I voice my disagreement. But when there are strong-willed people around, I find that there is a certain amount of respect. I can disagree, but the mentor will explain his position."

Barclay and her mentor engage in arguments, but since in this way Barclay is helping the mentor in the planning process, the mentor welcomes them.

One way for the protege to assess the quality of such intense mentor relationships is to observe how often the mentor is willing to credit and recognize his accomplishments. Dorwin is always encouraged by the fact that the mentor is quick to indicate improvement and progress in Dorwin's capabilities and in fact publicly advertised the part he played in Dorwin's promotion to vice president.

Another indicator of the quality of mentor-protege interaction is the extent to which the mentor will modify or correct his policy plans to take account of a logical and coherent presentation of fact by the protege. The mentor's refusal to change his views under any circumstances may indicate that he feels threatened by increases in the protege's input into policy decisions or that he does not respect the protege's viewpoint. These responses may portend conflict between the members.

Peer Relations

The executives interviewed felt that most of the problems existing in the mentor relationship emanated not so much from the members of the relationship as from the external environment. An environmental element with which the protege in particular must learn to come to terms is the organizational peer.

The protege is in a favored position, and he may be seen by his peers as a shooting star surpassing them in recognition, performance, and position, as an individual who is clearly identified with a member of a level of management that extends a helping hand to very few. Peer reactions to the protege will embrace a wide spectrum of attitudes, from admiration to disapproval, and the way the protege navigates through this ocean of opinion may determine how successful his career will be in the long run.

Although peer reactions to proteges in a mentor relationship vary considerably, most of them can be placed in one of three categories: neutrality, jealousy, and admiration.

Peer neutrality stems from a variety of organizational conditions. Peers are often unaware of the mentor relationship and thus cannot react to it. This unawareness is sometimes caused by the structure or physical layout of the organization, either of which can prevent employees from learning a great deal about co-workers' activities, work habits, or political maneuverings. At other times, the work style involves such a lack of interdependence that co-workers really are unaffected on a direct level by the protege's political maneuvering. Hence, they exhibit neither a positive nor negative reaction to the mentor relationship. In sales, for instance, the bottom line is often defined by how much the saleperson brings in to the company on a month-to-month basis, and though mentoring can have a tremendous effect on the protege's technique and on the number of his sales contacts, the process is so sub rosa that peers are unlikely to perceive the cause and effect relationship between having a mentor and sales results.

But most proteges report that there is some peer resentment regarding their mentor relationship. The protege's career seems to be moving at a faster pace than that of his peers, and since co-workers are typically unwilling to admit that the protege deserves to be mentored, they are likely to believe that favoritism is involved. The protege appears at meetings of senior executives, makes presentations on policy-related matters, has access to information that his peers cannot get, and seems to be emerging as a power within the organizational planning process. It is therefore natural for peers to ask, "Why is this person, and not I, becoming a corporate star? Could favoritism be the reason?"

Such jealousy, if unchecked, can wreak havoc with the career of a rising corporate star. It must be remembered that peers generally represent this middle manager's future power base, so even if he achieves a high position, resentment and bitterness generated early on can return to haunt him when he does. And excessive peer jealousy can insidiously destroy morale if the mentor relationship is perceived as unabashed favoritism. In addition, the protege's failure to establish credibility on the peer level can leave him vulnerable if the mentor retires, dies, or falls out of favor.

Proteges have developed many methods for assuaging peer resentment, but the one that repeatedly emerges is the demonstration of competence in the eyes of peers. (See Table 7–4). In this way, the protege undercuts the belief that he owes his position to favoritism. The mentor can help the protege to demonstrate his competence by giving him a highly visible, highly independent, and extremely responsible position in which performance can be directly measured. Thus the protege has an equal opportunity to fail or succeed. A senior manager describes how he overcame peer resentment when he was a protege.

> "It took me time to establish good relations with peers. I really think that until that time, until I went away a couple of years and left directly reporting to him to go become head of sales and marketing for one of our operations, and did it in the trenches and slugged it out, I don't think the respect existed for me. Today I legitimately have my own power base, and if he gets hit by a bus, I'm in no danger."

Most proteges learn not to boast about their mentor relationships. Bragging about his relationship with the chief executive officer caused Kevin Jones, the manager described in Chapter 6, to undermine his position in the company, his relationship with the mentor, and the mentor's credibility.

A big danger for proteges is to forget that their relationship with the mentor is informal, usually unstructured, and not legitimized by an organization chart. Keeping in mind that he is still a middle manager, the protege must interact on a day-to-day basis with his peers. He ignores at his own risk informal interactions among peers, such as coffee breaks and lunches. The greatest danger for a protege is to spend all his time with the mentor, acting more like a senior executive than a middle manager. In short, the protege must not veer too far in action and attitude from his formal role.

Another source of jealousy among peers, mentioned earlier, is the protege's access to privileged information. But the skillful protege can convert this career detriment into a positive force by sharing some of this information with his peers. While much of the information he

TABLE 7–4
Assuaging Peer Resentment
1. Demonstrating competence, establishing credibility.
2. Downplaying relationship whenever possible.
3. Continuing regular interaction with peers.
4. Becoming source of information for peers.
5. Serving as upward conduit of peer ideas, plans, and information.

receives consist of "state secrets" that the mentor told him in confidence and expects not to be repeated, some of it is "unclassified" and can be shared with peers and middle-management colleagues. Often rumors about shake-ups in the organization, the creation of new departments, unannounced holidays, and plans for the future are loosely defined as unclassified information, and by sharing such information, the protege can demonstrate to peers that his position as protege can benefit them. Instead of considering him a threat, peers will begin to think of him as a person with information useful to their own careers and job planning and performance.

Therefore, although resentment toward the protege is sometimes inevitable, the "star" status of the protege also inevitably pulls peers close to him, especially since this star possesses much information inaccessible to them. Michelle Ross described how she made use of this perception.

> *"I do find that a lot of peers, especially those on shaky grounds, do make it a point to see me at least once a day. They like to make it a point to have coffee with me, ask me out to lunch—people that I don't feel I have very much in common with. So I think that they think I must know what's going on."*

Before Michelle's peers met with her mentor, they would ask her opinion on the subject of the meeting, apparently believing that Michelle had insights into the workings of the mentor's mind.

The protege's position as information source can also be utilized in an upward direction. As easily as the protege can transmit information to peers, he can convey ideas, plans and information from peers to the mentor and senior management. As mentioned in the Mutual Benefits Model, one of the benefits that the organization derives from the mentor relationship is communication—between the mentor, the protege, peers, and senior management. As the protege's peers perceive that his role as protege enhances their ability to get their own ideas heard at upper levels, they will feel less resentful toward him.

Another problem in the protege's peer relations arises from the fear that he will inform the mentor of any problems that come up in his department. Charles Clancy, the vice president at the Eastern Investment Bank, feels that this fear can be addressed by the protege.

> *"I think that some people were a little wary of me because they felt that I kind of had his ear, or worked so closely with him they wouldn't want to say anything that would offend him through me. I mean, some worried, I suppose. But for the most part, I thought it was great, because the people that could get close to the vice president would ask my opinion on things because they knew we worked so closely together."*

But can all peer problems be solved? After all, being a protege means being in a state of transition from one reference group to another, from middle management to senior management, from follower to leader. The sociological literature on reference groups is filled with accounts of the pains of leaving one group to join another. Even on the societal level, the pursuit of the American dream of upward mobility, of movement up the class ladder, entails a separation from friends who fail to exhibit the same speed of mobility. In the same way, the protege, regardless of his intentions, is in the process of redefining his loyalties, of transferring his identification from one group to another. As he assumes more responsibilities of the higher group and abandons his ties to the lower group, a period of discomfort occurs. A product manager who was being groomed for the divisional director position found the transition period disorienting, since while he was becoming one of the upper management "ins," he was still a nominal member of a lower level. His movement to upper management was part of a major divisional reorganization at the Goodbrands Corporation, and one of his first priorities was to help management reorganize the staff.

> "In fact, it became very uncomfortable for me because people I knew were getting fired that week and I had to deal with them today. It put me in a very funny position, and people knew I was in this position."

In spite of the ambiguous status of the protege role, most of the respondents, realizing that it is part and parcel of their career advancement, seem able to establish peace with the organizational environment. Doreen Tokama brings the discussion back to the issue of competence. Once competence is established, there is less room for peer jealousy. Though people can be envious of the protege's opportunity to perform, once he does perform well, the issue of favoritism is largely resolved.

> "I was always aware of the jealousy, which is why I felt it very important to do my homework—to keep everything strictly professional, never to be seen as if I were favored."

Upward Relations

Important as it is for the protege to maintain a smooth relationship with peers, it is equally important for the protege to establish his legitimacy in the eyes of those in upper levels.

Geraldine Links, the business manager at the Steel Corporation, worked for some years at the Blue Pharmaceutical Corporation and met her mentor early in her tenure there. He left the pharmaceutical company to become a group vice president at the Steel Corporation, and soon after joining his new company, he hired Links as manager of business planning.

At the Steel Corporation, however, Links is not in a direct reporting relationship to her mentor. Her direct supervisor is not only unaware of the mentor relationship but is also convinced that hiring her was his own idea. She had sent her résumé to him and had become part of the small group of candidates from which he planned to fill the position. The selection process was monitored by the mentor, who had final approval, and when the supervisor and mentor "agreed" that she was the best candidate, the supervisor thought that he had been engaging in a joint selection process.

Hence, Links's direct boss does not understand her close relationship with the mentor, a person she supposedly never met before she applied for the position. All the supervisor knows is that an ease of interaction exists between her and this group vice president which he does not have.

"And he has expressed his nervousness among his peers. These are the people I have to get things done with and through."

In fact, Links claims that "it makes people in this organization very apprehensive that I have a direct line to him." Since many juniors are mentored from a level above that of the direct supervisor, this is a not uncommon reaction. But the supervisor's reaction affects not only the protege's relationship with him but her relationship with the entire membership of the department's rungs between the protege and the mentor.

The sources of tension between a supervisor and a protege are numerous. Many of the respondents claim that as their relationship with the mentor deepens, the mentor encourages them to assume more and more responsible jobs, many of which may conflict with the supervisor's assignments.

Most of the mentors and proteges I interviewed were very careful not to encroach on the work relationship between the supervisor and the protege. The extra assignments of the mentor were initially performed when the protege was free of formal obligations. Of course, the supervisors, who are below the mentor in rank, always feel an informal pressure to allow the protege more time to interact with the mentor. The problem of cross-loyalties is very difficult to confront and solve.

A potentially great source of friction involves the ultimate career path of protege and supervisor. At some point, it becomes apparent that the protege, and not his direct supervisor, has been chosen to wear the upper-management mantle, and unless the direct boss is himself mentored, he will resent that. This may lead to attempted sabotage of the mentor-protege relationship. We observed an example of this in Chapter 6, where a direct supervisor attempted to intercept and monitor communications between the mentor and the protege.

Lawrence Garibaldi, our financial analyst at the manufacturing conglomerate also experienced problems with his supervisor. Lawrence is in a division that serves as internal consultant to all the other manufacturing divisions. The organizational structure above Lawrence's level includes only director, vice president, and divisional president, and since there is little room at the top, people at the director level and below may never attain senior management status.

Lawrence's immediate boss is the director of his functional unit, but Lawrence is being mentored by a vice president. He is most obviously being groomed for upper management.

> *"Basically I work on a dotted line for the vice president and on a solid line for my boss. I spend half of my time working for my mentor and half working for my boss. He outranks my boss and when necessary will pull rank on him."*

If the vice president thinks it necessary for Lawrence to go on a business trip or attend an important meeting, he pulls him off projects. Though these are extreme actions, Lawrence feels that there is no other way to get ahead in this division, since the lack of mobility for directors has made them wary of their subordinates.

> *"My director doesn't want to be challenged. He doesn't want to be outshined by an underling. He will give you projects that will not show your capabilities and exclude you from the meatier projects, the projects where exposure will be at the higher levels instead of at your peer level."*

The mentor short-circuited this sabotage by quickly establishing the legitimacy of the protege among various levels of the organization, especially among the direct supervisor's peers.

> *"My direct boss has to recognize my potential because I have been recognized throughout the organization. It's very clear, and people will question him about me. 'Why is it that so many people have recognized this person and they are offering him the responsibility, and you keep saying that he shouldn't be offered the opportunity?'"*

Lawrence feels that his boss is "coming around," as evidenced by a quick increase in salary. But at one point the director attempted to sabotage the mentor relationship by requiring Lawrence to gather financial data on one of the mentor's projects, data that would threaten the mentor's position and cast doubts on his competence. Although his job required Lawrence to gather and present an accurate analysis of this information, his doing so would have been disapproved by the mentor. Lawrence resolved the problem by confronting the director with his feelings about the motivation behind the assignment. He expressed his willingness to carry out the assignment but also informed the director that he would tell the mentor that unfavorable information was being collected. The director quickly relieved him of the assignment and eventually aborted the entire project.

"The director finally agreed that it was a rotten thing to put me in that position. And that he wouldn't want the tables to be turned either."

But the moral to be drawn from this incident is that the situation should not have been allowed to reach this stage in the first place. If it is obvious that peer relationships are primarily the protege's responsibility, it is equally obvious that the mentor must adequately prepare all levels of upper management for the protege's ascendancy. As shown in the Mutual Benefits Model, the mentor must advertise and market the protege successfully, so that public opinion supports the protege's promotion and dampens the objections of the direct supervisor.

However, the mentor must also avoid undermining the supervisory function. Pulling someone off assignments is just poor politics, and the supervisor's resulting sense of threat and encroachment is not unexpected. Perhaps communication between the mentor and the supervisor regarding the protege's allocation of time could have averted some of the more political maneuvers of Lawrence's supervisor.

The material in this chapter suggests that a manager must understand and adhere to a set of rules in order to find and retain a mentor or protege. The respondents have become aware of the nuances and subtleties involved in initiating and maintaining a mentor relationship, and demonstrate a keen insight into the variables involved in this career mechanism.

The advice offered in this chapter was gathered with two aims in mind: first, to assist managers who are not currently in a mentor relationship and need to know how to enter one; and second, for managers who have already entered into such a relationship, to suggest ways of improving or maintaining the level of interaction in the relationship.

8

Mentoring and the Future of the Corporation

The mentor relationship will continue to contribute both to the growth of the corporation and to the careers of the participants in the relationship. But several recent developments suggest that mentoring will become even more important for the progress of the American corporation than it already is.

Because of the growing complexity of the corporate environment, today's manager is expected to master an increasingly broad array of skills. However, the new manager does not always know what skills are most needed in his corporation. The mentor can help him in finding out what these skills are and in obtaining the training that will enable him to acquire them as quickly as possible.

Part of the increased complexity of the business environment is the expansion of organizations. That expansion is a further burden on the corporate novice. A new manager is recruited by a Fortune 500 company, shows up at personnel on his first day on the job, is shown a large chart, and is politely informed by the personnel director with pointer in hand that "you are here." Bewilderment quickly follows, because it may take months before the young manager learns not only the location of "here" in the power structure but the real meaning of "here" in the overall scheme of things. If in the past a mentor was needed to guide the young manager from "here" to "there," certainly in the increasingly complex and puzzling modern corporation this function of the mentor has become even more necessary.

In addition to being ever more intricate, the business environment that the new MBA is entering has acquired a notable instability. The chief culprit in many cases has been the merger, a phenomenon which seems to be occurring in almost every field with alarming consistency. It was recently estimated by a consulting company that on average fully 20 percent of the people in top management lose their jobs when a merger occurs. In a business environment that has become ever more unpredictable due to acquisitions and mergers, managers will look for methods to anchor their positions, to be part of the "inner group" that maintains its position, and perhaps increases its power, when the big change occurs. Connection to that inner group is most easily made through a mentor.

And the unpredictability in the corporate environment will not disappear when the current troubles of the economy are behind us. Technological advances, new manufacturing methods, and changing consumer tastes and needs all seem to serve as catalysts for deep business disturbances. Thus the much heralded recovery will not serve as an antidote to instability. In short, even good times may not provide job security, because prosperity may signify rapid changes in the relative value of various types of companies, managers, and knowledge. Hence, companies may have to quickly change direction, products, and emphasis, removing themselves from familiar fields and entering wholly alien areas of activity.

To some extent, the mentor can insulate the protege from career disaster as the protege adjusts to the new requirements of an expanding economy. We all become obsolete, if only momentarily, until we upgrade our knowledge and skills, but the trick is to retain our positions during the adjustment period. A mentor can provide the necessary breathing room within the organization. Given a changing organizational, corporate, and business structure, the protege requires a mentor in order to ensure survival and growth.

Other influences will also necessitate the spread of mentor relationships in business. There is an expanding awareness among managers of the utility of such relationships as a career anchor. My interviews suggest that an increased sensitivity to the role of mentoring in career advancement is evolving among executives at various levels. And there seems to be an increased willingness to pursue mentor relationships and to persevere in them through their problem periods.

But perhaps the most significant reason for believing that the mentor relationship will win more acceptance and encouragement is the increased awareness among organizations of how the relationship contributes to their growth. The organizational benefits that derive from the mentor relationship—management development, ease of managerial succession, and reduction in turnover—inevitably suggest to the organization that it is worthy of encouragement. What companies need now are good managers, able people who are loyal to the organization and their profession and are functionally and psychologically integrated into the hierarchy. The American corporation regards with justifiable envy the success of the Japanese system in imbuing employees with a sense of loyalty, and in an attempt to emulate that success it has embarked on a frantic "search for excellence," experimenting with various organizational techniques, the Theory Z's, and corporate cultures.

But the point here is that we already have within our grasp a format for both the development of skills and the integration of the individual. The mentor relationship serves the organization and at the same time takes into account the executive's prosperity for pursuing self-interest, the desire of managers for career growth and expansion of power within the corporation.

Hence, the mentor relationship is necessary, important, and increasingly integral to the development of industry and the manager. Yet it has occurred only randomly. However, as we shall observe, there have recently appeared programs that encourage the establishment of mentor-protege relationships on a more formal basis than has existed in the past.

FORMAL MENTORING

Now that the benefits of mentoring have been established, the question that must be asked is whether a relationship that is at bottom spontaneous and subject to the vagaries of any human relationship can in fact be successfully fostered, established, and developed in a more formal manner. Can a large organization establish a system or program through which prospective mentors and proteges can somehow interact? Can the mentor connection be formalized?

To answer this question, I investigated firsthand the functioning of formal mentoring programs in both private industry and government.

The Government Program

The federal government's Federal Management Program (FMP), some of whose participants I interviewed, is a management development program with a mentoring component. The program was established to bring into government a higher caliber of manager who would eventually fill the senior executive slots, a so-called elite corps of executives culled from the best public administration degree programs and developed on a particularly fast track.

Entrance into the program is highly selective. To even be considered a candidate for recruitment, the applicant must be recommended by the dean of his or her graduate school. The selection process entails multiple interveiws and written tests. Each year about 100–200 individuals are selected nationwide for the program.

The program provides a three-year internship in which the new manager comes in at the senior trainee level, is given a core position, and is periodically assigned rotational positions within his functional area.

Since the participants represent an elite corps, the government wants their training to be as personalized and closely guided as possible. The development of these managers is not left to chance. Each intern is provided with a mentor to oversee his development.

Choice of Mentor After the intern has been assigned to an agency and an office, he is given four to six months to establish a relationship with a mentor. He meets with several participating senior managers on an informal basis, and he finally "signs on" with a mentor. The program is alerted to the establishment of the formal relationship, and an interagency formal approval process occurs. The stated role of the mentor is as follows:

1. The mentor is expected to help establish a training program for the protege, including the rotational training schedule among different agencies.
2. The mentor is expected to explain the organization to the protege, to show him the ropes, as it were.

The mentor, then, is expected to be responsible for the development of the protege for the duration of the program.

The proteges have various reasons for selecting a particular mentor. One protege chose his mentor on the basis of the mentor's perceived power:

> "He was the deputy regional administrator, in effect the lowest-level manager in the region. But I chose him because of his reputation for being able to exert power beyond his position, and his extreme interest in the program."

The functions of these mentor relationships have unofficially expanded over a period of years, and many participants claim that the mentors now perform functions other than establishing a training program or explaining the organization. In fact, the mentors have informally extended their activities into the Level III domain.

The mentor functions that have evolved are:

1. Within their scope of control, the mentors allow the proteges to assume supervisory positions for short periods of time.
2. The mentors use personal influence to help the proteges gain exposure to special training.
3. The mentors facilitate travel and mobility within and among departments and agencies for the protege.
4. The mentors arrange for the proteges to attend high-level meetings not ordinarily attended by "trainees."

Hence, the mentor program has gone beyond the stipulated formal duties and obligations of the mentor, but since the "finished product" has met expectations, the powers that be seem willing to allow this expansion of the mentor role.

Because of the influence of mentoring, the progress of the interns has far outdistanced that of peers who came in with the same title at the same time. One protege states:

"I would say that FMP proteges have risen to levels they could never have risen to without assistance. We have people who are operating as number three and number four men in the organization, as special assistants or special advisers. We have people operating very far ahead of their grades."

It should be noted that the mentor also receives benefits that are not specifically mentioned in the FMP handbook. One respondent said that a positive effect of the program was the mentor's sense of pride in his ability to change or affect the system in a way that helped the federal government in the fulfillment of its tasks. Also, since association with a protege reflects well on the mentor's ability to judge character and develop managers, power and influence flow from the mentor relationship.

But perhaps most important here are the mobility of the protege and his concomitant exposure to other parts of the agency and other agencies, a mobility and exposure that the mentor does not usually have. The protege's access to such conduits of information as central office, private agency, and private business networks transforms him into a source of information and intelligence usually denied the mentor.

Mentor's Role as Advocate Since the Federal Management Program is regarded as a method for attracting and quickly promoting the "best and the brightest," it has evolved into an elite training ground, a development that has not enthralled supervisors and regional managers. The program stipulates that proteges are to be rotated from function to function. Therefore, they are perceived by many agency heads as being "on loan" from the federal government and as representing no substantial return on investment. If the training plan requires that an intern change departments at Month 11 of Year 2, that intern will depart, regardless of the work he is currently performing. Consequently, departments begin to view the interns as trainees, not workers.

Since the program provides trainees with opportunities not available to nonparticipants, the conditions for peer resentment are present. The formal mentoring program enables proteges to receive training in 3 years that the average employee would not get in 10. And whereas regular employees receive additional training only in their own specialty, FMP participants can be trained in three or four program areas. One program protege went to Washington on a temporary assignment in personnel, a function totally unrelated to his main area.

The program representative tries to help the mentor understand that there is going to be resentment toward the protege and that as the protege's advocate it is his responsibility to explain the program's goals and operational rationale to other members of the organization. For instance, non-FMP employees might have various questions about why an FMP trainee who goes off to the Ford Foundation or the New York City government for six months of additional "exposure" can draw a paycheck while not directly contributing to the work of the agency.

The mentor can help most here by explaining to the protege's peers and supervisors that the aim of the program, the development of new managers, will eventually help improve the ability of the agency to perform its functions. While this may not completely eliminate the resentment and jealousy of peers and supervisors, it will at least indicate to them that the mentor is aware of the questions and doubts they have about the program.

Drawbacks of Program As just described, one obvious drawback of the Federal Management Program is that the agencies utilizing proteges often fail to see the value of having them. A high official at a local agency complains that while he realizes that the caliber of the proteges is quite high, he does not think that the agency will ever get a direct return on the time the mentors spend on developing them. Because of the personnel cutbacks his agency has suffered over the last several years, he indicates that he would be just as satisfied with four new permanently slotted clerk-typists as with a management trainee. In other words, the interns do nothing to directly facilitate the day-to-day operations of the agency.

Second, the program may be giving the proteges a false set of expectations about the type of work they will perform during the intern period. The protege is psychologically prepared for working on the "big project," but he is often confronted with the routine immediate needs of his agency. Unless the mentors can help the proteges tolerate the frustration of initially participating in lower-level jobs and projects, departures from the program, and possibly from government employment, are unavoidable.

A third drawback of the program is that the promised post-program slots may be eliminated before the intern can finish the program. The mentoring program, though correctly regarded as an effective method for developing a managerial elite destined for the top positions, is not in step with the long-range personnel needs of the federal government. Mentoring can create capable managers, but it cannot in and of itself provide jobs. This creates difficulties for mentoring programs in private industry as well as in the public sector.

Programs in Private Industry

Two of the private sector programs that I studied were those of the Wall Street Investment Company and the Northeast Insurance Company. These programs, in place for about three years, illustrate both the strengths and weaknesses of formal mentoring programs as they are currently conceived.

The scope and purpose of the Wall Street Investment Company program are limited. New recruits entering the company are routinely assigned a "mentor" who remains in that role for a six to nine month training period.

One weakness of the program is that its purpose has never been fully explained to the mentors. As one mentor in the program tells it, the parameters of this "formal" program are surprisingly informal.

> "They basically said, 'We're going to try something new. New people will be assigned to a mentor. You are to guide them through the six to nine month introductory period in the firm.' "

But it has never been made clear to the mentors what this guiding process actually entails. One mentor felt that the purpose was "to make them feel part of the corporate family, get them thinking the way we do in our business," but the interviews disclosed that there was little agreement among the mentors about the Investment Company's corporate culture. Hence, the proteges were obviously receiving different versions of corporate expectations and goals.

A second weakness involves the commitment of the mentors to the program. Though there is no direct pressure to participate, the upper managers perceive that noncooperation could have an adverse effect on their careers. Thus, although many agree to participate, their sense of coercion results in a halfhearted commitment of time and energy that definitely diminishes the quality of the program.

"After several months, some proteges didn't feel that they even had a mentor. The mentors didn't play the roles they were supposed to play."

Hence, the overall success of individual interactions varies greatly. In some instances, solid relationships develop in which the mentor fulfills numerous instructional and support functions; in other instances, the protege sees the mentor only for a periodic chat in the mentor's office. Moreover, the evaluation format is so loosely defined that mentor relationships can deteriorate without the knowledge of the program administrator.

The very structure of the program seems to contain the seeds of its own malfunctioning. Most of the training takes place at corporate headquarters, though the proteges will be relocated to regional offices around the country for permanent assignment. Since both the mentor and the protege are aware that their relationship is only temporary, both seem to have a low commitment level.

Another weakness of the program is the lack of choice in the selection of mentor or protege. Since participants are assigned by specialty, not according to common values, common goals, or the other selection factors mentioned in Chapter 7, clashes and a lack of interest permeate the program. One female participant found it difficult to adjust to the organization because everyone, regardless of prior business experience, was brought in as a "new recruit," at least for the initial orientation period. Because she had had several years of investment experience, she soon came to resent her novice status and began to exhibit a hostile attitude. If she had been allowed some say in the selection of her mentor, as in a normal mentor relationship, common goals and other "attraction factors" would have served as the foundation for a relationship that could have helped her in this transitional phase. Her ego would have received the necessary stroking, and her fears and outrage could have been expressed to the mentor in complete confidence and trust. In short, her mentor would have been functioning at Level II.

But it is hard to ensure that a measure of personal support will emerge from a formal relationship in which people are given no choice in the selection process. There is a Level II type of interaction that cannot be manufactured or assigned. This woman—capable, bright, and an obvious asset to the company and the field—left the Investment Company before her training period was even half over.

The mentoring program of the New Jersey division of the Northeast Insurance Company, one of the largest insurance companies in the United States, is intended to reduce the well over 50 percent turnover rate among young managers. Unfortunately, this program is plagued by many of the same problems that plague other attempts at formalized mentoring by private industry: lack of participation choice; inadequate definition of mentor and protege roles, duties, and expectations; and lack of continuity from training program to posttraining career.

One of the drawbacks of the Northeast Insurance Company program is that it is conceived as largely a local function. As in some other private industry programs, the original planning was done without the cooperation and participation of the national organization as a whole. Since the mentors know that the relationship will continue only for the duration of training and will for all practical purposes terminate when the protege is given a permanent assignment elsewhere, their level of commitment is somewhat tentative.

One solution at Northeast and other organizations would be to train the protege and establish the mentor relationship in the same agency or branch where the protege will eventually pursue his career. The mentor must know that he will receive a return on his investment if his commitment to the program and the protege is to be assured. Another solution might be to introduce the program, not in the training period, but in the early posttraining phase that occurs during the first agency or branch assignment. In that way, a real mentor relationship can develop around the permanent issues of job performance, politics, and promotion. The training period could be devoted to the group orientation procedures currently in operation around the country.

In several respects, the federal government seems to be a step or two ahead of private industry in the development of a coherent formal mentoring program. A three-year training program is vastly superior to the short-term approaches employed in private industry, and the free choice of partners has definite advantages (though this is a recent improvement over the government's earlier attempts). But the programs of both the public and private sector have serious flaws. In the next section, I will offer several suggestions for the development of a formal mentoring program that can overcome the problems present in the corporate and government systems currently in operation.

TOWARD THE DEVELOPMENT OF A FORMAL CORPORATE MENTORING SYSTEM

If any clear message emerges from this book, it should be that the mentor relationship has positive implications for the organization. It hastens managerial development, serves as a mechanism for senior-level managerial succession, enhances organizational communication, and prepares the young manager for the assumption of broader responsibilities and power.

But the mentor relationship is at best a random occurrence. The average manager spends most of his career without the guidance, direction, and help that derive from the mentor relationship. As we have just observed, sporadic attempts have been made to institute formal mentoring programs, but evaluations of these programs have been unsystematic as best. The overall effectiveness of the programs is uncertain.

However, regardless of their shortcomings, these pioneering attempts are forerunners of what will surely become an accepted mechanism for managerial training and organizational development. Hence, an attempt will be made here to establish what the data on these programs suggest are the parameters of a formal mentoring program suitable for the modern corporation (see Table 8–1).

TABLE 8–1
Guidelines for a Formalized Mentoring System
1. Establish clear goals of the program.
2. Communicate the program's goals to all participants.
3. Determine the organization's ability to absorb program "graduates."
4. Enlist the cooperation of the entire organization.
5. Make the selection process as autonomous as possible.
6. Be assured of the commitment of the mentors.
7. Give free rein to the mutual benefits accruing to both parties.
8. Permit withdrawal from the program.
9. Evaluate the program continually.
10. Give the program a long-term test period.
11. Anticipate extraneous effects of organization's perception of participants.

1. Establish Clear Goals of the Program One of the more confusing elements of the formal mentoring programs that have been established thus far is that the participants do not have a uniform understanding of the goal or guiding principle of the programs. Some perceive their program as an elaborate "buddy system" to help familiarize the new recruit with the practices and requirements of the organization. Others view it as a vehicle for promotion. This difference in perceptions results from the fact that specific, unambiguous goals were never established by the formulators of the program. As the Hierarchy of Mentoring indicates, mentoring can take place on any number of levels, with benefits and mentor investments varying at each level. The organization has to determine early on whether it wants the mentor program to fulfill a teaching function, a counseling function, or a promotional function. If it wants the program to fulfill all of these functions, this must be expressly stated.

2.   Communicate the Program's Goals to All Participants As mentioned earlier, the proteges and mentors in the various programs studied seem to be confused about their roles in the programs and about the goals of the programs. Both the mentor and the protege can fulfill their functions better if they are informed beforehand that the goal of the program is to teach the protege his job, or to expose the protege to an array of different operations, or to introduce the protege to administrators and divisional presidents.

3.   Determine the Organization's Ability to Absorb Program "Graduates" If promotion is the goal of the mentor program, the future growth of the organization is the predominant determinant of the program's ultimate success. The existence of such a formal program implies that advanced slots exist in the company, that all of the training and mentoring has as its purpose the eventual promotion of the trainee to a higher position. In such situations, a rapidly contracting organization can frustrate the good intentions of all involved.

If the formal mentoring program is instituted in order to develop a highly trained, elite cadre of supermanagers, make sure that your organization can utilize and absorb them.

4.   Enlist the Cooperation of the Entire Organization The underlying theory of this book is that mentoring is a three-way partnership of the mentor, the protege, and the organization. It was shown that the failure of informal mentor relationships often originates in organizational sabotage. My research on the operation of formal mentoring programs suggests that this also holds true for these programs. If the peers, managers, and supervisors who are not directly involved with the formal mentoring program do not understand the rationale for its existence, their noncooperation can undermine the program. The rationale, goals, and mechanics of the formal mentoring program must be explained to the entire organization, through official materials, group discussion, and organization-wide meetings. Be clear about the benefits of the program to the organization; solicit suggestions about the operation of the program; and ask employees what problems they foresee.

In the government agency I studied, it was felt that the mentoring program benefited the participants but not the employing agency. But there seemed to be no centralized method for listening to non-participants' complaints and responding to them.

Whenever possible, return some participants in the program to the cooperating departments, so that the departments can experience a direct benefit for the time and energy they devote to the mentoring program.

5.   Make the Selection Process as Autonomous as Possible The program must allow for as free a selection of mentors as possible. To the extent that industry programs exhibit a tendency to assign a mentor to an incoming recruit, these programs are less progressive than the government program. One government agency allows the protege a period in which to interview prospective mentors before making a decision, so that the mentor and the protege can explore each other's values, career goals, and ambitions.

One mechanism for facilitating the mentor-protege connection would be a cocktail party or other social gathering at which free intermingling of senior managers and recruits is encouraged.

6.   Be Assured of the Commitment of the Mentors The selection of mentors for the program must be as carefully conceived as the choosing of proteges. Programs that coerce senior managers into participating, however subtly, are doomed to failure. A less than enthusiastic participation by the mentor can severely reduce the training benefits of the mentoring program.

In the original communication of goals to the organization, it should be clear to senior management that the mentor's participation is not conceived as strictly a labor of love but that benefits can accrue to the mentor as well as the protege.

7.   Give Free Rein to the Mutual Benefits Accruing to Both Parties The mentoring program must be conceived as a formal manifestation of the informal mentor-protege relationship, and the possibility that mutual benefits will accrue to both parties ought to be recognized. Thus the program must be conceived as a mechanism for allowing each party to utilize the relationship to his own advantage.

Since we have observed that the mentor relationship increases the organizational "clout" of participants as well as their job and interpersonal skills, career advancement and corporate power accruing to both parties must be seen as a normal complement to the management development benefit that the organization receives.

8.   Permit Withdrawal from the Program If either party feels that the mentor relationship is not serving his best interest, he must be permitted to terminate it. However, there should be a closed review of the rationale behind the withdrawal from the formal program. This will provide the developers of the program with feedback that can enable them to modify the program if necessary. At the very least, a structured exit interview from the program should be required.

9.   Evaluate the Program Continually My interviews with program participants and program formulators reveal that mentoring programs have a tendency to take on a life of their own: goals change, participation varies, and dissatisfaction develops, often without the knowledge of those supposedly overseeing the programs.

The evaluation should involve the following aspects:

1. The mentors and proteges should be interviewed at set points to get general and specific feedback regarding satisfaction and dissatisfaction.
2. Channels should always be available for anonymous and confidential airing of grievances.
3. Suggestions for change and improvement should always be solicited.
4. A quantitatively based organization-wide survey should be made at regular intervals. The questionaire used need not be long or complicated, but it should be comprehensive enough to monitor the attitudes of both participants and nonparticipants toward the program.

10.   Give the Program a Long-Term Test Period A half-hearted attempt at developing a formal mentoring program is doomed. The mentoring program must be evaluated by the same criteria that are used to judge any mentor-protege relationship, that is, according to the long-term development patterns and their effects on the participants. Mentor relationships develop in curious ways, and the organization and the participants must be informed early on that time will be allotted for these relationships to mature and progress.

11.   Anticipate Extraneous Effects of Organization's Perception of Participants Two of the unintended consequences of formal mentoring programs are that those chosen for such programs acquire a "star" quality and that those not chosen are sometimes stigmatized as persons who are considered inadequate material for the programs. Personnel problems can occur as a result of any management development program, but the possibility of their occurrence is greater in formal mentoring programs, since these give participants the opportunity, denied to nonparticipants, to work with—and hence be identified with—successful managers. Thus, in order to ensure peace among peers, access to such programs must be as equitable as possible.

But the most important point is that any formal mentoring program must be tailored to operate within the structure and culture of the given organization. Hence, formal mentoring programs will have to be modified to meet the needs of particular companies.

The rationale for formal mentoring programs is obvious. The development of managerial talent is seen as crucial by those in positions of power in the modern corporation. This fact is demonstrated by the explosive growth of MBA programs, seminars of all kinds, and elaborate management training programs.

But mentoring signifies more than a development of skills. It represents an attempt to establish a humanized environment within the corporate structure through one-to-one relationships between junior and senior members of the organization. Yet such relationships, which have been a cornerstone of managerial and organizational development, unfortunately occur only randomly. The formal mentoring programs attempt to transcend this limitation.

There are indications that mentoring in the modern corporation will increasingly occur within a more formal framework. American industry as a whole will be the ultimate beneficiary of that development.

THE PROCESS IN RETROSPECT

We have finally completed our exploration of the mentoring process. In that exploration, I have attempted to locate the common threads that run through what are often highly individualized relationships. Though there have been great differences in the career patterns of the respondents, both mentors and proteges, several general conclusions about the mentor relationship and its place in the modern corporation can be drawn from their accounts.

First, the mentoring process emerges as a powerful factor in the corporate promotional structure. As some previous examinations of the process have suggested, mentoring provides a "road to the top." When I questioned my respondents about the promotional processes within their corporations, they described an organizational upper stratum that was characterized by many chains of mentoring relationships. In other words, the higher the manager's location in the corporate structure, the greater is the likelihood that he is part of a mentoring relationship.

Another finding of this investigation is that the literature on the mentor relationship overemphasizes personality fit as an underlying motivation in the decision to enter such relationships. In fact, the respondents attach much less importance to personality characteristics than to the perceived ability of the members of the relationship to fulfill each other's career needs. To that extent, the Mutual Benefits Model is a clearer representation of the rationale behind the formation of relationships than the various "psychological needs" paradigms currently popular in the literature.

The accounts of the respondents do not support the "life cycle" formulations that view the protege period as a "stage" in the development of the manager. These formulations portray the protege period as an early stage in the manager's development that inevitably leads to adoption of the mentor role when the manager is sufficiently mature. But the picture that emerges from the respondents' accounts is that managers enter into mentor relationships, not because of their stage in the life cycle, but because of career and organizational goals originating in the requirements of their work life. Since having a mentor can be useful throughout the manager's career, he does not automatically shed his protege role as he advances through the life cycle. In fact, many advanced managers are simultaneously both mentors to junior managers and proteges to managers farther up the corporate ladder.

Moreover, the mentoring process does not follow easily predictable stages, as has been suggested in several books and articles. Many "stage" theories of the process attempt to chart the "typical" progression within the relationship and to identify a beginning, a middle, and an inevitable termination. While for purposes of explanation it is helpful to subdivide the benefits of the mentor relationship and rank them according to their importance, it is stretching the data to suggest that such relationships invariably move from a teaching stage, to a personal support stage, to an intervention and promotion stage. Some functions of the mentor relationship may be performed simultaneously, or never at all, and their "order of appearance" varies according to the needs and goals of the particular mentor and protege.

An especially interesting finding is that the mentoring of women by both male and female managers is definitely on the rise. Because women face additional obstacles to the attainment of career success, such as their weak image in the workplace and their isolation from informational and social corporate networks, the mentor's investment of time and energy on behalf of a female protege is usually greater than it would be for a male protege. It is a definite sign of social change that upper managers have been increasingly concerned with helping women rise through the corporate ranks. What is particularly relevant here is the fact that the mentoring process works as well for women as for men, that traditional barriers against woman can be overcome with the help of a concerned senior manager.

Possibly the most novel finding of this investigation concerns the role of mentoring in organization development. In addition to enhancing the careers of the mentor and the protege, the mentoring process humanizes the environment for the protege and functions as a mechanism for integrating the protege into the corporate structure and culture. It also serves to increase the skills and effectiveness of both the mentor and the protege. As we have observed, these processes in combination can contribute to an increase in productivity and a reduction in turnover.

Although mentoring represents a form of management training and organizational development that is essential to the growth of the modern corporation, until now it has occurred only haphazardly. Senior and junior managers have had to form mentor relationships on their own, often in an organizational environment that does little to encourage or stimulate such relationships.

But as it becomes increasingly evident that mentoring ultimately benefits the employing organization, formal programs to accelerate the formation of mentor-protege dyads are being established. Hopefully, as further research is done on the intricacies of the mentor relationship, the findings will be utilized to improve the effectiveness of the current mentoring programs and to serve as a foundation for mentoring programs as yet unborn.

NOTES

Chapter 1

1. Eugene Jennings, *Routes to the Executive Suite* (New York: McGraw-Hill, 1976).

2. F. S. Lunding, C. E. Clements, and D. S. Peskins, "Everyone Who Makes It Has a Mentor," *Harvard Business Review,* July–August 1978.

3. Charles D. Orth and Roderick Jacobs, "Women in Management: Pattern for Change," *Harvard Business Review,* July–August 1971, pp. 139–47.

4. Michael Wachter, "Demographic Changes and Economic Challenges," in *Work Decisions in the 80's,* ed. Eli Ginzberg et al. (Boston: Auburn House, 1982).

5. "Manager Malaise: Middle Managers Grow Unhappy with Their Companies," *The Wall Street Journal,* October 26, 1982, p. 1.

6. "Middle Managers Are Getting Squeezed Out," *New York Times,* October 17, 1982, sec. 12, p. 10.

7. Merger Mania Adds to Executive's Woes," *New York Times,* October 7, 1982, sec. 12, p. 10.

8. Gerald R. Roche, "Much Ado about Mentors," *Harvard Business Review,* January–February 1979, pp. 14–28.

9. Woodlands Group, "Management Development Roles: Coach, Sponsor, and Mentor," *Personnel Journal,* November 1980, pp. 918–28.

10. G. Shapiro, F. Hazeltine, and M. Rowe, "Moving Up: Role Models, Mentors, and the Patron System," *Sloan Management Review,* 19 (1978), pp. 51–58.

11. Daniel J. Levinson, et al., *The Seasons of a Man's Life,* (New York: Alfred A. Knopf, 1978).

Chapter 3

1. Terrence G. Deal, and Allan A. Kennedy, *Corporate Cultures: The Rites and Rituals of Corporate Life.* (Reading, Mass.: Addison-Wesley Publishing, 1982), p. 4.

2. Thomas J. Peters, and Robert H. Waterman, Jr., *In Search of Excellence: Lessons from America's Best-Run Companies.* New York: Harper & Row, 1982), p. 37. This point, of course, appears in many current books on management. The best known is Ouchi's *Theory Z* (Reading, Mass.: Addison-Wesley Publishing, 1981).

3. Rosabeth Moss Kanter, "Power Failure in Management Circuits," *Harvard Business Review,* July–August 1979, pp. 65–75.

Chapter 4

1. Rensis Likert, and Jane Gibson Likert, *New Ways of Managing Conflict* (New York: McGraw-Hill, 1976), p. 187.

2. Ibid., pp. 190–91.

3. Thomas J. Peters, and Robert H. Waterman, Jr., *In Search of Excellence: Lessons from America's Best-Run Corporations* (New York: Harper & Row, 1982), p. 26.

Chapter 5

1. Linda Keller Brown, "Women and Business Management," *Signs*, Winter 1979, pp. 266–88.

2. Allan Cox, *The Cox Report on the American Corporation* (New York: Delacorte Press, 1982), p. 284.

3. "White Collar Cutback Are Falling More Heavily on Women than Men," *The Wall Street Journal*, November 9, 1982, p. 37.

4. Brown, "Women and Business Management."

5. Cynthia Fuchs Epstein, "Women's Attitudes toward Other Women," paper presented at the Twentieth Emil A. Gutheil Memorial Conference, Association for the Advancement of Psychotherapy, New York, November 17, 1978.

6. "Female Bosses Say Biggest Barriers Are Insecurity and 'Being a Woman,' " *The Wall Street Journal*, November 2, 1982, p. 31.

7. "Sex and Romance in the Office and Plant," *The Wall Street Journal*, November 29, 1982, p. 31.

8. *New York Times*, February 20, 1983, sec. 3, p. 27.

Appendix A:
Research Methodology

The respondents were drawn from the middle and the senior management of companies in the Fortune 500 manufacturing groups, the top retail corporations, and the largest banks in the Northeast. The industries represented included pharmaceuticasl, steel, petroleum, advertising, photographic equipment, communications, and computers. The companies range in size from very large conglomerates to small single-owner operations.

The age range of the respondents is from the young 30s to the 60s. Hence, this book taps the experience of several cohorts. The salary range of the respondents is from $30,000 to as high as several hundred thousand dollars (including stock options, etc.).

The sample of more than 100 managers and executives was obtained in several phases. I originally enlisted the cooperation of the alumni departments of several major MBA programs. Each of these departments sent letters from its offices to a randomly selected group of pre-1974 graduates. This cutoff date was used because it guaranteed that the respondent would have been in the work force for a minimum of eight years, thus increasing the likelihood that he or she would have acquired a mentor. The letter format employed was designed so as not to discourage unmentored managers from participating, since I was also interested in their career experiences.

If the recipient of this letter was interested in participating, he or she returned a preprinted response sheet in a prestamped envelope to the sending institution. The sending institution then forwarded the names of the volunteers to me. (In some cases, the respondents sent their forms directly to me.)

This complex system of processing respondents was employed in order to ensure the confidentiality of the respondents.

I also enjoyed the support and cooperation of the Association of MBA Executives (AMBA), which sent several mailings to its illustrious members.

The research instrument was designed to tap several dimensions of the subjects' mentoring experience, including the positive and negative aspects of mentoring, sex-related issues, the history of the mentor relationship, and strategies of acquiring a mentor and maintaining relationships with peers. But while I constructed the research instrument to ensure that all dimensions of the mentor relationships would be adequately covered, I kept the questionnaire and the interview itself as fluid as possible to ensure that the richness of mentor-protege interactions would be captured.

This open-ended method liberates the interviewer from his own preconception about the object he is studying. Much of the important information conveyed in this book—the attitudes of respondents toward the mentor or protege, the power of respondents in the organization, and the functional importance of the mentor relationship in their careers—emerged only because the respondents were allowed to interject as they saw fit facts or thoughts that they considered necessary to explain their case. The subjects, though not encouraged to ramble, could within limits tell their story as they perceived it.

This structured, open-ended technique permits the interviewer to freely explore the whole story with the respondents while ensuring that no important dimensions are omitted. The technique has obvious advantages over the multiple choice type questionnaire, which forces the subject to limit his responses to those items that the reseacher deems critical.

Allowing the respondent a somewhat freer rein within the structured interview format produced some unexpected findings. For instance, I originally equated the mentor's formal position with his actual organizational strength, but as I researched the corporation more deeply through the open-ended questionnaire, I became more sensitized to the informal hierarchy operating within the organization—influence and loyalty transcending such commonly acknowledged sources of power as organizational title. These subtle factors often gave a division manager, functionally connected to the day-to-day operations of the corporation, greater power over people's careers than that possessed by a senior vice president with authority but little influence.

The richness of informal organizational processes was often communicated, not as a response to a particular question, but as a by-product of allowing the subject to "talk through" his relationship.

Appendix B:
Study Questionnaire

Author's Note: The following questionnaire was administered to managers who are currently proteges. When mentors were interviewed, the questionnaire was changed slightly. The major modification usually involved substitution of the word *mentor* for *protege*, and vice versa, whenever required. Several questions directed specifically at mentors appear at the end.

INTRODUCTION

I am going to interview you about a number of issues related to your job and career. I wanted to interview you because my research interest involves people who are or were involved in a mentoring relationship, either as a mentor or as a protege.

The questions are "open-ended," which means that there are no preset responses. Merely respond to the questions in your own way; there are no right or wrong answers. Take as much time as you want. Make your answers as detailed as you feel is necessary.

The interview should take about an hour. Of course, all responses are confidential.

I would like to mention that preliminary results of these interviews will be available within the next year, and I will be happy to share some of these results with you at that time. At the end of the interview, I'll give you my address and phone number. Again, this interview is strictly confidential. You will not be identified in books or articles that may be produced as a result of this project. Your name and the name of your company will be changed.

CAREER INFORMATION

As a start, I would like to ask you some background questions about your job and career.

1. What is your current position?

2. What are the general functions, duties, and responsibilities of the job?

3. Could you fill me in on some of the particulars about your career, where you've worked, what your jobs were?

HISTORY OF MENTOR RELATIONSHIP

1. A mentor has been described as a person who takes a personal interest in another person's career, guides that person, and perhaps sponsors him for a job or position. Have you ever had a mentor?
    (Probe extensively.)

    (If the person has had more than one mentor)
    Well, I would really like you to relate the following questions to the main mentor or adviser in your career. But if you have had more than one, you can answer the questions with regard to both whenever appropriate.

    a. When did you first come in contact with this person? Was it during your schooldays, your first job, this job? How long ago was this?

        (1) What was your position at this time?

    b. What was your mentor's position at that time? Is it the same now as when you first met him, or did that person change positions since you first met?

    c. How exactly did you meet your mentor, and who actually took the first step in establishing this relationship? Please discuss.

    d. And then how did the relationship proceed? *(Continue with like questioning until exact chronology is established.)*

    e. What qualities in the mentor attracted you to him?

    f. And conversely, what qualities do you think your mentor first saw in you that encouraged him to pursue this relationship?

    g. *(If there was more than one mentor)*
        Have you maintained contact with former mentors?

FUNCTIONS OF MENTOR RELATIONSHIP

2. I would like to explore this relationship with you a little further, and I have some specific questions for you about the benefits of having a mentor. But before I get specific, I would just like to ask you the following question:

    a. What would you say has been the outstanding benefit that you have received from being in a mentor relationship? This can refer to career benefits, personal benefits, or any other positive results that come to mind.

    b. One mentor function, which you might have covered in your last answer, is in the area of teaching. What has your mentor taught you?

    c. I suppose that one of the reasons people look for mentors is because they think that this is an important part of building a career. How instrumental has your mentor been in directly affecting your chances for either promotion or career advancement?

        (*Lead:*   Career building can involve everything from the mentor giving the protege a clear picture of the career structure inside the organization to the mentor recommending the protege for a job.)

    d. I guess that part of career success is the ability to successfully weather such factors as "office politics." Sometimes a mentor can be very helpful to a budding protege by providing a "protective shield" when organizational pressure becomes too overbearing. Do you remember any instances when your mentor felt it necessary to run interference between you and the organization?

    e. Mentors have been known to provide psychological help to their proteges. Do you remember any times when you relied on your mentor for personal strength or warmth in the form of confidence building, pep talks, etc.?

    f. What expectations do you think your mentor has of you?

        (1)   Do you think you have fulfilled all of his expectations?

    g. What do you think your mentor gets from this relationship, either professionally or personally?

        (*Probe:*   Intelligence/information.)

    h. Does your relationship extend beyond the office?

    i. Mentoring, like any other relationship, changes over time. If you were comparing your relationship to your mentor from the initial stages to where it is now, what would you say have been the biggest changes? (*Are you closer, friendlier, etc.?*)

    j. How long do you perceive your relationship lasting?

DYSFUNCTIONS OF THE MENTORING PROCESS

3. *a.* So far we're been speaking about mentors from a relatively positive perspective. But can you think of any instances where having a mentor can actually be detrimental?

    (*Lead:* For instance, when someone ties his career to a downwardly mobile or out-of-favor mentor).

    b. Sometimes when a person develops a mentor relationship with a superior, the opinions of peers change. What have been the effects, if any, of mentoring on your relationship with co-workers?

    (*Lead:* Admiration or jealousy.)

    c. This leads me to another question. I'm sure that in some organizations there is more than one person with a mentor. Is anyone else in your immediate organization being mentored, and if so, is there any rivalry?

    (*Lead:* One mentor wanting to advance his protege over all others. Or same mentor with two or more proteges.)

    d. I would like to get a feeling for the position of the organization itself on mentoring. Would you say that mentoring is encouraged or discouraged by your organization?

    e. One writer equated the mentor-protege relationship with that of teacher and student, parent and child. He observed that "an intense mentor relationship ends with conflict and bad feelings on both sides." I wonder if you have found this to be true either in your own experience with mentors or in other relationships that you may have observed.

SEX ROLE–RELATED ISSUES (modified according to whether relationship is male-female or female-female)

4. *a.* Some of the studies suggest that one of the drawbacks for women entering management is the fact that the social and occupational networks are not as accessible for a woman as they are for a man. Based on this fact, would you say that a mentor is more important for success for a woman than for a man?

    b. In your opinion, does being a woman affect your relationship with your mentor?

    (*Lead:*)
    (1) Do you think your relationship with your mentor would be different if you were a man?
    (2) Does the fact that this is a male-female relationship act to hinder communication or interaction?

    c. What about the reaction of spouses to this relationship?
    (1) Mentor's spouse.
    (2) Protege's spouse.

d. The issues of sexual innuendo and sexual involvement are often viewed as problems in the male-female mentor relationship. I would like you to address these issues. Are these a problem in your relationship? Can you discuss the innuendo issue with your mentor?

MENTORS AND SUCCESS

5. *a.* All things considered, do you think having a mentor really makes much of a difference in career success?

   (*Lead:* As compared to such factors as ability to make decisions, ability to lead, energy level, ability to complete assignments, willingness to work long hours, luck.)

   b. Let me ask a related question. Is it having a mentor that leads to success, or is it actually that the person who seems to have potential, who is perceived as a "person on the way up," who demonstrates ability, has a better chance of attracting a mentor?

   c. It's obvious from this interview that having a mentor can affect a person's career. If you had to give advice to a budding young businessperson, how would you tell him to get or attract a mentor?

   (*Lead:* Is it at all possible for a person to choose a mentor?)

SPECIAL QUESTIONS FOR MENTORS

A. What would you say you learned from your own protege period that you've applied to your current mentoring?

B. Do you think that demands from your own organization or department interfered with your relationship with your protege?

C. Have you ever sponsored or been a mentor to a woman? How does this differ, if at all, from being a mentor to a man?

D. Why did you get involved in a mentor relationship?
   (*Lead:* Was it for the company, yourself, the protege?)

FOLLOW-UP QUESTIONS

a. Is there anything on this issue that you would like to add, that I perhaps haven't covered in this interview?

b. By the way, do you know of anyone who would be interested in participating in this project?

   (1) How about your mentor?

c. Could I call you, say, six months from now, if I have any additional questions?

BACKGROUND DATA

1. Current title⸻
2. Length of time holding that title⸻
3. Type of organization⸻
4. Number of people supervised⸻
5. Highest level of job ever attained⸻
6. Position you expect to get after current one (and where)⸻

7. Highest position that you will ever attain in your career⸻

8. When do you think this will happen?⸻
9. Type of undergraduate school attended (e.g., Ivy League, small private college, state university)⸻
10. MBA year of graduation⸻
11. MBA major⸻
12. Cumulative grade index (MBA)⸻
13. Other graduate degree⸻
14. Would you classify the environment you grew up in as small town, suburban, city, or rural?⸻
15. Father's main occupation⸻
16. Mother's main occupation⸻
17. Highest educational level of father⸻
18. Highest educational level of mother⸻
19. Marital status⸻
20. Age⸻
21. Number of children, with ages⸻

22. Your income⸻
23. Highest expected personal income⸻
24. Military service⸻
25. Spouse's occupation⸻
26. Spouse's income⸻

Index